A Lowfat Lifeline

for the '90s

How to survive in a fat-filled world

Valerie Parker, M.S.

Published by Lowfat Publications, Port Townsend, Washington

A Lowfat Lifeline for the '90s.
Copyright© 1990 Valerie Parker, M.S.

For information, contact:
Lowfat Publications
PO Box 1889, Port Townsend, WA 98368
(206) 379-9724

Note: It is not the intent of this book to provide medical advice, but only to offer information to complement the advice of your own personal health consultant. Anyone contemplating a major change in diet or exercise should consult a qualified health professional. The author and publisher have researched reliable sources to ensure the accuracy and completeness of the information in this book, however they assume no responsibility for errors or omissions.

Printed and bound in the United States of America
First printing 1990
Second printing 1991

Publisher's Cataloging in Publication
(Prepared by Quality Books Inc.)

Parker, Valerie

A lowfat lifeline for the '90s: how to survive in a fat-filled world/Valerie Parker.–
p.cm
Includes index.

1. Low-fat diet–Recipes. 2. Nutrition. I. Title
RM237.7   641.5'638   90-61458

Perfect binding: ISBN 0-9626398-0-X
Comb binding: ISBN 0-9626398-1-8

This book is dedicated to my husband, Ron, with special thanks: It wouldn't have happened without your unwavering support and encouragement.

About the author

Valerie Parker, M.S., is the owner of **LOWFAT LIFELINE**®, a marketing and distribution company specializing in educational materials for health professionals. For several years she wrote a nationally distributed monthly newsletter of the same name and is the co-author of the book *"The Lowfat Lifestyle."* All publications have been designed to show that it is possible to cut down on fat and still enjoy good food and have been applauded by health educators and fat-conscious consumers nationwide.

With both undergraduate and graduate degrees in Physiology, Valerie spent several years in cancer research at Stanford University, followed by further study at the University of California, Los Angeles. She has been a member of the medical support staff at a health maintenance organization, specializing in blood disorders. Valerie lives with her husband, Ron, in Port Townsend, Washington, where she enjoys fresh Pacific Northwest foods, hiking, camping, picnicking and reading mystery novels.

Contents

Introduction

Low fat for life

If you are at all interested in how you eat, in how you look and in your health, this book is for you. Why? Because dietary fat is beginning to be seen as *the* leading contributor to excess weight and chronic disease. Most of us eat about *six* pounds of it every month.

While trimming the obvious fat is now second-nature to most people, many still do not appreciate how much fat is disguised in foods. Fat lurks almost everywhere. The majority of the fat in our diet is invisible, hidden in meat, dairy products, nuts, bakery goods, snacks and restaurant meals.

"A Lowfat Lifeline for the '90s" shows you where the fat is and how to eat less of it. Our message is a simple one: Cut the fat! Not just saturated fat, not just cholesterol, but fat – plain, ordinary fat. You will discover easy ways to make changes in how you shop and eat and find new ideas for cooking tasty, good-for-you meals.

This book is an all-new outgrowth of *"The Lowfat Lifestyle"* which was published in 1984. The success of that book and of the *"Lowfat Lifeline"* monthly newsletter, which I wrote from 1985 through 1989, told me that a new book on how to cut fat and eat well in the '90s would be welcomed.

The book is divided into three sections. The first section gets you right into practical tips and techniques to help you make the change to a lowfat lifestyle. It's an eye-opening discussion of where all that fat really comes from, how to make smart choices in restaurants, what labels can tell you and how to cut fat when cooking by making simple changes.

The second section includes over 150 new and delicious recipes, all family-tested, with calorie content and grams of fat included. Additional cooking tips and fat-reducing suggestions are scattered throughout this section.

The last section contains background information on the relationship between fat and disease and explains the role of fat in dieting, the differences between fat and cholesterol, the effects of exercise and information on general nutrition.

Much more than a cookbook, *"A Lowfat Lifeline for the '90s"* can be used as a light read, as a guide for eating out or as a textbook in a weight control class. I encourage you to dip in and out of it, reading a few pages here and there to get started. It is not necessary to begin at the front and read through to the back. Waiting for a pot of water to boil is a perfect time to read a page on fat in fast foods!

Recipes have been developed with busy cooks in mind. Many of the recipes take just a few ingredients and a few minutes at the stove; others include make-ahead instructions and are designed to be refrigerated or frozen. They use basic products that most people have on hand, not exotic or unusual ingredients. In acknowledgement of smaller household units, most recipes serve two people instead of the more common four or six. Of course they follow general dietary guidelines of increased fiber and decreased salt and sugar, in addition to decreased fat.

It's not a love of cooking that created this book but the enjoyment of eating well while eating less fat. The fight against excess fat comes down to knowledge and common sense. There are no "no-no's" in sensible lowfat living; reducing, not eliminating, high fat foods is the best approach. The goal is to know where that fat is, know how much of it you're eating and cut down as much as possible. It's a lifestyle that is easy to follow as long as you keep it in perspective.

Calories do count

Ounce for ounce or gram for gram, you will consume more calories per mouthful of fat than per mouthful of protein or carbohydrate: 4 calories per gram of protein, 4 calories per gram of carbohydrate, but 9 calories per gram of fat. You don't have to be a math whiz to see that eating the same amount of fat gives you more than twice as many calories. Or to understand why eating too much fat can make you fatter.

Decisions, decisions

Every time you make a decision on what to pick up at the store, drop into your lunch bag or put into your mouth, you're making a decision about fat. Since it is sometimes difficult to find out how much fat is in foods, we have included several pages of fat and calorie content in different foods (look for *"Choices"* in the index or table of contents).

Although we can show only limited examples of all the food items you could eat, the lists, by themselves, will open your eyes to where some of that fat is hiding. Numbers for calories and grams of fat come from different sources, including USDA publications, product labels, manufacturers' information and health organizations (see *"Resources"* for a partial list). Cooking techniques, ingredients in processed foods and updated values because of new measuring techniques will all affect final values.

We list calories to the nearest five and grams of fat to the nearest half. Numbers that are more detailed than this suggest an impossibly precise way of eating and serve only to confuse the reader. The average consumer does not weigh and measure each portion of food that accurately. Recognize that these numbers are for comparison purposes only. We suggest that you use all published numbers as reference guidelines rather than absolutes.

Numbers to remember

How much fat is too much? Dietary guidelines recommend that we eat no more than 30% of our total daily calories in the form of fat. This translates into approximately 60 to 70 grams of fat per day for most people. We encourage you to remember this number because grams are listed on the labels of many prepared foods and for many recipes. That way, when you see a product with 30 grams of fat, or a recipe with 45 grams, you'll have a fairly good idea of how it fits into your whole day's eating plan – probably not very well! This is discussed in more detail in the next chapter.

We started the introduction by stating that the average American eats about six pounds of fat each month. You don't think you eat this much fat? Even if you ate only 2100 calories a day at the current national average of 37 percent of calories from fat, that would add up to over 23,000 fat calories in a month. That's almost 2600 grams of fat, or close to six pounds – and a lot of people eat more than 2100 calories and get more than 37 percent of their calories from fat.

Keep the picture of these pounds in mind as you begin to read *"A Lowfat Lifeline for the '90s"!*

Where's the Fat?

Check your fat facts

Fat is everywhere! In frozen meals, canned foods, at fast food restaurants, in bakeries and delicatessens – it is on our plates and in our mouths several times a day. Unfortunately, fat is not just the "white stuff" around a raw steak. If you want to cut your fat intake, you need to start by knowing where the fat is found; only then can you begin to make smart changes. Take this short quiz before you read on.

1. One cup of margarine contains the same number of calories as two cups of cooked white rice, true or false?

2. Main dish recipes without meat are always lower in fat than recipes using meat, true or false?

3. Rank these fast foods for fat content, from highest to lowest: (a) double hamburger (b) taco (c) half of a 10-inch pepperoni pizza (d) 2 pieces of crispy fried chicken (e) fish and chips (2 pieces of fish).

4. What should we eat less of, according to the dietary guidelines – total fat, saturated fat, cholesterol?

5. One tablespoon of butter has much more fat than one tablespoon of margarine, true or false?

6. Imitation sour cream is better than the real thing if you're concerned about cholesterol and calories – true or false?

7. Omega-3 fatty acids are found in extra-pure Greek olive oil, true or false?

Answers to quiz

1. False. It takes eight cups of white rice to equal the calories in one cup of margarine (about 1600).

2. False. Many non-meat recipes are loaded with cheese or nuts to provide protein, often resulting in a high fat content.

3. (d) Crispy fried chicken, 46 grams, (a) double hamburger, 30 grams, (e) fish and chips, 26 grams, (c) pepperoni pizza, 22 grams, (b) taco, 11 grams.

4. Dietary guidelines encourage us to reduce fat to no more than 30% of total calories, saturated fat to less than 10% and cholesterol to less than 300 milligrams per day. For an 1800 calorie intake, this translates into 60 grams of total fat with less than 20 grams coming from saturated fat. See *"Fat and Cholesterol"* chapter for a discussion of saturated fat.

5. False. Butter and margarine have approximately the same amount of fat (butter has 12 grams, margarine 11 grams per tablespoon). The type of fat is different, but the total fat is almost the same.

6. False. Imitation dairy products are often made with coconut oil, a highly saturated fat which raises cholesterol levels possibly more than the missing cholesterol. And, while imitation sour cream doesn't have cholesterol, as does dairy sour cream, it contains more calories. Imitation has 30 calories and 2.7 grams of fat, real sour cream has 26 calories and 2.5 grams of fat per tablespoon.

7. False. Omega-3 fatty acids are a type of polyunsaturated fat found primarily in fish.

Dietary guidelines recommend that no more than 30% of our calories should come from fat and at least 55% should come from carbohydrates (the rest from protein).

Hidden fat

The real problem with reducing the fat in our diet is that so much of it is invisible. Visible fat is fairly easy to reduce, primarily requiring a change in attitude, such as using less oil when frying meat, trimming the fat around the steak, cutting down on greasy fried chicken. Decreasing this visible fat is necessary, but not sufficient. The next step is to search out and eliminate as much hidden fat as possible.

Fat is a natural component of many foods, but its presence is not always obvious. It is easily hidden in meat, cheese, sauces, nuts and dairy products. You don't see all the fat inside those nuts (1 teaspoon in six almonds), or the fat sliding down your throat every time you snack on some cheese (2 teaspoons in an ounce of Cheddar cheese).

The major source of hidden fat, however, is the fat that is **added** to foods, from snacks to fast foods to frozen dinners. Consider the hidden fat in commercial baked goods. While a small, plain cookie may have as little as a teaspoon of fat, it's an easy ride up the scale through doughnuts with **2 teaspoons** each, cakes with **3 teaspoons** per serving and pies with **4 teaspoons** per piece. Even a "healthy" bran muffin may pack 2 to 3 teaspoons of fat inside its oatmeal cover.

> Maybe you think that the problem of eating too much fat doesn't apply to you, like the person who said, *"I don't have to worry about any of this – I've been taking the skin off my chicken for years."* That's good, but when that same person covers the skinned chicken with a cheese sauce, or makes it into a sandwich with mayonnaise, you know she doesn't have the whole story.

Fat is in many more foods than you may think. Take a look at the list on the next page to see how many times you eat high fat foods, possibly without being aware of it. The first step in reducing fat is to know where it is hidden. Then you can begin to look for lower fat alternatives.

Face the fats

Are you positive that you eat as little fat as you think you do? Think about how often you eat the following (seldom or never, once or twice a week, three to five times a week, almost daily):

Pan-fried, deep-fat fried or breaded foods,

Fatty meats such as bacon, sausage, fat-marbled meat and luncheon meats,

Whole milk, high fat cheese, rich ice cream,

Rich sauces or gravies,

Oily salad dressing or mayonnaise,

Whipped cream, sour cream, table cream,

Butter or margarine on vegetables, sandwiches and toast,

High fat desserts such as pastries, rich cakes, icings,

High fat snacks such as chips, nuts, crackers.

If you eat several of these more than once or twice a week your fat intake may be much higher than you realize. One of the main problems with excess fat consumption is that people don't realize where the fat is coming from.

Spoon that fat

Dietary guidelines recommend that no more than 30% of our total daily calories should come from fat. The chart below shows the **maximum** amount of fat we should eat at different calorie intakes to stay within the 30% limit for the day.

Daily calories	Fat calories	Grams of fat	Teaspoons
1200	360	40	10
1500	450	50	12
1800	540	60	15
2100	630	70	17
2400	720	80	20

The chart above shows that a person eating 1800 calories a day, with 30% of them from fat, consumes 60 grams of fat per day. However, studies indicate that most Americans eat not 30%, but closer to 40% of their daily calories in the form of fat. Some eat considerably more of both calories and fat, so it's easy for people to eat in excess of 100 grams of fat per day.

You may be thinking, *"That's interesting, but I've never seen a gram of fat, it's just another number."* Well, if you can't relate to grams, think of teaspoons. A teaspoon of fat contains approximately 4 grams. Those 100 grams of fat represent about 25 teaspoons of fat; that is like eating the equivalent of a cube of butter or margarine or half a cup of oil every day!

> Picture half a cup of oil, ready to pour; 25 pats of butter, piled in a stack; a margarine cube, with the paper peeled back, ready to munch. That's a lot of fat. That's 100 grams.

Pick the visual image that means the most to you. Every time you eat a cookie, for example, the mental picture of pouring a teaspoon of oil down your throat may deter you just a bit.

The balancing act

Once you know where the fat is coming from, you need to have some idea of how much of it you eat. If you are like most people, you don't really have any idea. Take time right now to think about it. Is your usual breakfast high in fat? Do you take a sensible sandwich to work or grab something from the cafeteria? What do you have in the house for snacks?

Write down the food you expect to eat in the next two days; not every cookie or glass of juice, but total meals. Be realistic. A quick look may tell you that one, two or all of tomorrow's meals appear to be high in fat. Does this mean you have to give up your plans? Not at all. The key is to balance high fat meals against low fat meals over a period of time.

Is there a way to modify your favorite breakfast so it will offset some of the snacks you know you'll eat later? Can the high fat lunch be balanced by a low fat, nutritious dinner?

Look at some of our suggestions below. You'll see how well you can eat even if you're watching calories, once you learn where the fat is and how to cut it. Note that our high fat examples are for very typical meals; you may be surprised at how much fat is contained in them. (Remember, you are aiming for about 60 to 70 grams per day or no more than 30% of your total calorie intake.)

Breakfast: Want pancakes and sausages? Make pancakes in a nonstick pan with half the fat called for in the recipe, substitute broiled light ham for sausages. Result – 10 grams of fat instead of 38. Rather have a cheese omelet? Instead of two eggs, one ounce of mild Cheddar cheese and a teaspoon of butter, use one egg, one egg white and half an ounce of sharp Cheddar – 11 grams of fat instead of 25.

Lunch: You just want soup, crackers and cheese? If it's black bean, Ry-Krisp and Mozzarella, instead of cream of mushroom, Ritz crackers and Swiss, you'll eat 9 grams of fat instead of 28. Prefer a pizza? Choose half a medium cheese pizza plus lowfat milk instead of a cheeseburger and milkshake – 19 grams of fat instead of 36.

Dinner: Pan-fried chicken, salad with blue cheese dressing and pound cake for dessert sounds great. Change it to oven-fried chicken, salad with light Italian dressing and sponge cake for dessert – 19 grams of fat, not 39. Hungry for beef? Prime rib and baked potato with sour cream and butter adds up fast. Substitute 6 ounces of flank steak, keep the potato and sour cream, omit the butter and eat 17 grams instead of 35.

Seeing the light

Once you learn how much fat some foods have you really will have a reluctance to eat them in the quantities you used to. I never thought I'd change my desire for rich, creamy guacamole and tortilla chips, even though I knew it was a high fat treat. However, once I really understood that one avocado contained about 9 teaspoons of fat, it just wasn't worth it to me.

Now I'll still have an occasional handful of tortilla chips, but this time they're dipped into a spicy salsa – at least there's no fat in the dip. Being in control of your own decisions about fat consumption means that you're not doomed to a life of carrot sticks, as most diets make you feel.

We like grams! Grams of fat are printed on all product labels that have nutritional data and are listed in many recipes. Even if you don't know what a gram is, it's not hard to remember that most of us should be eating about 60 per day.

Fast fat

I had a sudden desire for an ice cream bar one hot day. Unfortunately, once it was in my hand, it was gone almost instantly. After it was eaten, I took a look at the label and realized that in less than 3 minutes I had slurped down 3 teaspoons of fat, 20% of my day's supply! (And this wasn't even one of the super-rich brands.) Was it worth it? Hardly. When I eat fat, I like to feel that it's a rewarding experience and this one left me feeling sort of gypped.

It's amazing how much fat we can eat in a very short time. Although many food products contribute fat to our diet, there are some in which the "mouth-time" is extremely short compared with the fat intake. Take a look at this list and think about how quickly you could consume these teaspoons of fat.

Fast fat	Grams of fat	Teaspoons
Ice cream bar, super-rich	26	6
Macadamia nuts, 10	21	5
Peanut butter, 2 tbsp.	16	4
Avocado, half	15	4
Whipped cream, ¼ cup	11	3
Snickers fun size bar	5	1

Moral: If you're going to eat a lot of fat, at least try to make it last a while.

Analysis paralysis

Do you spend hours in the supermarket figuring out the percentage of fat in every potential purchase? Do you shiver and shake in front of the freezer section while you multiply and divide grams and calories? If so, you're suffering from analysis paralysis, the indecision caused by not being able to quickly determine how much fat is in food.

The dietary guideline of eating no more than 30 percent of our calories in the form of fat is excellent, but putting it into practice leads to confusion. To many, this means that every food should be analyzed to find out its "percent fat" and that any food that has more than "30% fat" is a no-no. (From now on, we will use the commonly accepted "percent fat" term instead of the more precise "percent calories from fat.")

Endless lists, charts and graphs of foods have appeared, classifying items into low, medium and high fat foods, based on this magic 30% number. People express shock when they see a food listed as (gasp) 50% fat. This approach to monitoring food intake has been taken to an extreme by many people who analyze every bite to make sure it's less than 30% fat. While there is no doubt that in some cases the percent fat does represent the fat content accurately, there are other situations where this percentage is overly simplistic and misleading.

For example, whenever sugar and fat are present in high quantities, the percent fat may look somewhat acceptable yet may actually mask a high amount of fat. Dessert #1 with 150 calories and 5 grams of fat is 30% fat; dessert #2 with 700 calories and 23 grams of fat is also 30% fat. Yet the second dessert has more than four times the fat and represents approximately one-third of your day's fat quota.

A similar problem with concentrating on percent fat is that some foods and recipes are wrongly classified as high in fat. Using the previous example of dessert #1, we could make the same dessert with artificial sweetener and drop the total calories to 75. Now the dessert, which still has the same 5 grams of fat, is suddenly 60% fat and supposedly should be avoided. This doesn't make any sense.

One valid reason to calculate the percent fat of a specific food is to be able to recognize products that are primarily fat. For example, regular cream cheese has 10 grams of fat and 100 calories per ounce, making it 90% fat. While ten grams of fat may not sound like a lot, 90% fat certainly does. However, you may fool yourself if you ignore the actual fat content. Light cream cheese can also be 90% fat, but it has half the calories and half the fat content, making it a better choice.

> A meat, bean and cheese burrito has 200 calories and 10 grams of fat. That works out to 45% fat. If you add an extra handful of beans, you will increase the total calories, let's say to 250, but still have the same amount of fat. Although the fat content has not changed, the percent fat has decreased to 36%. You're now eating the same fat surrounded by more calories. Wouldn't it be better to take out some of the fat?

Articles that rank foods by their percent fat instead of their total grams of fat can lead the reader to some incorrect conclusions. In a list of different brands of popcorn, packaged caramel popcorn with 53% fat and 288 calories ranked "better" than plain popcorn with 76% fat and 130 calories. But the caramel popcorn contains 17 grams of fat, whereas the plain contains only 11. The first brand just **appears** lower in fat because total calories are higher. I know which one I would choose.

If you want to analyze products for fat content, be sure you understand what the numbers tell you. The total grams of fat will tell you what the fat content really is.

Think about it: You can bring any food to under 30% fat...if you add enough sugar!

Basic arithmetic

Obviously it is wise to keep the overall percentage of calories from fat within reasonable limits wherever possible. We prefer to concentrate on the total grams of fat eaten each day rather than the percent of fat calories in individual foods. However, for those who want to understand the calculations, and figure out our examples for themselves, we include the following instructions.

To calculate percent fat calories, given grams of fat and total calories, multiply grams of fat x 9 calories per gram, divide by total calories, and multiply by 100.

Regular cream cheese: 10 grams of fat x 9 = 90 fat calories divided by 100 total calories x 100 = 90% fat. Light cream cheese: 5 grams x 9 = 45 fat calories divided by 50 total calories x 100 = 90% fat. Note that the light cream cheese has the same percent fat, but less total fat.

Regular burrito: 10 grams x 9 = 90 fat calories divided by 200 total calories x 100 = 45% fat. Burrito with extra beans now has 250 calories and the same 10 grams of fat. 10 x 9 calories divided by 250 total calories x 100 = 36% fat. Percent fat is lower, total fat is the same.

To calculate grams of fat, given total calories and percent fat, multiply calories by percent fat and divide by 9.

Caramel popcorn: 288 calories x 53% fat = 153 fat calories divided by 9 calories per gram = 17 grams of fat. Plain popcorn: 130 calories x 76% fat = 99 fat calories divided by 9 calories per gram = 11 grams of fat. The plain popcorn has a higher percent fat, but less total fat.

Which contains more fat, a product with 36% fat and 25 calories or one with 26% fat and 35 calories? Each has 1 gram of fat. Don't be fooled by percent fat.

Weigh the fat

One problem with relying on percent fat is that the term has a different meaning on product labels. A lunch meat that says it is 20% fat means that it contains 20% fat by **weight**, not by calories. This same meat may actually have over 70% fat by calories, but you have to calculate this number or look it up in a book. A glance at the total fat content of 6 grams per ounce is quicker. If you then pick up another package, listing 1 gram per ounce, you can see that this number is easily compared from product to product.

Milk labeled as 3.3% indicates the **weight** of the milk solids. Since milk is mostly water, the milk solids are only a small portion of the total amount. However, its percent of fat calories works out to about 50%. The label tells us that each glass of milk contains 8 grams of fat; that's what we want to know.

Tub o' Lard Award

Many times you don't need to analyze a lot of numbers to know that a recipe is loaded with fat; all you need to do is read it. That's the case with **Microwave Lemon Dessert**. Since it came from the cover of an egg carton, it's understandable that it would encourage the use of lots of eggs. However, every ingredient is in excess, making it a truly horrible example of how to eat.

> For ten people, it requires 10 eggs, 1 cup of butter, 1 cup of whipping cream and 3 cups of sugar, plus lemon juice and peel. This filling is poured into a graham cracker crust, also made with butter, of course. The result is a pan full of sweet grease – **42 grams of fat plus 720 calories** in each serving.

This works out to 53% fat, a number that doesn't accurately represent how awful it is!

Changing Habits

Keep it in perspective

"Perspective: The ability to evaluate information with respect to its...comparative importance." (Webster) The amount of fat in the American diet has been the subject of hundreds of articles, thousands of classes and countless discussions – why you should eat this, why you should not eat that, what to choose, what to avoid. For the person determined to do the right thing, conflicting statements and suggestions result in confusion. Add strongly held conviction to half-understood facts and it's small wonder that some people lose perspective.

In the rush to get rid of fat some consumers over-react, until they've gone past what we call the lifestyle approach into a rigid and often unrealistic situation. Cutting down some of the fat in a favorite recipe is an achievement in itself, especially if you've retained the original taste. To cut it all out, and possibly ruin the recipe, isn't necessary. If it's already down to 1 teaspoon per person, will getting rid of another ½ teaspoon really matter? Keep your perspective.

The person who says he hasn't eaten a piece of bacon in over a year, and still misses it, gets our sympathy, not our praise. How much damage would be done by a couple of strips of crisp fried bacon on special occasions? He needs perspective, as does the person who's determined not to let a gram of saturated fat pass her lips. She refuses a bowl of lightly buttered popcorn, then munches her way through a bag of peanuts instead. True, she avoids saturated fat, but ends up eating much more total fat. She lacks perspective.

Losing perspective is easy to do, especially if you're a recent convert to low fat eating. In the end, it often leads to frustration with the new chosen path, which in turn can result in quitting. The real key to low fat success is to stay alert to where the fat is hiding, keep an eye on how much of it you're eating, and cut down where possible. Keep your life and your fat in perspective!

Tips for getting started

When you start to make changes, focus on what you like to eat and start with an easy change. Recognize that it may not be the same solution for everyone. Maybe you don't care about dessert each day, but know you'd miss those crackers and cheese you have each evening. Another family member may not care about the cheese, but wants something sweet after a meal. You decide to have no dessert and a low fat cheese; he has no cheese and a smaller portion of dessert. Each of you has saved fat in a way that is acceptable to you.

Instead of focusing only on what you will subtract from your diet when you make changes, concentrate on what you will add; make those new additions healthier choices – fruits and vegetables, whole grains, beans, legumes. Think of adding fruit to your dessert, not giving up a cookie. Think of adding a whole grain roll to your salad lunch, not giving up white bread. Look on developing new eating habits as opportunities for new taste adventures.

Know thyself

To achieve healthy eating habits, you need to start by understanding yourself – what, how, when, where and why you eat (the last may be the most important). Take a pencil and paper and answer this excellent, self-assessment quiz developed by the USDA Human Nutrition Information Service. List as many as apply.

What do you usually eat? (A varied, balanced, moderate diet; deep-fried foods; high fat snacks; sweets and rich desserts; extras such as gravy, spreads, salad dressings; cocktails, wine and beer; anything.)

How much do you usually eat? (One small serving; one large serving; more than one serving.)

When do you usually eat? (Mealtime only; after supper; coffee breaks; while preparing meals; while cleaning up; anytime.)

Where do you usually eat? (At the kitchen or dining room table; in front of TV or while reading; at restaurants or fast food places; anywhere you are when you're hungry.)

Why do you usually eat? (It's time to eat; you're starved; food looks tempting; everyone else is eating; you're bored, tired or upset; don't want to waste food.)

Your answers will show personal problem areas and give you clues to where your extra calories are coming from. Identifying your own habits is the first step to modifying them. Armed with a better understanding of yourself, you can then approach the fat control battle with good ammunition.

> *Do you nibble while you cook? Do you automatically eat a doughnut at work when everyone else does? Before you eat, stop and ask yourself if you're really hungry.*

It's war

Most habits are hard to change, eating habits possibly the hardest of all. Even though you know how you should be eating, and want to change, it isn't easy to translate good thoughts into action. That's why we call it war – with yourself, your family and the outside world. Temptations are many and the will is often weak.

The first battle is with yourself. Sometimes it's hard to stick with new changes. Don't beat yourself up. It is natural to backslide now and then, especially when you're tired, stressed and short of time. If you plan for such times by having nutritious, low fat food all ready to eat, you'll be able to survive.

The next and larger battle is with your family. Although it can seem like a thankless struggle to get others to change, recognize that they, too, find it easier to stick with their own old habits. If you try to persuade others to follow your path when they're not convinced, you may find that you win some battles but lose the war. They must understand why fat reduction is important and believe that change is worthwhile to them personally. Food habits are individual decisions; you have to choose for yourself and so do your family members.

Battling the temptations of the outside world is a war in itself, addressed in *"Eating Out"* and *"Shop Smart"* chapters. Don't underestimate your resistance to change; patience is essential. You can't expect to alter the habits of years in just a few days or weeks. After all, most battles aren't won overnight. Since this is a psychological war, any forward progress is commendable. Take a tip out of marketing and aim for a 10% change at a time, but be supportive of any change, no matter how small.

Tally the tallow

When you begin to cut the fat, it is important to look at the amount of fat you consume over a long period of time, instead of just in the meal in front of you. In keeping with that, for one month we want you to keep a record of the amount of **obvious** fat you bring into the house. Every tub of margarine, every block of cheese, every bag of chips, etc. Don't worry about smaller amounts of fat, just these gross (!) sources.

As soon as you've finished reading this chapter, make a list of the usual fat-filled items in your house. Some items to look for are listed on the next page. Look in your refrigerator and on your shelves right now for other possibilities.

List all these sources down one side of a piece of paper and next to each one show how much you have on hand, e.g. ½ pound butter, 4 ounces of Cheddar cheese, two chocolate bars, etc. Each time you bring home groceries, check the list quickly and add the new amounts to each line. Don't worry about how much fat is in each product, just list the total amount you buy.

Keep adding to the list all month long, then subtract what you have left in the house at the end of the month. This will tell how much you've consumed in each category. Then spend a few minutes looking at how much fat was eaten by you and your family from just these obvious sources. Visualize the tubs and bags and blocks of fat and think about where they are now!

Some of you may be pleased, but we predict that many will be horrified. For example, it is easy to think you are cutting down on cheese consumption, because you tend to forget how long it's been since you last bought some. Keeping a tally for a month may point out that you have been buying, and eating, more of it than you thought. We hope this simple exercise will help guide some of your food choices in the future.

Life in the fat lane

The following table will give you a rough idea of how much fat is contained in some high fat supermarket items.

Food	Calories	Grams of fat
Mayonnaise, 32 oz. jar	6400	710
Salad oil, 16 oz. bottle	3840	425
Butter, 1 pound	3520	390
Margarine, 1 pound	3260	360
Ice cream, ½ gallon	4230	280
Peanut butter, 16 oz. jar	3000	260
Potato chips, 16 oz. bag	2400	160
Cheddar cheese, 1 pound	1820	150
Mixed nuts, 8 oz. can	1400	128
Chocolate kisses, 14 oz. bag	2070	116
Whipping cream, ½ pint	830	90

Tub o' Lard Award

Fat can be found in the most unlikely places. A fresh apple is certainly not on your list of high fat items, but even such a healthy fruit can be destroyed by the inventiveness of cooks. **Chocolate-Caramel Apples** may be the most amazing thing to happen to fresh fruit that we've ever seen.

Remember caramel-coated apples? This recipe takes that idea to an absurd level by coating four wholesome apples with 12 ounces of chocolate chips, 14 ounces of caramels and 2 cups of chopped nuts.

Total per apple, an unbelievable **1330 calories and 74 grams of fat**.

An apple a day may keep the doctor away, but not when it's ruined like this!

The sliding scale

We assume that after adding up your month's fat consumption, you have resolved to cut down on fat! One of the best ways to get started is to find lower fat versions of the foods you already eat. To make this easier, visualize different groups of food placed on a sliding scale, from high fat at the top to low fat at the bottom. When you're about to choose something to eat (e.g. crackers, snacks, sweets, meats, cheese), think about all the choices you have. You don't always have to choose the lowest fat item at the bottom. Your goal is simply to slide down that fat scale as much as possible.

Choices in sweet treats show how to use a sliding scale. The morning coffee break at the cafeteria presents you with a typical range of choices. The sliding scale of fat ranges from Danish pastries (high) down through doughnuts, muffins and bagels. The further down you can go, the better off you are. Even if you break down and have a doughnut one day, you can comfort yourself with the thought that it's a better choice than the Danish pastry.

Milk choices give another illustration of how the sliding scale works. Milk products can be arranged on a scale from heavy cream at the top through light cream, whole milk, 2%, 1%, down to skim milk at the bottom. You know you should drink skim milk but you've tried and just don't like it? Maybe 1% will be where you end up; maybe 2% – both have less fat than whole milk, don't they? Although skim milk has less fat than 1%, 1% still has less fat than 2% and 2% has less fat than whole milk. Any change in the direction of less fat is worth applauding.

> For different people there are different choices. If everyone in your family is trying to change his or her milk-drinking habits, each may end up in a different spot on this sliding scale and that's fine.

One way to make the slide easier is to mix high and low fat ingredients until you find the one you're willing to stick with. For example, mix your regular, high fat mayonnaise with equal parts of a lower fat brand and try it. You don't like it? Then mix just one part low fat with three parts regular. You're already using the lower fat brand straight and like it? Then mix it with plain yogurt.

The point is to keep sliding down that fat scale as much as you can, always making the next change a gradual one. Once you start ranking your own food choices from high to low fat you'll quickly see that you do have options. If you try to make more of your choices from the lower end of the fat scale, you'll find that you will automatically cut down the fat you consume each month.

Does this week look familiar?

Early morning meeting (grab a donut), working late one evening (too tired to cook), out one evening for a class (no time to cook), lunch meeting (with hamburgers sent in), a friend's birthday lunch (uh oh, dessert) – and company's coming for dinner on Friday.

Fatigue, shortage of time, stress and special events can often threaten to overwhelm our good intentions about eating sensibly and watching our fat intake. How can anyone survive this week and eat well? The key is planning.

We all know we should plan ahead it but it's easy to forget as pressures mount. However, a short time spent thinking through your coming week's activities will save both fat and calories. Planning doesn't mean that you have to figure out every meal in exact detail, but it will give you the opportunity to balance high fat meals with lighter ones.

One day at a time

Too many people focus on the amount of fat in a particular food or meal, then eat it anyway and feel guilty. *"I really shouldn't have had...but I wanted it"* or *"I guess I can't ever have...again"* may sound familiar. Resolve to put such thoughts out of your head. The problem is that your fat focus is too narrow. Concentrating on the fat in every mouthful is not the way to change your fat habits.

Give your thinking a quarter-turn and look at the food you eat over a longer period of time. Learn to focus on at least a whole day's consumption (better yet, a whole week). If a high fat meal can be offset by one that's low in fat later that day, or even the next day, you know you are cutting down fat yet still enjoying favorite foods.

> We interpret the dietary goals of eating less than 30% fat to mean eating less than 30% over an extended time period, not worrying about whether each item in the meal has less than 30% fat in it. What's wrong with a low calorie dessert that is 50% fat if the rest of the meal is 15%?

What you want to achieve is an awareness of how much fat confronts you every day and then begin to strip it away here and there. By looking at everything you eat over a period of time, you'll find ways to lower your fat intake in general, rather than giving up some favorite foods completely. The fat total of most meals can be decreased with just some minor changes. These small changes will move you from a temporary, weight-loss mentality to a permanent shift in the way you eat.

Remember, if you "de-fat" one meal a day, you've made progress. The objective, after all, is to make a lifetime change instead of worrying about every bite that goes into your mouth.

Add and subtract

Learn to think before you eat. While many meals might be acceptable by themselves, too often the total day's intake is not: too many calories, too much fat, simply too much food. Look at these menus and note how quickly the calories and fat can add up. Replacing even one or two of the loaded meals with the leaner option makes quite a difference.

Breakfast: 1 cup of orange juice, one apple Danish pastry, a pat of butter, coffee with 2 tablespoons half and half (*"At least I'm getting lots of fruit in my diet"*). 430 calories, 18 grams of fat.

> Better: A whole orange (with half the calories and more fiber) plus a bowl of cereal with blueberries and lowfat milk gives you more food value at less fat cost. 210 calories, 4 grams of fat.

Morning snack: Bran muffin, pat of butter (*"Maybe that breakfast wasn't too smart, I'd better smarten up and get the muffin instead of the donut"*). 260 calories, 13 grams of fat.

> A toasted bagel spread with jelly is safer than a big bran muffin. Calories are less, fat is much less. 210 calories, 1 gram of fat.

Lunch: Bowl of chili, crackers, glass of whole milk (*"I usually get some fries, too, but I'll eat crackers instead today"*). 490 calories, 18 grams of fat.

> Bring your own lunch to work occasionally; make a filling tuna salad sandwich with water-packed tuna, light mayo, two slices of bread, and some cherry tomatoes on the side. Add a glass of lowfat milk and some gingersnaps. 485 calories, 12 grams of fat.

Mid-afternoon pickup: Chocolate bar (*"I need a little energy boost, probably because I passed up the cake at lunch"*). 250 calories, 14 grams of fat.

> Too many empty calories. If you must have chocolate, munch a couple of chocolate-coated graham crackers. For lasting energy, add a small apple. 205 calories, 6 grams of fat.

Dinner: Frozen Lasagna entree, buttermilk biscuit, tossed salad with Thousand Island dressing, dish of ice cream (*"Only a small dish of that fancy ice cream, dear, I'm kind of full"*). 1060 calories, 72 grams of fat.

> Both the lasagna and the ice cream contribute 25 grams of fat each. Substitute a lower fat but equally pleasing "winter warmie" such as *Italian Pasta Shells*. Add a whole wheat roll, pat of margarine, broccoli with lemon, then finish up with ½ cup of one of the new ice milks. You'll still be full. 690 calories, 21 grams of fat.

Evening snack: A few nuts and a soft drink (*"These dry roasted nuts aren't nearly so greasy as the other ones"*). 310 calories, 14 grams of fat.

> Both dry-roasted and regular nuts are loaded with fat. Try popcorn and a glass of sparkling water instead. 50 calories, no fat.

Grand total for the high fat day: **2800 calories, 149 grams of fat** (37 teaspoons). Grand total for the low fat day: **1850 calories, 44 grams of fat** (11 teaspoons). Still loads of food, but a third fewer calories and two-thirds less fat.

Long term lowfat living depends on balance, moderation and variety. We believe in gradual changes on the path toward a lowfat lifestyle.

Be a starch starter

One of the best ways to cut the fat is to be a "starch starter." Too often we decide what to make for dinner by looking in the refrigerator or freezer to see what meat or poultry is available. Instead, look on your shelves for rice, pasta, barley, beans, vegetables, and start your meal planning with one of these. Make the starch, not the protein, the main focus.

A dinner of steak plus a baked potato emphasizes the high fat meat. A baked potato topped with meat sauce puts the emphasis on the potato. Four ounces of potato has 100 calories and no fat, four ounces of steak can have over 350 calories and 20 grams of fat.

Some starch-starting suggestions:

Breakfast: Dry or cooked cereal; a piece of whole grain toast added to your usual coffee and grapefruit; a whole grain muffin instead of a sweet roll (one offers starch, the other sugar).

Lunch: Cup of minestrone, barley or other hearty soup; bean tortilla; vegetable-topped pizza; sandwich with two slices of whole grain bread, sprouts, lettuce and a small amount of protein-rich filling. A standard tuna sandwich may have as much as 24 grams of protein, or half your daily supply. Cut down on the tuna and fill up on that starch-rich bread.

Dinner: Brown rice topped with stir-fried vegetables and a small amount of meat; barley pilaf with mushrooms and green onions, plus cubes of cooked chicken; pasta primavera, with assorted fresh vegetables bought at the local supermarket salad bar; winter squash stuffed with bulgur and a bit of ground lamb; vegetable lasagna; baked beans or bean soup plus cornbread; main-dish salad with garbanzo beans, corn niblets, raw vegetables, grated cheese, diced eggs or egg whites, croutons.

Snacks: Popcorn; whole grain crackers; pretzels; dry cereal (don't laugh, it's great to dip into); raw vegetables.

Holiday survival

The month of December seems to be everyone's excuse for eating big meals, baking favorite sweets, cooking high fat treats and generally indulging at every opportunity. Magazines are filled with glistening photographs of gluttonous excess, described as "holiday dinners for your loved ones." At every turn we're tempted with food.

How many teaspoons of fat do you think you swallow in the month of December? A prudent eater probably consumes 425 teaspoons; it's easy for a less-than-cautious holiday celebrant to gobble up twice that much. What? Eat 850 teaspoons of fat? Thirty-five cubes of margarine? Nine pounds of butter? Or three large cans of shortening? It can happen to you!

It's not hard to believe if you look at a few numbers. Let's make two assumptions, both very possible. Your normal 2000 calorie days will increase to 2500 calorie days and at least 40% of those calories will come from fat. In 31 days you will have eaten about 78,000 calories, with 31,000 from fat. 31,000 fat calories equal 3,444 grams of fat equal approximately 850 teaspoons of fat.

Unfortunately, these fat-filled temptations of the holiday season will not vanish. If you decide to suffer through the month with eyes and mouth shut tight against all treats, you'll only make yourself and those around you miserable. An occasional splurge won't hurt. The problem starts when people decide that every day and every meal is an excuse to eat something special.

Don't worry, we're not going to suggest that you should pass up these festive attractions. We do recommend, however, that you anticipate them with some advance planning. Look at the month ahead and write a big "H" on the calendar for every day you have a "High-fat Holiday Happening." Then plan on being very careful how you eat before, during and after that day. Take a look at our examples on the next page.

Do you have an office lunch coming up at a fancy restaurant? Plan on bean soup for supper, not grilled cheese sandwiches. Going to a neighborhood cookie exchange? Munch on an apple for a snack that day instead of sampling your own baking. Invited to two holiday parties in one weekend? Start each day with cereal for breakfast, rather than bacon and eggs.

As a general rule for sensible eating every day, ask yourself if it's worth it before you put it in your mouth. We all look forward to special tastes during the holiday season. However, those once-a-year treats may be accompanied by a lot of stuff that, quite frankly, isn't so special. Indulge in your friend's famous shortbread, but pass up the store-bought cookies. Save your fat allowance for truly irresistible goodies.

Decide, right at the start, that you'll choose to eat the things that are important to you and cut down on fat and calories where it doesn't matter. Understand where the fat is, eat those tantalizing foods in moderation and balance the treats with healthful, low fat meals. You will both look and feel better after the party's over.

If you don't plan ahead, you're likely to roll through the holiday season like an out-of-control snowball tumbling down a hill. And you may end up looking like one when it's all over. Unfortunately, it will take much more than a sunny day to melt you back to normal!

A word of advice about dieting for the holidays: If you can't fit into your new party dress on December 1, it's probably too late. Trying to lose a fast ten pounds in the following two weeks is not smart eating and will likely be a short-lived success at best. However, the dress that fits that day will still fit on New Year's Eve if you eat wisely in between holiday treats.

Loving gifts

Contrary to popular opinion, the best gifts are not always those that are highest in calories. Food magazines would have us believe otherwise, that the way to show your friends how much you like and appreciate them is to give them a special gift from your kitchen, full of fat and calories. Many of us fall into this trap at the holiday season, even though we cook perfectly sensibly the rest of the time.

Why not show your friends and family how much they really mean to you by giving them "good-for-you" gifts? You can still give them special treats, but you'll have the pleasure of knowing you're adding to their lives rather than harming them.

Pass up the suggestions for making butter pecan chocolates, double chocolate squares, nut-covered cheese balls and peanut butter fudge. Is this a nice way to treat your friends? (Remember, beware of gifts bearing grease.) They will be just as pleased with gifts of cranberry conserve, pumpkin bread, flavored vinegars and fruit butter.

Holiday gifts don't have to be homemade treats. Unusual foods from the supermarket, cooking utensils, books and other items that focus on healthy living are excellent ideas. See some suggestions on the next page.

Gifts go both ways, of course, and you may not get the kinds of things you give. We don't expect you to throw out all the rich, sweet treats you receive. For many, they are a cherished part of the holiday season and a few won't hurt most of us. However, if you find yourself the recipient of several high fat gifts, which you know you'll eat over time, keep one or two and get the rest out of the house.

Gift suggestions

Mixture of dry beans in a pretty glass jar, plus a soup recipe to encourage some new cooking techniques.

Assortment of different pastas – various shapes, vegetable-flavored, whole wheat – in an attractive basket lined with a checked napkin.

Bag of mixed spices and cinnamon sticks for flavoring hot apple cider or tea.

Jar of popcorn plus an air-popper and a bottle of artificial butter sprinkles to use instead of melted fat.

Large nonstick skillet to help cut the fat in cooking – buy one for yourself, too, if you don't already have a good one.

New cookbook that is not a diet book but one that shows how to make delicious, healthful recipes.

One very good, very sharp, paring knife for trimming fat, new set of measuring spoons and cups for accurate measurement, kitchen scale, gravy skimmer, cheese slicer, mini food processor.

An "exercise-encourager" such as a stopwatch, headband, water bottle, fancy shoelaces, pedometer, thick socks, bright new tights, exercise class gift certificate. You get the idea!

Think about it – you will swallow four teaspoons of fat every time you drink half a cup of real eggnog made with heavy cream and eggs.

Gross out on grease

Presenting delicious, low fat food is the best way to get people to think that maybe, just maybe, they could enjoy this way of eating. However, be sure they realize what you're doing for them. While the person doing the cooking realizes how much fat can be eliminated, the eaters who see only the finished product may have no idea. It is no kindness to keep them in the dark.

Has anyone else seen the mound of skin you take off the chicken? If you remove the skin from several chicken breasts and thighs and pile it on a plate, that huge, sloppy white mass left for all to see becomes a very persuasive argument against eating it!

Trouble convincing someone to switch to lower-fat milk? Pour a glass of skim milk, float two pats of butter on top and give that glass to the person who insists on drinking whole milk. After all, that's what whole milk is – skim milk with two teaspoons of fat in it. This picture could save you at least a thousand words.

Drawbacks to a lowfat lifestyle!

The cheese keeps getting moldy
That cute bacon grease container never gets used
A pound of butter goes rancid before it's used up
People are always badgering you for your new recipes
Your favorite salad bowl cracks from lack of oil
You don't have enough empty margarine tubs for leftovers
You get tired of explaining that you're **not** on a diet
You have to buy new clothes, in smaller sizes
There are too many great, new foods to try out
All those old "magic-diet" books are getting dusty
You don't get invited out to dinner as much, because friends think you won't eat their high fat cooking

Choices: Every day

While there are no "no-no's" in a lowfat lifestyle, common sense suggests that some foods should be reserved just for an occasional splurge. The important thing to remember is that every time you decide to eat something, you have a choice.

Food	Calories	Grams of fat
Sandwich		
Grilled Cheese	430	27
French Dip	390	12
Soup, 1 cup		
New England Clam Chowder	160	7
Turkey vegetable	70	3
Deli		
Hot dog in bun	275	15
Smoked turkey breast, 2 oz.	60	1
Bakery		
Chocolate eclair	240	14
Cake donut	105	6
Brown bag dessert		
Snack Pie, 1	390	20
Canned pudding, ⅖ cup	110	3
Frozen dessert, ½ cup		
Gourmet ice cream	310	24
Frozen yogurt	130	4

Eating Out

Place your order, please

Eating out presents its own set of problems for the person trying to follow a lowfat lifestyle. Do you know how to eat well
when you eat out? At home it may be easy to decide that tuna
is a better choice than beef, or salad a better choice than
creamed soup, but in a restaurant that's not necessarily the
case. You must learn how to read the menus. Those flowery
descriptions can give you, the fat-finder, some important information if you take the time to read carefully.

Understand. You can pick your way through a potentially fat-
filled menu by knowing what the chef plans to do. For example,
fried foods can follow a sliding scale from amazingly high to
relatively low in fat. Everyone knows that "deep-fried" implies
a high fat content; in addition, you should be aware that the
kind of fat used may be highly saturated and definitely less than
ideal. However, "pan-fried" foods can be almost as high in fat,
while "sauteed" foods range from high to low fat depending on
the chef. "Stir-fried" meals often use little oil and are probably
your best bet.

What if it's out of the frying pan and over the fire? "Broiled"
food is usually reasonable, although most places will baste
with some fat. "Roasted," "steamed" or "poached" are good
starting points, but keep on reading to see if a sauce is put on
top. "Marinara" is a tomato-based sauce (and probably your
best choice), "Mornay" is a white sauce made with flour and
butter, "Au Gratin" implies a layer of cheese and often a cream
sauce. "Smothered" always sounds ominous!

Ask. The trend in many restaurants is for servers to tell you, often in excruciating detail, how a dish is prepared. Here's your chance to ask them to make minor modifications. If the fish is basted with nut butter, ask them to leave it off; if the salad is topped with their famous house dressing, ask for it on the side so you can dip into it instead of trying to eat around it. Restaurants want to please us and are receptive to making minor changes.

Trade. One of the tricks to good restaurant choices is balance. For every item in which you can't, or don't want to, avoid some fat, choose one where you can. If you want to order the chicken with cream sauce, choose rice instead of French fries to go with it. Either save some calories and fat for the special dessert or enjoy the nachos along with everyone else, but don't eat both. By thinking in terms of tradeoffs, you'll minimize the damage. There's always a choice of the lesser of two evils even if nothing seems particularly low in fat.

Appreciate. Eat slowly and stretch the meal out. Enjoy one plain roll or piece of French bread (easy on the spread); a good crusty roll eaten before the food arrives is an excellent way to begin satisfying your appetite with very little fat consumption. Order a bowl of clear or vegetable-based soup; by the time you get to the main course your stomach will know that it already has something in it.

Recommend. Whenever you find low fat items on the menu, keep a good thing going by telling the manager or chef how much you appreciate having healthful choices. Then tell your friends about this great place to eat.

Did you know that you can easily consume 250 calories and 13 grams of fat in a serving of fries? And 350 calories and 9 grams of fat in a large chocolate shake? That adds up to 600 calories and 22 grams of fat before you add the hamburger!

Menu magic

Every cuisine offers high and low fat choices, so no restaurant should be considered off-limits when it comes to dining out. For example, an Italian meal might be Seafood Lasagna or Pasta Primavera. The Primavera, with its fresh, lightly sauteed vegetables, would be a better choice than the lasagna; despite the low fat seafood, lasagna is usually smothered in cheese and ends up high in fat.

A French restaurant might offer Steak Bordelaise or Chicken Hollandaise. Bordelaise is a wine-based sauce, much lower in fat than the egg yolk and butter Hollandaise. In a Chinese restaurant you'd be better off with Beef Stir-Fry than with Sweet and Sour Spareribs. Despite the "fry" in the name, any added fat in the stir-fry is probably outweighed by the basic fat in the spareribs.

The way something is prepared is often more critical than its initial fat content. If you don't know how it's prepared, either ask or expect the worst.

Tub o' Lard Award

What could be a better choice than a huge bowl of chopped vegetables? Unfortunately, salads often bring you much more than you bargained for. Take a look at this **Chef's Salad** from a fancy restaurant.

> It starts with carrots, zucchini, celery, bell peppers, cabbage and lettuce; so far, so good. Plus more than 1½ pounds of ham and salami; hmmm. Then it is covered with a sauce made from 4 egg yolks, tuna in oil (with the oil added in), 1 cup of olive oil and ½ cup of sour cream; uh-oh. Served to six dieting patrons, those healthy vegetables have been changed into a salad containing **916 calories and 81 grams of fat** per serving.

Take it back to the kitchen, Chef!

Leave a little

How do you balance wise menu choices with the natural desire to treat yourself because it's a special occasion? If the night out at the fancy restaurant is an infrequent part of your life, don't worry too much; just plan ahead by eating lightly before and after the big meal. However, if eating out is a regular occurrence, you have to approach it differently. Over-indulging every day is not the best way to treat yourself.

Here's a tip that might help. When your meal arrives wait a minute before picking up your utensils and diving in. Look it all over and decide how much you're going to eat.

> Perhaps you often decide to eat only half the meat – but once you're into it, somehow it's hard to stop. This time, cut the meat in half right away and set one part of it to the side of the plate. When you have finished the first half you will have to make a conscious decision before you begin eating the rest.

Once you decide you have had enough, signal the waiter immediately to remove the food, even though there's still food on your plate and others are eating. Otherwise, we guarantee that you will just keep picking at it while you're talking, until suddenly it's all gone; what a pity to waste the calories and fat on food you didn't even notice. You don't have to eat everything just because you paid for it. Learn to leave a little.

Cut the fast fat

Most of us find ourselves in a fast food restaurant at least occasionally. They're quick, inexpensive, convenient and predictable. With the average family having less time but more money to spend, fast food restaurants are handy alternatives. We often feel vaguely guilty, however, knowing that these fast food meals are probably too high in calories and fat. Yet we don't want to give up the convenience. Can you keep the "fast" and cut the fat? Yes.

Not all fast food is fattening. For those who take the time to think about their selections, it is possible to make low fat choices in a high fat, fast food world. You just need to know how to make wise decisions and convince yourself that you are in control of your choices.

If you always choose "whoppers" and "doubles" and "fried," there's no question that you're getting a lot of fat. Watch out for the "house specials" and anything that sounds big: Super, Deluxe, Extra, Giant, Double (Triple!). You're guaranteed to get more of something – more cheese, more guacamole, extra bacon, twice as much meat – and that something is usually fat-filled.

Fat in fast food comes from the fat content of the original item plus the fat added in preparation. Compare roasted chicken breast with a piece of fried chicken and a chicken salad sandwich. When the original low fat chicken is roasted, you get 250 calories and less than 8 grams of fat. The fried version has 260 calories and 14 grams of fat, while the chicken salad sandwich can soar to 470 calories and 32 grams.

Baked potatoes appear to be healthy alternatives, but are they? A large, plain baked potato has about 215 calories and almost no fat; no problem. Topped with broccoli and cheese, however, it can become a big fat bomb with over 500 calories and 25 grams of fat – and that's not from the broccoli!

Do you think you can cut the fat by avoiding the hamburgers and eating fish instead? Not necessarily. A seafood platter can top 800 calories and 40 grams of fat. Even a simple fish sandwich generally starts out with fried fish, which is then topped with a fat-filled sauce to give you 400 to 500 calories and 25 grams of fat. Compare these numbers with a regular hamburger at about 350 calories and 16 grams of fat.

You must recognize the sources of fat. Just because a fast food item starts out low in fat doesn't mean it is still that way when the restaurant is finished with it. Look the menu over carefully and think about what will contribute most to your health. Remember the tradeoff principle: If you must have a triple burger, at least leave off the cheese; if you want cheese, don't pick the biggest hamburger. You can enjoy fast food without excess fat if you're willing to spend just a little time making smart decisions before you order.

Fast fat

Every restaurant has higher and lower fat choices. Here are a few typical selections to show you what you might end up eating. Your goal when you eat fast is to eat smart.

Food	Calories	Grams of fat
Double hamburger	560	30
Single hamburger	350	16
Chicken thigh, extra crispy	370	26
Chicken breast, regular batter	260	14
Pepperoni pizza, 2 slices	540	22
Cheese pizza, 2 slices	400	17
Beef burrito	400	17
Beef taco	185	11

Breakfast on the road

When you travel you leave behind your familiar, low fat kitchen and plunge into a fat-filled world. Breakfasts in particular are difficult for people who are faced with eating out several days a week. A few suggestions:

Order a la carte – if the bacon isn't on your plate you won't eat it.

Order carbohydrates – English muffins, toast and bagels are all basically low in fat, as long as you ask for them unbuttered. Spread them with jam instead. You can have two teaspoons of jam for every teaspoon of butter you avoid.

Order the best piece of fruit available – the melon in season, the bowl of berries, the pineapple wedge, etc. These will be much more satisfying than a glass of juice and you may be more content to follow them with a simple bowl of cereal.

While many people treat restaurant meals as opportunities to eat what they don't get at home, too often they seem to choose foods that would taste much better at home. A classic example is bacon and eggs. In a restaurant the bacon is likely to be cold and the fried eggs are seldom right. If you want to indulge in this treat, at least do it at home so the bacon is sizzling and the eggs are cooked the way you like them.

An increasing number of restaurants offer low calorie/low fat choices. Look for symbols on selected menu items which suggest that they follow nationally recognized dietary guidelines.

Think about it – a scrambled egg and sausage platter at a fast food restaurant can reach 700 calories and 50 grams of fat, with the rest of the day still to come. Even a simple egg breakfast sandwich can contain 350 calories and 16 grams of fat.

Grease 'n go

Lunch may be the most troublesome meal of the day if you are trying to reduce fat consumption. Every day you have to balance calories, money and time. A leisurely meal at a fine restaurant offers low fat choices but costs too much and takes too much time; a quick meal at a local cafe saves money and time, but not fat.

However, a poor lunch may cost you more than you think. Your lunch choice affects your productivity and energy level as well as your health. For a meal of such significance, too many give it very little consideration. It's so easy to say, *"I'll just have a...,"* giving your decision no thought beyond the quick physical and psychological satisfaction.

Your body deserves better treatment and your day's activities require it. If you expect quality output, in terms of accomplishment, you must provide quality input in the form of good nutrition. That means giving your body high quality fuel, not high fat. You're careful to put the right gas and oil into your car for maximum performance; give more attention to how you fuel your body and save the grease for the car!

Salad bar smarts

The all-American favorite salad bars fool many people. We start out by piling our plates high with low fat vegetables. Then we come to the salad dressings, where our smart choices suddenly become totally neutralized.

> The dressing is served with a ladle, described in the dictionary as a "long-handled utensil with a cup-like bowl." No wonder you can't get by with just a small spoonful on top of your gigantic plate of salad.

Be aware that every tablespoon adds 6 to 9 grams of fat. With a couple of scoops of the ladle you can easily add over 20 grams of fat to what started out as just some vegetables.

Lunch options

Select soups. Many soups are excellent choices. Watch out for the words "Cream of..." and choose "Hearty..." instead; the latter probably refers to a thick bean or vegetable soup, a much better choice. In addition to eating less fat, you will also get a good helping of fiber and complex carbohydrates.

Sample sandwiches. Their descriptions are often very informative, so read the ingredient list carefully. Avoid processed meats (e.g. pastrami, salami) and salad fillings which may have lots of mayonnaise such as chicken or tuna. Choose plain chicken or turkey, roast beef, etc., and ask the chef to go easy on the mayo.

Be adventurous when you look at the menu. Don't automatically choose the day's special or your usual clubhouse sandwich. You can open up your options and cut your fat with a little creative thinking. Why not select an appetizer, such as steamed clams or grilled shrimp, and a spinach salad? Or a small order of pasta with marinara sauce and a basket of French bread? Expand your thinking and your alternatives.

Quick lunch

Get your fast food lunch at a supermarket rather than a restaurant. You can be in and out in minutes with small, zip-top cans of water-packed canned tuna, whole grain crackers wrapped in individual packets, slices of processed low fat cheese, low fat lunch meats, fresh fruit, single serving cans of applesauce or juice-packed canned fruit, small cans or cartons of juice, small cans of baked beans.

Deli decisions

Many of us buy lunch items in a delicatessen where the dazzling selection makes us wonder if perhaps "deli" is short for "delicious." In the typical mouth-watering display, everything looks tempting. But when our fat-consciousness has been raised, we have to wonder if everything is also off limits. Not really, as long as you take time to look carefully at the choices before you order.

Meat and poultry selections have a fat content ranging from low to very high. Turkey, ham and roast beef are fine; salami, bologna and pastrami will all be loaded with fat. (Have you ever really looked at a piece of salami? What do you think all those white flecks are – decoration?!)

The cheese selection requires advance knowledge or the ability to read the label through the glass. Look for the words "part-skim" on the label. It won't always be a guarantee of less fat, that depends on whether they added back some cream, but it's your best hope.

Deep fried foods, such as chicken, onion rings, potatoes and corn dogs, have two strikes against them: extra fat and unknown fat, perhaps lard, beef tallow or palm oil.

Prepared salads in numerous forms are a big part of deli counters. If the dressing is an oil and vinegar marinade, as in mixed bean salad or marinated mushrooms, at least you can drain some of it off. Avoid potato and pasta salads that are glued together with mayonnaise; you can't eat the food without eating the fat.

If you buy a sandwich every day at a deli, consider this: If you threw out the little bag of accompanying chips four times a week you could save 2400 calories in a month. If you asked them to hold the mayo just twice a week you could save 1600 calories in a month. Little changes do add up.

Traveling snacks

The long drive presents its own set of problems, from quick stops at unknown restaurants to just plain boredom. We avoid both by carrying our own food with us. For ready-made meals the first day or two, we take some home prepared food, such as oven baked chicken or low fat sandwiches.

Fresh fruits and vegetables top the list of fast snacks, but there are other ideas. Some of our favorite on-the-road snacks: small cans of fruit and vegetable juices, cartons of milk, plastic containers of cold cereal to be eaten as finger food, zip-top containers of applesauce, reduced fat cheese wedges, packages of sliced turkey lunch meats, individual cans of water-packed tuna, low fat crackers, homemade bran muffins, bagels, rice cakes, small boxes of raisins, gingersnaps.

Note that these foods can be replenished along the way, so they're ideal for long trips. Don't forget water; we fill small, screw-cap soda bottles with fresh water daily and keep them chilled. A good drink of cold water is often hard to find.

Tuck in small pots of mustard and light mayonnaise and keep all food properly chilled in a small cooler. A picnic basket stocked with paper plates, utensils and lots of napkins allows you to stop at an attractive picnic spot and have a great meal ready to go.

Travel doesn't have to mean bad eating habits. The key to sensible, low fat eating on the road is to be prepared. You'll enjoy your trip more and return home feeling good about yourself.

Choices: Soups and sandwiches

Since each restaurant creates these menu items according to
its own recipes, it is impossible to state exactly what is in them.
However, there are some generally accepted ingredients. For
example, a Patty Melt with beef and cheese is almost certainly
going to be a high fat choice. Note that the "worst" soups are
lower in calories and fat than almost any sandwich.

Food	Calories	Grams of fat
Sandwiches		
Patty Melt	640	42
Reuben	530	30
Grilled cheese	430	27
Hot roast beef and gravy	430	25
Clubhouse	590	21
Ham salad	320	17
Ham and cheese	370	16
Bacon, lettuce and tomato	280	16
Chicken and tomato	300	14
Tuna salad	280	14
French dip	390	12
Corned beef on rye	300	11
Soups		
Cheese	230	15
Cream of mushroom	200	12
Bean with ham	230	9
Chili beef	170	7
New England clam chowder	160	7
Split pea	190	4
Minestrone	130	3
Manhattan clam chowder	130	3
Turkey vegetable	70	3
Chicken noodle	70	3
Black bean	120	2

Shop Smart

Labels don't lie, but...

Supermarkets are filled with thousands of items, many of them tempting, lots of them fattening and all of them vying for your food dollar. While many companies produce nutritious foods, concerned consumers must be wary of what they're buying. Package labels promise sizzling plumpness, juicy goodness and delicious taste, but what do they really tell you? Often less than you need to know and sometimes more than you may want to know. Test your knowledge before you read further.

1. Compared with regular olive oil, "lite" olive oil has less fat and fewer calories. True or false?

2. The claim of "100% natural" means nothing has been added. True or false?

3. The label says one serving has 4 grams of fat. Is this a low fat food?

4. If the cheese is labeled as "imitation" it is not as good for us as the original. True or false?

5. Does a product labeled "sugar-free" have fewer calories?

6. Any kind of "oil" in the ingredient list makes that product a better choice than one listing "lard." True or false?

7. The new brand of cheese labeled "reduced fat" has to be substantially lower in fat than regular cheese. True or false?

Answers to quiz

1. False. In olive oil, "lite" refers only to lighter color and milder flavor – and a higher price. Calories, fat and cholesterol remain the same: per serving, 120 calories, 13½ grams of fat, no cholesterol.

2. True only when applied to meat and poultry products, where "natural" means that the food is minimally processed and that it contains no artificial flavors, colors or preservatives. Otherwise, the word "natural" is not regulated.

3. Not if the serving size is 1 ounce and you usually eat 3. This is a clever way of making fat content appear low.

4. False. If a standardized food is modified so that it no longer complies with the standard it must be labeled as "imitation." This doesn't mean that it isn't a good product – a lower fat imitation cheese product may be just what you want. This is a case where the manufacturer and the consumer may be hurt by the label.

5. Not necessarily. A sugar-free candy may contain sorbitol, a sweetener with the same calorie content as sugar.

6. False; it depends on the oil. Coconut oil is 87% saturated, lard is 41%. Much better than either of these are canola oil at 6%, or safflower, sunflower, corn, olive and soybean oils, ranging from 10% to 15% saturated.

7. False. "Reduced fat" or "lower fat" or "low fat" are words that can mean anything the manufacturer wants. However, if a food label suggests that calories have been cut, it has to back up that claim with numbers, so the small print will help.

It's difficult to think that manufacturers have our best interests at heart when their labels can be so misleading. When does hiding the truth become a profit-making lie?

What's in a label?

For most foods, the **ingredients** must be listed on the label and must be identified by their common or usual name. What's common to the manufacturers, however, may not be recognized by the consumer! Ingredients must be listed in order of concentration, from most to least, but there's no way to tell how much of each there is. Some products, such as mayonnaise and catsup, are made according to government-set standards of identity; the ingredients are mandatory, so don't have to be listed.

US government regulations require that **nutrition information** must be included for food to which a nutrient has been added or for which a nutritional claim is made. Nutrition labeling includes serving size, servings per container, calories per serving, protein, carbohydrate and fat (in grams), sodium (in milligrams), plus Recommended Daily Allowances (US RDAs) in percentages for protein, five vitamins (A, C, thiamine, riboflavin and niacin), and two minerals (calcium and iron).

Producers may also list information about cholesterol, saturated fat and polyunsaturated fat, but most do not. Even if these are listed, monounsaturated fat is not, so it must be calculated. They don't make it easy.

Descriptive information is where the fables really begin. You think "light" always means fewer calories? You think "natural" always means nothing has been added? You think "no cholesterol" means it's a great food for your heart-healthy body? Think again. Many of these words and phrases are not yet regulated by any government agency, meaning the manufacturers can say what they want, hoping you will not notice the misrepresentation.

We're not saying that the large print found on labels is untrue, only that it is not adequate. To get a good mark in "Advanced Label Reading," you must take the time to go beyond a brief look at the basic words and read the entire label.

At first glance many of the words in ingredient lists appear to be foreign. Let's do some translation.

Additives: *Butylated hydroxyanisole (BHA), disodium inosinate, sodium erythorbate, benzoyl peroxide, calcium propionate, guar gum* – amazing names for some of the hundreds of potential additives. Some are preservatives and stabilizers, others are coloring agents and flavor enhancers. Some may be of questionable value, some are necessary for the storage that consumers demand. Books have been written just on this subject.

Fat: *Vegetable oils, partially hydrogenated oils, lard, shortening* are fats in different forms. See the next page for a more detailed discussion of fat labeling.

Salt: *Sodium, soda, Na, monosodium glutamate* are words to look for if you're salt-conscious. "No salt added" doesn't necessarily mean no sodium has been added.

Sugar: *Sucrose, dextrose, glucose, lactose, fructose, maltose, syrup, honey, molasses* are all forms of sugar. *Sorbitol* or *mannitol* are sweeteners that appear in some "sugar-free" foods; while not sugar, they still contribute calories.

Vitamins: *Retinol (A), pyridoxine (B), ascorbic acid (C), alpha tocopherol (E)* – some of the longest and most puzzling names may actually be vitamins, so don't make snap judgments about a product just because there are a lot of strange-sounding ingredients listed on the label.

A frozen ice-cream dessert labeled "Sugar-Free" doesn't necessarily mean it is low in calories or fat. We saw one with 140 calories and 12 grams of fat. Makes you wonder what the extra-rich bars add up to, doesn't it?

Fat and fiction

Where fat is concerned, ingredient listings can be extremely confusing, if not downright misleading. Look at some of these common phrases and what they don't tell us.

"No cholesterol" – doesn't tell you anything about fat content.

"100% vegetable oil" – what kind? Some are better than others; it could be highly saturated palm or coconut oils, not an improvement over animal fat.

"Hydrogenated" – tells us that an unsaturated fat has become saturated.

"Partially hydrogenated" – even less useful; how much has been hydrogenated?

"May contain any of the following oils or shortening..." – the most frustrating statement of all to those who want to or must avoid certain fats; many will pass up the product altogether rather than take a chance.

Product example: The label on the front of the shortening can says "No cholesterol" and "Contains the finest all-vegetable shortening." The back label says it is "made from the finest vegetable oils (soybean and palm) which are partially hydrogenated for freshness and consistency." The front label is correct, but the back label tells you more, doesn't it? You can learn a lot from product labels, as long as you read the small print!

> *Quick question: Is a product with safflower oil lower in fat than one with butter? No – fat is fat is fat. If you're also looking at cholesterol content or degree of saturation then of course you will make a distinction. But remember that using oil instead of butter does not make a product lower in fat.*

Descriptive definitions

Shelves bulge with products to help fight your bulge. There are diet versions of traditional favorites such as pancake mixes, syrups, puddings, cheese, mayonnaise, lunch meats, ice cream, etc. Be sure that you understand clearly what the labels tell you. The Food and Drug Administration (FDA) looks after us to some extent and its rules do affect products that claim to be low or reduced in calories:

"Low calorie" – each serving must have no more than 40 calories and 0.4 calories per gram,

"Reduced calorie" – food must be at least one-third lower than a similar food in which calories are not reduced, and must not be nutritionally inferior.

To see how these rules work in real life, take an example of diet blue cheese dressing. One tablespoon, a serving, of diet blue cheese dressing has 40 calories. This works out to 2.5 calories per gram, too many to be called "low calorie." However, the dressing could be called "reduced calorie" since it has at least one-third fewer calories than regular blue cheese dressing at 75 calories. Note that "reduced" or not, it still has 40 calories per tablespoon.

Labels of foods that are naturally low in calories, such as mushrooms, are not permitted to use the term "low calorie" right before the name of the product. "Low calorie mushrooms" would suggest that they are lower in calories than other mushrooms. They can, however, be labeled "mushrooms, a low calorie food."

Watch the stated serving size. If it's not what your family normally eats, you could be fooling yourself about how many calories you're consuming. Obviously, the food will appear to be low in calories and fat if the serving size is unusually small.

Many other terms, such as "lean, extra-lean, lower fat," imply fewer calories, but be careful. The only place that these terms have any regulated meaning is on meat and poultry, where the FDA has specific requirements:

> **"Extra-lean"** – no more than 5% fat; amount of fat must be indicated on the label,

> **"Lean"** or **"Lowfat"** – less than 10% fat; amount of fat must be indicated on the label,

> **"Light," "Lite," "Leaner," "Lower fat"** - 25% less fat than similar products on the market.

Be aware that these percentages refer to percent fat by weight, not by calories. Read the small print to find out how many grams of fat are in each serving.

In foods other than meat and poultry, these same words can mean just about anything. The words "light" or "lite" may just refer to the color of the product. Many products, of course, are truly "light," such as light mayonnaise (diluted with water), light margarine (same thing), light cream cheese (diluted with skim milk and cottage cheese). Nutrition labeling on packages of light or lowfat dairy products such as milk, yogurt, cottage cheese and sour cream shows that these are all genuinely lower in calories and fat.

"Reduced fat" is not a regulated term, but a subjective one that is often misinterpreted by the customer. Cheese is a product where this is often found. Brand X makes a claim of "reduced fat" prominently on the front of the label. However, in the small print, you find that 1 ounce contains 8 grams of fat where its original counterpart contained 9 grams. Well, it is reduced, but saving one gram seems hardly worth bragging about to us. This "saving" usually costs more, too.

Conclusion: Keep reading.

Smart shopping

Every time we choose a product, we make a decision that affects our health, our pocketbooks and the profit of the manufacturer. While many companies make excellent products, others aren't so responsive to consumer demands. Take the time to make smart choices and support the companies that manufacture better products, such as:

The cracker company that uses very few ingredients (e.g. only whole rye, corn bran and salt), instead of making crackers with lard, sugar, salt, etc.,

The cookie bakers that have replaced highly saturated fats with healthier oils,

The pasta producer whose label provides a sodium-free, herb-seasoned pasta salad recipe which uses yogurt instead of mayonnaise,

The muffin mix maker whose directions suggest using egg whites instead of whole eggs.

Conversely, why give your support to products like these?

The canned cake frosting made with "vegetable and/or animal shortening (one or more of partially hydrogenated soybean oil, cottonseed oil, beef tallow and/or palm oil)." You won't need birthday candles – just light the cake!

The "No Cholesterol" popcorn which uses coconut oil and the "Real Buttered" popcorn that lists butter fat plus coconut oil,

The non-dairy creamer which is promoted as a healthful alternative to cream but contains highly saturated coconut, palm or palm kernel oil.

Comparison shopping

From Webster's Dictionary: *"Tallow – the solid fat taken from the natural fat of cattle, used to make candles, soaps, etc."* One of the "etc." Webster doesn't mention is tallow's use as a fat in processed foods! No secret, tallow is a listed ingredient (in small print, mind you) and many of us have eaten a lot more beef tallow than we might like to think. That's why it is so important to take the time to read labels thoroughly.

We suggest making a goal of reading at least five new labels every time you shop. Start with your favorite foods, the ones you buy every week, and for each favorite brand you pick up, read the label of a competing brand to see if there is any difference. Test your skills by reading the front of the label first and making a quick judgment as to whether you think it's a healthful product. Then read the back. If you're not used to reading labels, practice on the foods you have at home first. We guarantee that you'll find it a fascinating, occasionally pleasing, sometimes horrifying, exercise.

Tub o' Lard Award

Some of the worst examples of high fat recipes come from product manufacturers. In an attempt to get us to buy more of their product, they combine it in some truly outrageous combinations, such as this **Ft. Knox Pie.**

After starting with a fine product, the gelatin, the recipe quickly deteriorates with the addition of 2 cups of whipping cream, a bag of chocolate chips, a cup of caramels, eggs and butter. That's just the filling.

The chocolate mixture is then poured into a crust made of chocolate wafer cookies, pecans and butter. We estimated that this concoction has about **750 calories and 55 grams of fat** per serving.

This Ft. Knox treasure is best left unclaimed!

Stock up and save (fat)

Fact: You will eat what you have on hand. If the only crackers around are a high fat variety made with coconut oil, that's what you'll eat when you want a cracker. Make your life easier and healthier by surrounding yourself with low fat items. Below are the basics of our low fat kitchen.

Chicken breasts, skinned and frozen
Water-packed tuna
Lean ham or turkey ham
Flank steak, frozen flat for quick thawing, thin slicing
Canned or dried beans – pinto, kidney, white, pink
Dried split peas and lentils
Eggs, primarily for the whites
Brown rice, potatoes, onions
Scandinavian flat crackers

Plain lowfat yogurt – for cooking, even if you don't like it by itself
Buttermilk – same comment as above
1% cottage cheese – to blend, as well as eat
Part skim Mozzarella cheese
Parmesan cheese – a little goes a long way

Lemons and limes
Dijon mustard
Worcestershire sauce – low salt, high flavor
White, wine and malt vinegars
Extra-virgin olive oil – stronger flavor so you can use less
Salsa, fresh or bottled
Chicken broth – preferably homemade
Cornstarch – for thick sauces without added fat

When you stock a low fat larder, you can fill it with low cost as well as low fat staples; dried beans and peas, rice, lentils, barley, canned water-packed tuna, chicken, seasonal fruits and vegetables are not expensive. Incidentally, a low fat **lard**er is the only positive use of the word "lard" that we can think of!

Super shopper tips

There's no doubt that the concerned consumer has to be edu-
cated, well organized and full of resolve to concentrate on
foods for a healthy lifestyle. While we advocate a policy of no
"no-no's," with this freedom to eat anything comes the responsibility of knowing where the fat is so you can make wise
choices.

Keep close to the original food. Buy plain frozen green beans
to serve with lemon juice instead of beans frozen in butter or
cream sauce; buy dried fruit for your brown bag lunch instead
of something labeled "fruit snack" with its added sugar and
missing vitamins.

Look for the leanest variation of a particular food. Buy lean
sandwich meats, e.g. turkey breast instead of salami; choose
lowfat milk to drink with it.

Compare label ingredients and choose the brand with the least
damage. Because you know you should eat more fish doesn't
mean you should reach for any brand of frozen fried cod.
We've found brands ranging from 13 to 29 grams of fat in a 4-
ounce serving.

For all types of food there are more acceptable choices: frozen
yogurt instead of ice cream, top sirloin steak instead of prime
rib, water-packed tuna instead of oil-packed, fresh baked potato instead of frozen deep-fried.

Smart shoppers make lists. They keep you from buying things
you shouldn't and help you buy the things you should.

One of the oldest and truest statements is still, *"Don't shop
when you're hungry."* This is more critical than ever with the
rise of the super-stores with all their ready-to-go foods that
smell and look so enticing (see next page).

Choices: Temptations

It used to be safe to say that if you stayed on the outside aisles of the supermarket you could avoid most high fat foods. Now these aisles are filled with enticing attractions. Deli counters are piled high with fried chicken, fat-filled salads and fancy sandwiches and the fresh bakery section offers tantalizing pastries, cookies and muffins. Take a look at some in-store fat packages waiting for you.

Food	Calories	Grams of fat
Bakery		
Butterhorn	330	18
Super-muffin	370	16
Big cookie	340	16
Chocolate eclair	240	14
Carrot cake	260	11
Apple pie	250	11
Cake doughnut	105	6
Deli		
Pastrami-cheese sandwich	560	40
Fried chicken, 1 piece	370	20
Corn dog	330	20
Hot dog in bun	275	15
Egg salad sandwich	280	13
Potato salad, ½ cup	180	12
Coleslaw, ½ cup	115	8
Snacks		
Peanuts, 1 oz. bag	170	14
Ice cream bar	160	11
Pepperoni stick, 1 oz.	125	11
Chips, 1 oz. bag	150	9

Cook Smart

Back to basics

In the fight against excess fat, how you cook is as important as what you cook. Unfortunately, with busy days it is sometimes difficult to cook at all, never mind properly. It's a rare family where the refrain of *"Hurry, let's eat"* isn't heard at least a few times every week. With both energy and enthusiasm in short supply, it's too easy to fall back on quick deli pickups, fast food meals and frozen dinners.

The problem with buying prepared meals is that much of the fat is hidden, so you don't know what you're eating. When you buy these foods, you hand over your fat fate to others. In contrast, every time you cook something yourself, you retain control of your fat intake.

Sounds good, but how do you find the time to cook? Even one who knows better finds it too easy at the end of an exhausting day to say, *"Let's just have a grilled cheese sandwich."* For busy days you need ready-to-go meals that almost cook themselves. Our answer is to plan ahead and practice fast scratch cooking. We apply the term "fast scratch" to a meal that takes just minutes to prepare or to one that can be made ahead of time so it's fast to finish.

Shelf-ready meals come from the cupboard, refrigerator or freezer, almost ready to go. Keep some low fat convenience foods on hand, such as marinara sauce, beans, tuna, etc. By combining them with a few ingredients you'll be able to come up with something more than just a meal from a can.

Make-ahead meals are those you work on when you have time and energy. A big pot of soup made on a quiet day ensures that you'll eat well on a busy day. Double the recipe and freeze extras for the future. Some meals can be partially prepared ahead of time, leaving only reheating; we indicate these in our recipe instructions.

We can't emphasize enough that planning is the key. Make a list of your most commonly used, nutritious foods and be sure that you always have them on hand. That way, when you're hungry and harassed, you'll at least have some choices. See *Stock up and save (fat)* in the previous chapter.

> There is nothing quite so supportive of a lowfat lifestyle as having the chicken already skinned, or the casserole already made. Trying to be a sensible lowfat cook when you're tired just doesn't work.

The benefits of scratch cooking are many: satisfaction – providing well-balanced, healthy food, safety – avoiding unknown handling and dubious preparation techniques and simplicity – making a great meal with just a few ingredients. Most important, cooking from scratch allows you to control what goes into your mouth. Busy lives, hungry families and good nutrition can co-exist happily if you get in the habit of planning ahead.

Think of teaspoons, not tablespoons, of fat for browning food, use lowfat dairy products wherever possible, substitute egg whites for whole eggs, part-skim Mozzarella cheese for higher fat Swiss or Cheddar.

Making change

People tend to cook the same few familiar recipes over and over, never questioning how they're doing it, where they could make changes or whether there is a new and better way to prepare the same food. With old favorites, you rarely analyze how you cook it, because it's always been done that way.

Is your roast turkey always basted with butter just because that's how your mother did it? No, switching to margarine isn't enough improvement.

Do you always brown your meat in $1/4$ cup of fat? You might have had some excuse before nonstick pans appeared, but not anymore.

Do you always dip your chicken pieces into melted butter before coating with crumbs? The coating will stick just as well to milk. Of course, you remove the skin first in any case – don't you?

You don't need to change every ingredient and you certainly don't have to give up most of your favorite meals. If you understand how to make small changes you'll be delighted at how these slight modifications can save a lot of unnecessary fat. It may take a little more of your limited free time, but it can have a big effect on your fat intake. It's worth it.

Obviously, you need to experiment with some changes. Make small modifications and keep your substitutions close to the original taste. We saw one list that suggested substituting grapefruit segments for avocado in a salad. Sorry, folks, when the recipe, and your mouth, calls for creamy avocado, grapefruit will not be satisfactory. The goal is to maintain the basic flavor as much as possible while saving your fat for times when it is absolutely required.

Start by asking several questions about each recipe. Is the high fat ingredient essential to the taste of the dish, or are you just accustomed to using it? Do any of the ingredients have a lower fat version? Will the recipe turn out all right if you reduce the amount of the high fat ingredient? Is it impossible to cut the fat? We see several ways to make changes.

Eliminate higher fat ingredients altogether. Ask yourself if the ingredient is essential or just extra fat. Is it really necessary to put butter pecan frosting on the cake? Sprinkle the cake with powdered sugar instead and you may find it is just as tasty.

Substitute lower fat ingredients for similar high fat ingredients. Replacing regular sour cream with light sour cream will save calories and fat and will make no difference in a casserole.

Reduce the amount of higher fat ingredients if no substitutes are available. In a recipe where both the taste and look of Cheddar cheese are critical, keep it in, but switch to sharp instead of mild and use half as much.

Recognize total fat content and simply eat less of the food. If you're not willing or able to eliminate, substitute or reduce, the only choice left is to cut the serving size or the number of times you eat that meal. If top sirloin will never replace a New York cut in your estimation, enjoy a smaller New York steak occasionally and don't worry about it.

While it is easy to read that you should modify your favorite recipes to cut the fat, it may be difficult for some cooks to translate that advice into revised recipes. On the next page are a few ideas to show you how we do it. We've chosen party foods as examples, since many cooks prefer to stick with their old favorites rather than risk any changes. Remember that our goal is to end up with a taste and texture that is similar to the original.

Examples of recipe modifications

Cheese ball: Original was made with mild cheddar cheese, cream cheese and blue cheese, all rolled in pecans. Per tablespoon, 65 calories, 6 grams of fat.

Now made with half the cheddar (sharp, instead of mild) and light cream cheese, but the same blue cheese (no good low fat substitute for that flavor). Rolled in chopped parsley instead of pecans, a tablespoon now has 30 calories, 3 grams of fat. We substituted and reduced.

Molded salad: Original had shrimp, avocado, black olives, celery and green onion in a tomato base made creamy with mayonnaise. Per serving, 160 calories, 16 grams of fat.

Revised version still has celery and green onion, but more shrimp, less avocado and just a few chopped black olives. We tried it with and without light mayonnaise; both were excellent. Per serving without mayo, 60 calories, 2 grams of fat. We eliminated and reduced.

Turkey stuffing: Our old favorite had both sausage and butter, lots of each. Per half cup, 250 calories, 15 grams of fat.

First we cut both sausage and butter in half, later we eliminated the sausage altogether, cut the butter again and replaced it with margarine. Made up the loss of "juice" (i.e. melted fat) with chicken broth, made up for some loss of richness by adding chopped, cooked chestnuts (no fat). Now, per half cup, 100 calories, 3 grams of fat. We eliminated, reduced and substituted.

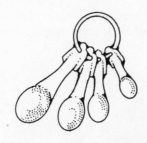

Sneak it to 'em

The person who cooks is usually the one who decides how and what the whole family is going to eat. Choices made in the supermarket and cooking techniques used in the kitchen control the final result. But just because you are prepared to make big changes doesn't mean that other family members will agree.

A better way is to make minor, sometimes even hidden, changes instead of obvious ones. Remember that the important thing is to avoid feelings of deprivation. If the food still tastes and looks the same, or if the substitution is equally delicious, your family won't care a bit that the fat content has been lowered. Become a little sneaky, in a good cause.

Obvious: Replace the usual cheese and cracker snack with raw vegetables, period. **Not obvious:** Replace the high fat cheese with a low fat cream cheese and keep the favorite crackers.

Obvious: Remove the skin from the chicken breast, poach the chicken and serve it on a white plate, announcing firmly, *"We don't eat chicken with skin anymore."* **Not obvious:** Remove the skin and brown the chicken breast or oven-fry it with a seasoned flour coating. Forget the announcement!

Obvious: Put a pot of yogurt on the table for topping baked potatoes. **Not obvious:** Combine half sour cream and half yogurt in a serving bowl and don't say anything.

Obvious: Cancel the bubbling fried mushrooms for the steak and instead steam them in water and serve limp. **Not obvious:** Brown the mushrooms in a nonstick pan, then add a small amount of oil so they sizzle and really look, and taste, fried.

Obvious: Serve apple slices for dessert instead of their favorite apple pie. **Not obvious:** Make a deep-dish apple pie, with top crust only.

Kitchen necessities

To get by with a minimum of fat in cooking and eating, we suggest adding the following to your shopping list:

Good nonstick pans – these are a must for a lowfat lifestyle. If you can buy only one, get a large skillet with a lid. You can fry, simmer, cook a meal for one or four in it, all with a minimum of added fat. Don't be too cheap; this one pan will save you so much fat that it's worth its weight in gold. New nonstick coatings are much better than the old ones. Silverstone Supra* is my favorite and I recommend it highly.

Very sharp knives – for trimming the fat right to the edge of the meat, skinning the chicken, dicing, slicing and chopping. As with the nonstick pans, your best bet is to buy a good set.

Small kitchen scale – despite all the cooking I do, I still rely on the scale to be sure of how much we're eating. The eye is unreliable when the tummy is growling. Conversely, it gives you a great feeling when the family pronounces itself satisfied with supper and you know that you got away with just a few ounces of meat per person.

Cheese slicer and grater – if you're a fan of cheese and crackers, you'll be pleasantly surprised at what a cheese slicer can do for you when an ounce of cheese turns into 10 slices. To make your cheese go even further in cooking, grate it. A small amount of cheese seems like more in a casserole or grilled cheese sandwich when it's grated instead of sliced or diced.

Hot air popcorn popper – saves time and fat. By avoiding extra fat when you pop the corn, you can reward yourself by melting a bit of margarine to toss over the finished product, where you will appreciate it more.

*Silverstone and Supra are registered trademarks of DuPont.

Treat them right

Do your good, low fat intentions go out the window when guests are coming over? If you've been changing your eating habits in private, go public and show off your new cooking skills. Too many people think cutting down on fat means giving up all the things they like, so this is the perfect opportunity to prove that the lowfat lifestyle is worth living.

> You can serve your friends chips and a dip, but instead of potato chips and a sour cream dip, give them tortilla chips and salsa. For every ounce of tortilla chips and $\frac{1}{4}$ cup of salsa, your friends will eat 7 grams of fat, instead of 19, and save 12 grams, or 3 teaspoons.

> Don't revert to your famous fat-filled creamed chicken, complete with skin, just because you think they'll want to eat "real" chicken. Go ahead and prepare your best new, sauciest, low fat, skinless chicken recipe. Then wait for the rave reviews.

> You don't want to serve overnight guests a bowl of bran cereal for breakfast, but a fancy meal of sausage and eggs could put over 30 grams of fat in front of each person. That isn't friendly. A basket of hot homemade muffins, good jam and fresh fruit would surely be more appreciated.

The quickest way for your friends to learn how tasty this low fat food can be is to eat it. One tip: Serve it without comment. If you say, apologetically, *"Try this, it's a low fat recipe,"* some people immediately become critical experts and assure you that they can tell the difference.

The best compliment I can receive after serving a low fat meal is, *"This was delicious – I'm sure glad you didn't give us any of that low fat stuff tonight."* Make this kind of compliment your goal. Your first response should be to thank them but your second should be, *"Guess what?"*

The festive dinner

You can eat a real turkey dinner during the holiday season, complete with all the trimmings, if you just think it through before you start. The goal is to blend traditional family expectations with an en**light**ened approach. Read your own recipes before you do your shopping and see where you can cut fat down, not out.

Does the dip have to be made with regular mayo and sour cream? Low fat mayo and yogurt won't even be noticed if the dip has other strong flavors.

Do you have to use 2 tablespoons of oil to brown the onions for your special casserole? They'll brown just as well in 2 teaspoons if you have a nonstick pan.

Does the stuffing recipe really need all that butter? Replace at least half the butter with chicken broth; the stuffing will still be moist and have a rich flavor.

Do you have to put in all the nuts the dessert recipe calls for? Cutting the amount in half won't hurt it and every half cup not added saves about 30 teaspoons of fat.

Analyze the fat content of your favorite holiday recipes and watch out for the automatic fat trap. Just because you've always made it with lots of fat doesn't mean it needs it. We recognize that traditions are important and familiar tastes define much of the holiday season. All we ask is that you try to make at least a few changes in how you prepare your traditional meals. Check your own recipes before you start cooking and make smart choices where you can.

Tub o' Lard Award

Here's a Santa-sized tip of the tub for all the magazines that print those amazing menus for holiday dinners. Glorious pictures make the food look so tempting that you can hardly wait to eat it. However, a look at the recipes shows that most of them are loaded with fat; no wonder the photographs look so shiny! The following example of a **Fat-Filled Feast** tells the tale.

The main event is turkey, not just roasted but heavily basted with butter; with it is rich gravy, of course, and a sausage-filled stuffing. A serving of this turkey plus only half a cup of stuffing gives you 910 calories and 49 grams of fat.

Then you add one serving each of the accompaniments, most of them laden with fat: vegetable tart, mashed potatoes with butter and cream, bacon and bean salad and a biscuit (only one). Another 970 calories and 60 grams of fat.

Total for one serving of everything: **1880 calories and 109 grams of fat**. No seconds. If you are still tempted, close your eyes to these glistening pictures and visualize, instead, a plate containing a cube of butter topped with a tablespoon of oil.

This meal is a fat attack waiting to happen. And it doesn't even include dessert (such as coconut custard pie, nesselrode pie or praline pumpkin pie, with calories ranging from 400 to 500 per serving, fat from 24 to 33 grams). Season's Greasings!

Read all recipes through carefully. Scan the ingredient list for high fat alarm signals such as oil, butter, margarine, cheese, cream, etc. Stop and analyze before you start cooking. Cut the fat where you can, reject the recipe if you can't.

A note about yogurt

I like to cook with plain yogurt because of its creamy texture and minimal fat content. Our recipes generally call for lowfat yogurt because it is easier to find than nonfat, however the latter can certainly be substituted for a fat saving of 3 to 5 grams per cup.

Brands vary in taste and texture and some are much better than others. Have a "taste-off" and try several at one time. If your preferred one has a thin consistency, add a teaspoon of cornstarch to each cup of yogurt that you plan to heat.

If you're new to yogurt, mix it with sour cream or light sour cream initially. As you get used to that mixture, try more yogurt and less sour cream until you find the lowest fat combination you're willing to use.

Cooking spray

Using margarine, butter or oil to keep food from sticking in the pan is a fast way to add a lot of calories. Many recipes start with the instructions to add 2 to 4 tablespoons to the pan before you do anything else and too many people do this out of habit. The use of a nonstick vegetable cooking spray will help you cut this unnecessary fat. In our recipes, we coat the pan with a quick spritz of cooking spray if the food to be cooked is very low in fat, then sometimes add a teaspoon of oil for flavor and "sizzle." (Mushrooms just don't sound exciting frying in cooking spray.)

The primary ingredient in nonstick vegetable cooking sprays is fat, but one quick spray, about 1½ seconds, gives you only 7 calories and less than 1 gram of fat. Note that we said "quick" – don't keep spraying until you have a thick white coating over the pan. Read the instructions and be sure not to spray it on heated surfaces or near an open flame.

Choices: Substitutions

In many recipes a lower fat substitute can be made without changing the texture or taste of the final product. While you may not enjoy drinking skim milk, you won't notice its use in a muffin recipe. Plain lowfat yogurt on your baked potato may be hard to take, but it can be used in a sauce that will pass inspection. Note how much fat you can save in cooking and baking by simply choosing a lower fat ingredient.

Ingredient	Calories	Grams of Fat
Fats, oils and spreads, 1 tbsp.		
Vegetable oil	120	14
Butter	110	12
Regular margarine	100	11
Mayonnaise	100	11
Diet margarine	50	6
Light mayonnaise	50	5
Vegetable oil spray, 1½ seconds	7	1
Artificial butter buds, 1 tsp.	6	0
Cream and milk products, ¼ cup		
Imitation sour cream	120	11
Regular sour cream	105	10
Light sour cream	80	7
Lowfat yogurt	35	1
Nonfat yogurt	30	0
Eggs and egg substitutes		
Whole large egg	80	6
Scramblers, ¼ cup	60	2
2 large egg whites	30	0
Egg Beaters, ¼ cup	25	0

Munchies

How did this get on my plate?

Delicious treats that most of us love, appetizers seem to leap off trays right into our mouths. Since these tiny morsels are often a major source of calories and fat, controlling the appetizer assault requires some planning.

A loaded party table can be a dazzling sight and most people eagerly line up, plate in hand, and start cruising along, picking up one, at least, of everything. We suggest a different approach. Before you join the line, walk casually around the whole table, staying two feet away. Look at all the different dishes and decide, in advance, what you're going to sample.

If the stuffed mushrooms look great, go ahead; but why add olives to your plate? You know what they taste like. A crab dip may be worth sampling, but a basic onion and sour cream mix is not. Most of the cheese balls in the world taste the same, and chips and nuts you can have any day. By passing up the ordinary foods that you're familiar with, you'll have fat and calories to spare for something really special.

After you've looked at everything, make your choices, limiting yourself to two or three items. If you ignore the plates and use your cocktail napkin instead, you'll find there's an automatic limit to the number of goodies you can carry on it! Then leave the table; don't stand beside it so that your hand can sneak back while you're talking. If you want more, make a conscious decision to go back. When you do, try only one new item on each repeat visit.

Alternate a high fat treat with carrot or celery sticks to spread out the time between "fat gulps." Notice we said "alternate" – low fat eaters aren't limited only to carrot sticks! Convince yourself that you are capable of making smart choices, then go ahead and enjoy the party.

If you're entertaining at home, avoid the temptation to make your all-time-favorite, high fat appetizer that "everyone loves." This is your chance to present a great little treat that tastes rich and fattening, but isn't. Don't say anything about it being low in fat, just accept compliments graciously.

Party pointers

Before you start grazing indiscriminately at the party table, check this list:

If the food is glistening, beware! Sardines, smoked clams, marinated mushrooms and olives all have something in common – a shiny glow of excess oil.

Fancy cheese spreads often contain a lot of cream cheese, sometimes even butter. You're better off with a slice of cheese so you know exactly what you're eating.

Cocktail meatballs will probably be all right, unless they're made of sausage. If you're lucky, they will have been broiled, so excess fat has dripped out.

Your best bet may be a sandwich from the deli tray. With good bread, low fat meat and mustard instead of mayonnaise, you can have a real treat. Select turkey, lean roast beef or boiled ham slices instead of fat-flecked salami.

If nibbling nuts is an important part of the holidays, at least buy them in the shell. It takes much longer to eat 12 almonds when you have to crack each one open. Keep those fingers busy shelling instead of putting more food in your mouth!

Garden Shrimp Dip

Your guests won't believe that this dip is made with yogurt instead of cream cheese. Mix it at least 8 hours before serving so the dried vegetables have ample time to burst with flavor.

makes about 2½ cups   per ¼ cup: 60 calories, 1 gram fat

1 envelope dried vegetable soup mix (about 1 oz.)	1 cup cooked tiny shrimp (about ⅓ pound)
2 cups plain lowfat yogurt	¼ cup chopped chives

Combine vegetable soup mix and yogurt, cover and refrigerate for 6 to 8 hours. Stir in shrimp and chives, cover and chill another 2 hours.

Deviled Clam Dip

This fat-trimmed variation of an old favorite shows that dips don't have to be made with sour cream and mayonnaise. Good with raw vegetables or thin Scandinavian crackers, this one should be prepared ahead of time for maximum flavor.

makes 1¾ cups   per ¼ cup: 100 calories, 4 grams fat

1 cup 1% cottage cheese	1 teaspoon Worcestershire sauce
½ cup light cream cheese	
2 cans (6½ oz. each) minced clams, drained	¼ teaspoon garlic powder
	¼ teaspoon dried dill
1 tablespoon lemon juice	¼ teaspoon salt or to taste

Place cottage cheese in strainer, rinse with water and press firmly against strainer until curds are fairly dry. Place in blender or food processor with cream cheese and blend at high speed until smooth. Scrape into bowl, stir in all other ingredients and refrigerate at least 1 hour.

Citrus Fruit Dip

This refreshing dip makes a pleasant contrast to the usual rich,
salty appetizers. Also great as a dessert sauce.

makes 1 cup dip   per ¼ cup: 70 calories, 1 gram fat

1 cup plain lowfat yogurt
2 tablespoons honey
1-2 teaspoons grated orange
peel (depends on how
tangy you like things)

fresh fruit segments such
as pineapple spears, apple
slices, tangerine wedges,
banana slices, melon cubes

Stir together yogurt, honey and orange peel. Place in a small
bowl and surround with fresh fruit speared with toothpicks.

Smoky Tuna Spread

The creamy texture of this spread will make your guests think
they're getting a real treat; only you know the fat is low. Make it
at least 2 hours before the party (or even the day before).

makes about 2 cups   per ¼ cup: 80 calories, 3 grams fat

1 cup 1% cottage cheese
½ cup light cream cheese
1 can (6½ oz.) water-
packed tuna, drained

1 tablespoon lemon juice
1 teaspoon liquid smoke
½ teaspoon onion powder
½ teaspoon salt

Place cottage cheese in strainer, rinse with water and press
firmly against strainer until curds are fairly dry. Place in
blender or food processor with cream cheese and blend at high
speed until smooth. Add all other ingredients and blend until
smooth. Chill for at least 2 hours or overnight.

Note: Use canned salmon for a delicious alternative.

The party bowl

Most families have a favorite dip that appears at every party. Is yours made with sour cream and/or mayonnaise? By substituting lowfat yogurt for the sour cream and light mayonnaise for the regular brand, you'll cut the calories by more than half. Many dips have strong flavors, such as onion, curry or blue cheese, so it won't make a difference in taste.

Choosing light cream cheese is another easy way to save fat and calories. Per tablespoon, regular cream cheese has 5 grams of fat, 50 calories; Neuchatel brick cream cheese, 3.5 grams of fat, 40 calories; light, soft cream cheese, 2.5 grams of fat, 30 calories.

> Tip: Put your new low fat treat on the table without any comment. Telling your teenager that it is low in fat, then asking for an opinion, is likely to bring you the answer you deserve!

Planning to surround your low fat dip with the usual potato chips? Maybe you'll think again when you realize that every time you eat five or six chips it's like swallowing a teaspoon of oil. Try some of our "little dippers" instead:

> Large cooked shrimp, cubes of ham or turkey, rye bread rounds, baked potato wedges, toasted bagel chips, snow peas, green pepper strips, small bread sticks, cooked artichoke leaves, sliced large mushrooms, toasted pita wedges, sliced broccoli stalks, jicama cubes or slices, oven-baked tortilla triangles, cooked potato slices, home-baked corn chips.

> *You'll eat one teaspoon of fat every time you eat: two walnuts or ten peanuts; 1 tablespoon of sunflower seeds or 200 pretzel sticks; 1/2 ounce of Cheddar or 1 ounce of part-skim Mozzarella cheese; one slice of salami or three slices of turkey ham; one piece of buttered French bread or four pieces of unbuttered bread. Conclusion: You can eat more if the fat is less!*

Salmon Mousse

This attractive molded salmon spread adds a colorful touch to your party table. What a pleasant way to get your omega-3s!

makes 12 appetizer servings   each: 40 calories, 1 gram fat

1 envelope plain gelatin
¼ cup water
1 tablespoon lemon juice
1 can (7½ oz.) pink salmon
½ cup peeled, chopped cucumber, seeds removed

½ cup plain lowfat yogurt
½ cup 1% cottage cheese
½ teaspoon dried dill weed
½ teaspoon salt
1 small bunch parsley

Soften gelatin in water. Add lemon juice and heat over low heat until gelatin is dissolved. Cool. Drain salmon well and remove all skin. (Leave the bones for added calcium.)

In blender or food processor combine cooled gelatin mixture, salmon, cucumber, yogurt, cottage cheese, dill and salt. Blend until smooth.

Coat a shallow, 1½-cup mold with cooking spray (a wide soup bowl works well). Pour in salmon mixture and refrigerate until set, 1 to 2 hours. Unmold onto a serving plate and surround base with chopped parsley. Serve with crackers.

DILL

Cheery Cherry Tomatoes

Make these attractive little morsels in minutes.

makes 36   each: 10 calories, almost no fat

2 boxes cherry tomatoes (about 36)	1 small carrot, shredded (about ¼ cup)
¼ pound cooked turkey	3 tablespoons plain lowfat yogurt
2 green onions, finely chopped (about ¼ cup)	dried dill weed and salt

Slice tops off tomatoes; slice a thin sliver off the bottom so tomatoes will sit upright. Hollow out pulp with a small spoon and turn upside down to drain. Dice turkey, mix with green onions, carrot and yogurt. Sprinkle with dill, add salt to taste. Stuff tomatoes and chill until ready to serve.

Quick Treats

Here are some speedy suggestions for last-minute nibbles.

Ham 'n Dills: Spread thin slices of turkey ham with light cream cheese and wrap around thin spears of dill pickle. Roll up, secure with toothpick.

Cocktail Reubens: Trim off crusts and cut slices of dark rye bread into quarters. Spread each with mustard, top with a square piece of turkey pastrami, a teaspoon of well-drained sauerkraut and a teaspoon of shredded part-skim Mozzarella. Broil until cheese is melted and serve at once.

Sardine Squares: Drain a can of sardines, blotting dry. Mix a teaspoon of horseradish into ¼ cup light cream cheese; spread on 6 slices of dark pumpernickel bread. Cut each slice into quarters, top with a small piece of sardine and place a thin slice of red onion diagonally across the top.

Tuna Tomato Bites: Prepare your favorite tuna salad (with light mayo, of course) and stuff it into hollowed out cherry tomatoes. Top with a sprig of parsley for color contrast.

Bacon-Mushroom Bits

We're not against using any food product, in moderation. Bacon is a case in point; a few slices of well-cooked bacon, divided among 32 mushrooms, is not going to hurt. We guarantee these will be a big hit. Easy on the cook, too, since they can be prepared ahead of time except for last-minute broiling.

makes 32   each: 15 calories, 1 gram fat

　3　slices bacon
32　small mushrooms, about
　　　1-inch diameter
½　cup finely chopped onion

1　tablespoon Worcestershire
　　sauce
½　cup grated Parmesan cheese

Trim excess fat from ends of bacon. (You can get rid of at least 2 inches of solid fat from most pieces.) Dice bacon into small pieces and cook until crisp. Remove bacon and all but 1 teaspoon of fat. Blot fat from bacon. Meanwhile, wash and dry mushrooms. Remove stems and set aside caps. Chop stems finely and add to bacon fat, along with chopped onions. Cook until soft. Remove from heat, add cooked bacon, Worcestershire and Parmesan cheese. Mix well.

Stuff mushroom caps with bacon mixture and refrigerate, covered, until ready to serve. Just before serving, preheat broiler and place caps on broiler sheet. Broil until stuffing is bubbly and mushrooms appear hot, 2 to 3 minutes. Watch carefully as these have a tendency to burn while you're off enjoying the party (voice of experience).

Note: Original recipe had more bacon, much more bacon fat, and chopped black olives instead of chopped mushroom stems. They were slippery little morsels!

Ginger Wings

Finger-lickin' good, these are perfect appetizers for a bunch of hungry skeptics who think you need fat to make food taste good. Can be partially prepared ahead of time.

makes 24   each: 25 calories, 1 gram fat

12 chicken wings	**¼ cup apricot jam**
¼ teaspoon powdered ginger	**2 tablespoons soy sauce**
1 cup orange juice	

Preheat oven to 375 degrees. Cut each wing into two pieces. Remove as much skin as possible (see Note below). Coat a 7x11-inch baking dish with cooking spray. Place wings in a single layer and sprinkle with ginger. Combine orange juice, jam and soy sauce. Pour two-thirds of this sauce evenly over the wings.

Bake 20 minutes, turn wings over and bake another 20 minutes. Remove from oven and turn on broiler. Pour over the rest of the sauce and broil 5 to 10 minutes until wings are dark brown and glazed. Serve warm or cold.

Make-ahead instructions: Bake the wings for 40 minutes, as described. Then remove from oven, cool and keep refrigerated until ready to cook. Preheat oven to 375 degrees and bake them for 10 minutes; then add the remaining sauce and broil as described above.

Note: See *"Poultry"* section for tips on how to remove skin. However you do it, get that skin off, then you can enjoy as many of these as you want. Obviously chicken wings vary in size, so nutritional information can only be approximate, but fat and calories have to be low once the skin is gone.

Sea Shells

The original recipe was a Tub o' Lard special, calling for a cup of butter, a butter-based white sauce and lots of Cheddar cheese. The low fat modification will still get rave reviews. Must be made ahead and frozen (cook from the frozen state).

makes 44   each: 55 calories, 2 grams fat

1 22-oz. loaf thin-sliced white bread
3 tablespoons margarine
1 tablespoon margarine
2 tablespoons flour
1 cup 1% milk
1/4 cup grated Cheddar cheese (1 oz.)
1/4 cup shredded part-skim Mozzarella (1 oz.)

1 tablespoon minced green onion
1 tablespoon lemon juice
1/2 teaspoon Worcestershire sauce
1/2 teaspoon Dijon mustard
1/2 teaspoon salt
1/8 teaspoon Tabasco sauce
1/4 pound flaked crab, (about 1/2 cup, packed)

Preheat oven to 450 degrees. Coat mini muffin cups (1¾-inch diameter) lightly with cooking spray. Flatten bread slightly with rolling pin and with a 2-inch round cookie cutter cut out 2 circles of bread from each slice. Melt 3 tablespoons margarine in small pan and remove from heat. Brush one side of bread lightly with margarine and press, brushed side down, into muffin cups. Bake for barely 5 minutes (watch carefully so edges don't burn). Remove from muffin pans immediately and cool. Shells should be golden brown and crisp when cool.

To make filling, melt remaining tablespoon of margarine, stir in flour and cook 1 minute, stirring constantly. Add milk gradually, 1/4 cup at a time, stirring with wire whisk until smooth before adding more milk. Boil gently until sauce is thick. Add cheeses and stir until melted. Remove from heat. Add all other ingredients. Fill shells with filling. Freeze immediately on flat baking sheet. When frozen, store in freezer bags until needed.

To serve, preheat oven to 400 degrees. Bake **frozen** shells for 10 minutes. Serve hot.

Tub o' Lard Award

This award goes to a suggested **Cocktail Party** menu featured in a holiday magazine. It is a classic example of how not to treat your friends. The problem with this selection is that everything is high in fat; there's no balance. Just picture your friends wandering along this table, happily grazing on the following fat:

Smoked Salmon Torte, made with cream cheese and butter, 8 grams of fat per tablespoon,

Phyllo pastry cups brushed with butter (lots) and filled with cheese and whipping cream, 8 grams in one,

Seafood dip made with cream cheese, olives, oil-packed sardines and oil-packed tuna, 4 grams per tablespoon,

Shrimp and mushroom roll, with the filling held together by cream cheese and sour cream, 13 grams of fat in two 1x3-inch slices,

Stuffed mushrooms, brushed with butter and stuffed with cheese and ham, 9 grams of fat in one,

More stuffed phyllo, this time stuffed with red and green peppers...and ricotta and Parmesan and Mozzarella cheese, 8 grams in 1 small triangle.

Just one of each of these adds up to **650 calories and 50 grams of fat**! That's close to a day's supply for most of us – and who eats just one? To make all these recipes, designed for sixteen people (who were expected to eat more than one of each) required 6 pounds of cheese, 1¾ pounds of butter, 1 cup of heavy cream, ¾ pound of high fat meat and several eggs. Welcome, dear friends!

Curried Turkey Spread

Combine turkey, water chestnuts and chutney for an easy, make-ahead appetizer to serve with crackers.

makes about 1 cup   per ¼ cup: 100 calories, 2 grams fat

1 cup chopped cooked turkey
¼ cup chopped, drained water chestnuts
¼ cup mango chutney
½ teaspoon hot curry powder
½ teaspoon salt
2 teaspoons lemon juice
2 tablespoons light cream cheese

After measuring turkey, blend in food processor until coarsely ground, so it starts to stick together when pressed. Add water chestnuts and chutney and blend for two or three short bursts. The final mixture should have some crunch to it, from the water chestnuts. (If you don't have a food processor, mince turkey finely and dice water chestnuts.) Blend in curry powder, salt, lemon juice and cream cheese. Cover and chill until ready to use.

Herbed Deviled Eggs

A traditional egg treat with less total fat than expected.

makes 12 halves   per half: 30 calories, 1½ grams fat

6 hard cooked eggs
3 tablespoons dry 1% cottage cheese*
2 tablespoons plain lowfat yogurt
1 tablespoon finely chopped onion
1 teaspoon Dijon mustard
½ teaspoon dried parsley
¼ teaspoon dried dill weed
⅛ teaspoon garlic powder
dash hot pepper sauce
salt and pepper to taste

*Buy dry curd cottage cheese or use regular 1% cottage cheese and rinse it in a strainer, pressing out excess moisture.

Cut eggs in half. Save all whites. Discard half the yolks, put the other half in a small bowl. Mash yolks together with cottage cheese and yogurt. Stir in remaining ingredients and stuff egg whites. Chill before serving.

Smoked Turkey Pinwheels

Bright colors make these an attractive party addition; you can prepare them early in the day.

makes about 50   each: 10 calories, ½ gram fat

½ cup light cream cheese
2 tablespoons chopped
   pimento
2 tablespoons chopped
   green onion

½ pound smoked turkey,
   sliced thin (about 8
   slices, 3x5 inches each)

Combine cream cheese, pimento and green onion. Spread 1 tablespoon of cheese mixture on each turkey slice, spreading right to the edges. Roll up turkey, starting at the narrow end. Place seam down on a flat plate, cover with plastic wrap and refrigerate for at least an hour. Slice each roll into ½-inch pinwheels. Place cut side down on serving tray.

Super Sippers

Flavored sparkling waters: In various fruit flavors, these make great thirst-quenchers, either alone or in combination with other liquids. Just be sure that they don't have added sugar or sodium.

Citrus sparkler: Fill a tall glass with crushed ice. Fill half full with unsweetened grapefruit juice, then add orange-flavored sparkling water and stir gently to mix.

Simple spa cooler: Cut wedges of lemon and lime and keep refrigerated in a glass bowl. Fill a glass with ice, add cold water, a sprinkle of sugar substitute, if desired, and a couple of citrus wedges. This refreshing drink somehow seems a much better treat than just a glass of water.

Sangria: Combine 2 parts of red wine with 1 part of orange juice. Add half an orange, thinly sliced, and refrigerate mixture for two hours. Fill a tall glass with ice cubes, pour two thirds full with sangria and top up with salt-free seltzer.

Choices: Party snacks

Even though you know that many foods contain fat, you may not realize just how easy it is to let excess fat slip down your throat. We're not saying that anything on this list is off limits; just be aware of how quickly fat can add up.

Treat	Calories	Grams of fat
Eat		
Liverwurst, 1 oz.	90	8
Cocktail sausage, 1	45	4
Sardine, 1	50	3
Smoked salmon, 1 oz.	50	3
Large shrimp, boiled, 2	15	0
Dip, ¼ cup	80-160	8-16
Tiny cheese crackers, 25	140	6
Cream cheese, 1 tablespoon	50	5
Wheat crackers, 3-4	70	4
Potato chips, 5-6	60	4
Black olives, 2 large	20	2
Pretzels, 1 oz.	110	1
Cocktail rye, 2 slices	50	1
Drink		
Eggnog, homemade, ½ cup	330	16
Champagne, ½ cup	85	0
White wine, ½ cup	80	0
And be merry.....		
Walnuts, 8-10 halves	100	10
Peanuts, 15-20	90	7
Cashews, 6-8	85	7
Chocolate-nut fudge, 1 oz.	120	5
Peanut brittle, 1 oz.	120	4
Pistachio nuts, 15	50	4

Soups

The perfect meal

We love soups! They're ideal for the fat-conscious fan and for the busy cook. Ranging from delicate broths to thick mixtures, they come in enough varieties for everyone to have a favorite. Thin soups make an excellent appetite suppressant before a meal, thick soups often are a meal in themselves. Remember that "hearty" doesn't have to mean "high fat." A steaming bowl of chowder or lentil soup can offer nourishment and satisfaction without excess calories and fat.

While many soups can be ready to eat in a short time, others need long slow cooking for maximum flavor. However, even with these, initial preparation time is usually quite short; after that, it just takes time on the stove, with an occasional stir. You'll end up with a lot of food for very little effort.

In addition to being low in fat, the ingredients for many soups are usually very inexpensive. For example, two pounds of dried split peas will cook up into approximately 12 cups. By the time you mix them with vegetables and liquid, you can feed a great number of hungry people for very little money.

All our soup recipes make at least four cups, because we haven't found a soup yet that isn't good reheated. They can be stored overnight in the refrigerator or frozen for longer storage. A pot of ready-to-eat soup is a life saver at the end of a tiring day. An added benefit of making soup ahead is that any excess fat is easily removed.

Cajun-Hot Tomato Soup

Sip a mug of spicy, super-easy soup half an hour before dinner to take the edge off your appetite. Only minutes to make.

---

makes 4 cups   per cup: 70 calories, 2 grams fat

1¼ cups chopped onion
  1 clove garlic, minced
  1 teaspoon olive oil
  1 can (14½ oz.) whole
    tomatoes, undrained

2 cups regular strength
  chicken broth
1 teaspoon hot chili powder
⅛ teaspoon cumin
  salt to taste

Cook onion and garlic in olive oil until lightly browned, about 5 minutes. Place in blender or food processor with tomatoes and blend until smooth. Pour into saucepan, add chicken broth, chili powder and cumin. Bring to a boil, reduce heat, cover and simmer for 10 minutes. Add salt to taste.

Spring Green Soup

Frozen small green peas make a very quick and tasty soup and the bright color is particularly appealing in mid-winter.

---

makes 4 cups   per cup: 150 calories, 1½ grams fat

4 cups regular strength
  chicken broth
½ cup chopped green onion

2 cups peeled, diced potato
  (2 medium)
2 cups frozen small peas

Combine broth, onion and potato in saucepan; bring to a boil, reduce heat, cover and simmer until potatoes are tender, about 15 minutes. Add peas and simmer 5 minutes more. Cool to room temperature. **Caution**: Mixture must be cool to avoid dangerous spatters when blending. Blend in food processor or blender and return to saucepan. Reheat gently.

Note: Soup is also excellent chilled, served with a tablespoon of plain lowfat yogurt on top.

Clam and Corn Chowder

Open a few cans and in half an hour you'll have a great meal.

makes about 6 cups   per cup: 110 calories, 1½ grams fat

2 **cups regular strength**
  chicken broth
1 **cup chopped onion**
½ **cup chopped celery**
1 **cup peeled, cubed potato**
  (1 medium)
¼ **teaspoon dried dill weed**

¼ **teaspoon dried thyme**
1 **can (16 oz.) creamed corn**
1 **cup 1% milk**
1 **can (6½ oz.) chopped**
  clams, plus juice
  salt to taste

In a large saucepan bring chicken broth to a boil. Add onion, celery, potato, dill and thyme. Reduce heat, cover and simmer about 15 minutes or until potatoes are barely tender.

Stir in creamed corn and simmer 5 minutes, then add milk and undrained clams. Simmer until heated through, about 5 minutes. Adjust salt, if necessary (depends on saltiness of broth and clams, so taste before adding anything). Serve hot.

We prefer to use homemade broth whenever possible but recognize that not everyone has that on hand. Therefore, our recipes have been tested with canned regular strength chicken or beef broth. Canned broths vary in saltiness, so leave final salt adjustment until the end of cooking.

Dead Head Soup

This cold soup makes use of those leftover lettuce leaves cooks often find in the bottom of the crisper. No one will know they were "over the hill"! Make ahead and serve cold.

makes 4 cups   per cup: 55 calories, 1½ grams fat

3 cups regular strength
 chicken broth
4 cups chopped lettuce

¼ cup finely diced onion
1 cup buttermilk
 salt to taste

Bring broth to a boil, add lettuce and onion, reduce heat and simmer for 5 minutes. Remove from heat and cool to room temperature. **Caution:** Mixture must be cool to avoid dangerous spatters when blending. Blend in food processor or blender. Add buttermilk and salt to taste. Chill.

Chilled Carrot Soup

This thick, colorful orange soup will delight the eye and the palate. Made ahead and chilled, it's a perfect "summer sipper."

makes 5 cups   per cup: 150 calories, 2 grams fat

4 large carrots, chopped
 (about 2 cups)
2 cups peeled, diced potato
 (2 medium)
1 cup chopped onion

¼ teaspoon hot curry powder
2½ cups regular strength
 chicken broth
2 cups buttermilk
 salt to taste

In a large saucepan, combine carrots, potato, onion, curry powder and broth. Bring to a boil, reduce heat, cover and simmer for 20 to 25 minutes, until vegetables are soft. Remove from heat and cool to room temperature. **Caution:** Mixture must be cool to avoid dangerous spatters when blending. Blend in food processor or blender. Add buttermilk and salt to taste. Chill before serving.

Note: If you absolutely refuse to try buttermilk in anything, you can substitute lowfat milk; the soup is excellent even without any milk at all.

Basic broth

Having a good supply of homemade chicken, turkey and beef broth on hand saves time, money and fat. The basic cooking principal is similar for all three, although beef broth will be richer in flavor if the bones are browned first. See "bare bones" instructions below or consult any general cookbook for specifics.

Easy Poultry Broth: Long, slow cooking is the secret. Cover bones and scraps of chicken or turkey with water. Add chopped vegetables for flavor – an onion, a couple of carrots, four stalks of celery plus tops, a bit of fresh parsley; toss in a bay leaf and sprinkle in a pinch of thyme. Simmer mixture at least three hours. Season to taste with salt and pepper.

After cooking, strain broth through colander to discard bones and vegetables. Refrigerate broth until thoroughly chilled and remove fat that rises to top. Freeze in small containers.

Momma's Turkey Soup

In winter, leftover holiday turkey comes along just in time for the sniffle season. Make a pot of turkey broth from the carcass, then put together this simple but satisfying "cold comforter."

makes 4 cups	per cup: 185 calories, 2 grams fat
4 cups turkey broth	½ cup thinly sliced green
1 stalk celery, sliced	onion (include tops)
1 carrot, sliced	2 cups cooked turkey, cut in
2 cups peeled, cubed	bite-sized pieces
potato (2 medium)	¼ teaspoon dried thyme

In a medium saucepan, combine broth, celery, carrot and potatoes. Bring to a boil, reduce heat, cover and simmer for 10 minutes.

Add green onion, turkey and thyme. Simmer 10 to 15 minutes more or until potatoes are fork-tender. Adjust seasoning.

Minestrone

On a cold night, what would be better to come home to than a pot of steaming minestrone soup? Best prepared ahead, it improves by being left in the refrigerator for a day before eating.

makes 8 cups   per cup: 260 calories, 5 grams fat

½ pound extra lean ground
  beef or ground turkey
1 small onion, chopped
½ cup chopped celery
1 can (15 oz.) white beans,
  drained and rinsed
¼ teaspoon garlic powder
½ teaspoon dried basil
2 tablespoons tomato paste

1 can (14½ oz.) stewed
  tomatoes
1½ cups regular strength
  beef broth
1 small zucchini, unpeeled,
  cut in 1-inch pieces
1 cup chopped cabbage
½ cup macaroni, uncooked
  salt and pepper to taste

Brown meat in a nonstick skillet; remove, blot dry with paper towel and place in a large saucepan. Add onion and celery to skillet and cook until lightly browned. Add to saucepan, along with beans, garlic powder, basil, tomato paste, tomatoes and beef broth. Bring to a boil, reduce heat, cover and simmer for 30 minutes.

Add zucchini and cabbage and simmer for 45 more minutes. Then add macaroni and cook an additional 15 minutes. It may be necessary to add water, but soup should be very thick when finished. Adjust salt to taste.

Rib-Sticker Soup

Make a big pot of delicious, low cost, high fiber soup and enjoy it for days; it also freezes well. Despite the number of ingredients, it goes together quickly; just remember to start it early so beans and peas can soak.

makes 8 cups   per cup: 160 calories, 1 gram fat

¼ cup dried navy beans

¼ cup dried red beans

¼ cup *each* dried yellow and green split peas (or ½ cup of either)

¼ cup dried lentils

1 large onion, chopped (about 1½ cups)

2 cups chopped celery

1 clove garlic, crushed

1 tablespoon dried basil

1 can (15 oz.) tomato sauce

1 can (14½ oz.) stewed tomatoes

4 cups regular strength beef broth

1 tablespoon Worcestershire sauce

1 teaspoon salt or to taste

Rinse and pick over beans and peas, discarding any debris. Place in a large pot and cover with water. Soak overnight. Or, bring to a boil, boil for 2 minutes, then remove from heat, cover and let stand for 1 hour. Drain off excess water in either case.

Place drained beans and peas in a 4-quart pot. Rinse and pick over lentils. Add to pot, along with all other ingredients, and stir to mix well. Bring to a boil, reduce heat, cover and simmer for 3 to 4 hours. If soup get too thick, add water.

See *"Pasta, Legumes & Grains"* chapter for more recipes and information about dried beans, peas and lentils.

Black Bean Soup

When nights are cold and dark, that's the perfect time to indulge in a hearty soup. This one gives you protein, fiber, vitamins and minerals. Make ahead so you can cool the soup and remove any fat.

makes 5 cups | per cup: 220 calories, 4 grams fat

1 cup dried black beans
1 smoked ham shank, about 1 pound
1 cup regular strength beef broth
3 cups water
1 cup chopped onion

1 cup chopped celery
½ cup chopped carrot
¼ teaspoon garlic powder
½ teaspoon dried cumin
½ teaspoon dried oregano
salt to taste

Rinse and pick over beans, discarding any debris. Place beans in a large pot and cover with water. Soak overnight. Or, bring to a boil, boil for 2 minutes, then remove from heat, cover and let stand for 1 hour. Drain off excess water in either case.

Place drained beans in a heavy 4-quart pot. Trim obvious fat from ham shank. Add shank to pot, along with all remaining ingredients except salt. Bring to a boil, reduce heat, cover and simmer for 2 hours or until beans are tender.

Cool soup. Remove ham shank, cool and trim edible meat from bone. Set aside. Skim off any fat and blend **cooled** soup in small batches, using food processor or blender. Place blended soup back into large pot; add reserved ham and salt to taste. Amount of salt depends on saltiness of ham bone, how much meat was on it, etc. Reheat soup gently to serve.

Note: Nutritional data for "1 ham shank" is hard to come by; a 1 pound bone with meat on it yields 4 to 5 ounces of trimmed meat, so it's not much anyway. If you prefer not to use a ham shank, you can add 5 ounces of diced lean ham or turkey ham.

Submarine Soup

Navy beans come to the rescue in the battle to win people over to low fat eating. This filling soup is easy and inexpensive to make. If you haven't bought navy beans before, you may be surprised to find that they are actually white.

makes 5 cups   per cup: 200 calories, 2 grams fat

1 cup dried navy beans	¼ teaspoon garlic powder
¼ pound diced turkey ham	¼ teaspoon dried marjoram
1 cup chopped onion	1 cup peeled, diced potato
1 cup chopped celery	(1 medium)
1 bay leaf	parsley, chives or green
6 cups water	onion (optional)
1 teaspoon salt	

Rinse and pick over beans, discarding any debris. Place beans in a large pot and cover with water. Soak overnight. Or, bring to a boil, boil for 2 minutes, then remove from heat, cover and let stand for 1 hour. Drain off excess water in either case.

Place drained beans in a heavy 4-quart pot. Add all other ingredients **except** the potato and optional parsley, chives and green onion. Bring to a boil, reduce heat, cover and simmer for 1½ hours. Add diced potato and simmer for an additional half hour.

Sprinkle a teaspoon of parsley, chives or chopped green onion on top of each serving for an eye-pleasing contrast.

Penny-Pincher's Pea Soup

The perfect winter energy-charger, split peas are packed with vitamins and protein. Combine them with cancer-fighting cabbage and you've got a tasty lunch for mere pennies.

makes 6 cups	per cup: 170 calories, 2 grams fat
1 cup dried split peas	3 cups regular strength
3 cups water	chicken broth
¼ pound turkey ham or	1 cup water
lean ham, diced	½ teaspoon dried thyme
1 cup chopped onion	2 cups shredded cabbage
1 clove garlic, minced	salt to taste

Rinse and pick over peas to remove any debris. Combine peas and 3 cups water in a 4-quart saucepan. Bring to a boil, reduce heat, cover and simmer for 30 minutes until water is absorbed. Set aside.

Cook ham, onion and garlic in a nonstick pan for 5 minutes until lightly browned. Add to peas. Add chicken broth, 1 cup of water, thyme and cabbage. Bring to a boil, reduce heat, cover and simmer for 45 minutes, until cabbage is tender. Adjust salt. Serve hot or cold.

The American Cancer Society encourages us to eat daily servings of cruciferous vegetables such as cabbage, broccoli, Brussels sprouts or cauliflower.

Split Pea and Barley Soup

South of the border flavors spice up this robust split pea and barley soup. With bread or muffins, it makes a filling meal.

makes 4 cups   per cup: 195 calories, 2 grams of fat

1 teaspoon olive oil	2 cups regular strength
1/2 cup chopped onion	chicken broth
1/2 cup chopped celery	1/2 cup dried split peas
1 clove garlic, minced	1/4 cup pearl barley
1 can (14 1/2 oz.) stewed	1/2 teaspoon chili powder
tomatoes, Mexican style	salt to taste

Coat a 2-quart pot with cooking spray and heat to medium-hot. Add oil and cook onion, celery and garlic until soft. Add tomatoes and chicken broth. Rinse and pick over peas to remove any debris. Add to pot along with barley and chili powder. Bring to a boil, reduce heat, cover and simmer for 1 hour.

Add water if soup appears too thick. Add salt to taste. Serve immediately or refrigerate and reheat later.

Note: Canned tomatoes now come with different seasonings. Look for Mexican or Cajun style; if you can't find either, you may want to add more chili powder or a tiny amount (e.g. 1/8 teaspoon) of cayenne pepper.

Split peas and barley are welcome additions to a healthful diet, since they are naturally high carbohydrate, high fiber, low fat foods. Even better, the fiber they contain is the water-soluble kind thought to lower blood cholesterol levels. In addition to fiber, split peas also contain significant protein, B-vitamins, iron and other nutrients, and are very low in sodium.

Cream of Lentil Soup

Plan ahead when making this soup. You need to cool it and skim off fat before finishing the cooking.

makes 6 cups   per cup: 200 calories, 3½ grams fat

1 cup dried lentils	1 smoked ham shank, about
5 cups water	1 pound
1 cup diced onion	2 cups 1% milk

Rinse and pick over lentils, discarding any debris. Place in 4-quart saucepan with water and onion. Trim obvious fat from ham shank. Add shank to water, and bring to a boil. Reduce heat, cover and simmer for 45 minutes.

Remove ham shank and cool. Cut meat off bone and dice into ½-inch pieces. Set aside. Allow lentils to cool, then strain through sieve, **saving all liquid.** Remove fat from liquid by skimming it off the top, or by refrigerating liquid until fat is congealed on top. Blend lentils in food processor or blender; return them to saucepan and add diced ham and defatted liquid. Stir in milk, reheat soup and serve. Add salt to taste, if necessary, depending on saltiness of ham bone.

Note: Calories and fat include estimated values for ham shank. (See *Black Bean Soup* recipe for ham shank information.)

Souper Lentils

For a double-barreled attack on cancer, make this low fat, high fiber soup with "fighting" vegetables – carrots and cabbage. Takes only 5 minutes to throw together, then cooks without any more effort.

makes 4 cups   per cup: 170 calories, 1 gram fat

¾ cup dried lentils	2 stalks celery, diced
1 cup regular strength beef broth	1 carrot, sliced
2½ cups water	1 cup peeled, diced potato (1 medium)
¾ cup chopped cabbage	¼ teaspoon dried thyme
1 small onion, chopped	salt and pepper to taste

Rinse and pick over lentils, discarding any debris. Place in medium saucepan with all other ingredients except salt and pepper. Bring to a boil, reduce heat, cover and simmer slowly about 45 minutes, or until lentils and vegetables are tender. Stir occasionally.

Season to taste with salt and pepper. Serve at once, refrigerate overnight or freeze.

Lentils are a high carbohydrate, high fiber, low fat food. As such, they fit right into the dietary guidelines. In addition, research suggests that their water-soluble fiber may be helpful in lowering blood cholesterol levels. A one cup serving contains 210 calories and essentially no fat. Unlike beans, lentils are quick to prepare as they require no pre-soaking.

Tub o' Lard Award

As a serious fat-finder, you would surely think twice about eating a creamy cheese soup – two words in that name give it away! But even you may be shocked at how much fat is in **Cream of Brie Cheese Soup**.

Many soups start with a few cups of good, low fat chicken broth and this one is no exception. Unfortunately, the remaining ingredients quickly make up the missing fat: ½ cup butter, 4 cups of half and half cream and 1½ pounds of Brie cheese.

Even worse than those ingredients is the suggested serving size. This amount is intended to serve only six poor souls, meaning each person will stare into a bowl containing **750 calories and 66 grams of fat!**

Those 66 grams of fat equal a whole day's ration for most of us, in just one bowl of soup. Don't fall victim to yet another trendy "gourmet treat" for your arteries.

Poultry

101 uses for a dead chicken

"A chicken in every pot...pan...oven...microwave...grill..." Is that how you view your weekly meal choices? If so, you have obviously discovered the many advantages of poultry. In addition to versatility, both chicken and turkey offer quick convenience, low cost and good nutritional value. Recommended by many government and public health associations, poultry fits well into dietary guidelines. A 3½-ounce serving has about 155 calories and 4 grams of fat; only 1 gram of that is saturated; cholesterol content is about 82 milligrams.

Because of consumer demand, there is a growing variety of raw cuts of both chicken and turkey which can be prepared in dozens of different ways and served hot or cold, winter or summer. As a quick rule of thumb, one pound of chicken breasts with bone and skin yields half a pound of raw, boneless, skinless chicken. The poultry producers figure you can get a serving of cooked chicken from one half breast, two thighs, two drumsticks or four wings.

If you're tempted to pick up fried chicken on the way home, because it's such a quick meal, you need a lesson in advance preparation. Having poultry "meal-ready," so that it is ready to cook when you are, is very satisfying and is easy to do. Turkey is now widely available in packages of fresh, skinless, boneless turkey breast slices all ready to go. You can skin and bone chicken yourself or buy breasts, and sometimes thighs, already skinned at the supermarket. You may also discover restaurant provisioners in your area that sell high quality chicken to the public in bulk packages.

If you would prefer to save money rather than time, a few minutes and a few fryers will get you set for several meals.

First, cut the fryers into individual pieces. Divide whole breast into two halves; cut apart thighs and legs – just wiggle them until you see where the joint is and slip your knife right between the two pieces; cut small tips off wings and cut apart the two remaining wing bones.

Skin all pieces right away and remove excess fat. (It's much more convenient to have the chicken skinned and ready to go when you thaw it.) Skin will pull off the thighs and breasts easily, with the help of a sharp knife. Skin the legs by inserting the tip of the knife under the skin at the top of the large end and slice up and away through the skin, then peel it down.

Wings are a bit more difficult but are worth it, since there is a lot of extra skin on them. Lay the wing on the cutting board, press the skin flap down on the board with the middle fingers of one hand, and hold the knife with the other hand, above your fingers and under the meat, at a 45-degree angle to the board. Push the knife against the wing and away from yourself, holding the skin flap firmly. The wing will roll away from the skin as the knife separates the two.

Important: Rinse hands, board and knife thoroughly with hot, soapy water to kill any bacteria. USDA surveys indicate that although salmonella poisoning from raw chicken is not unusual, it can be prevented by careful precautions.

Freeze the pieces individually – lay them flat on a baking sheet and freeze until solid. Then package similar pieces together so they're ready for specific meals. This method of freezing lets you pick out just enough pieces for the light or dark meat eaters in your family.

Make chicken broth with the back pieces. If you know you're going to want boneless chicken breasts, do it now and add the bones to the broth.

Paprika Chicken

This recipe makes lots of delicious sauce, so serve it over noodles or with rice. Takes only 20 minutes to prepare.

serves 2   per serving: 245 calories, 5½ grams fat

1 **whole chicken breast (1 pound), skinned, boned and cut in 1-inch pieces**
2 **cups sliced mushrooms (about ⅓ pound)**
1 **clove garlic, minced**
1 **teaspoon olive oil**
1 **tablespoon paprika**

½ **cup regular strength chicken broth**
¼ **cup white wine (or more chicken broth)**
1 **tablespoon** *each* **cornstarch and water, stirred smooth**
⅓ **cup plain lowfat yogurt salt and pepper to taste**

Coat a large nonstick skillet (one with a cover) with cooking spray and heat to medium hot; brown the chicken on all sides, about 5 minutes. Remove chicken from skillet.

Add mushrooms and garlic to skillet. Cook mushrooms until lightly browned. Add oil to skillet and stir mushrooms until they sizzle. Return chicken to skillet and immediately add paprika, stirring well to spread evenly. Add broth and wine. Bring liquid to a boil, reduce heat, cover skillet and simmer 5 minutes.

Add cornstarch mixture to sauce. Increase heat and boil sauce 1 to 2 minutes or until thick. Remove pan from heat and stir in yogurt; do not boil. Season to taste.

Serving tip: Toss chicken with cooked noodles and place in a large bowl. Surround the outer edge with a ring of bright green peas.

Chicken Mozzarella

So easy – just 5 ingredients and 30 minutes from start to finish.

serves 2   per serving: 275 calories, 10 grams fat

4 **chicken thighs (1¼
   pounds total), skinned
   and trimmed of excess fat**
½ **cup chopped onion**
½ **cup regular strength
   chicken broth**

¼ **cup mild salsa, fresh
   or bottled**
2 **tablespoons grated
   part-skim Mozzarella
   cheese (½ oz.)**

Heat a large nonstick skillet (one with a cover) to medium hot.
Brown chicken 5 minutes on each side, until golden. Add onion
to skillet and cook until soft. Add chicken broth, reduce heat,
cover and simmer for 20 minutes, or until chicken is cooked.
Spread chicken with salsa, then sprinkle cheese over top.
Cover again and cook 5 minutes or until cheese has melted and
salsa is hot.

The Chicken Caper

*The chicken takes only a few minutes to cook, so have the accom-
panying vegetables, etc., nearly done before you start. Good with
rice and steamed asparagus for color contrast.*

serves 2   per serving: 155 calories, 5 grams fat

1 **whole chicken breast
   (1 pound), skinned,
   boned and split**
⅛ **teaspoon *each* salt,
   garlic powder and paprika**

2 **teaspoons margarine**
1 **tablespoon lemon juice**
1 **tablespoon capers, drained**

Coat a large nonstick skillet with cooking spray and heat to medium-hot. Pound chicken breasts flat with a mallet and
sprinkle one side lightly with salt, garlic powder and paprika.
Brown quickly in the hot pan, 2 to 3 minutes per side, until
cooked through. In a separate small saucepan heat margarine,
lemon juice and capers. When sauce is hot, pour over the
cooked chicken and serve immediately.

Chicken Fajitas

If you're a burrito fan, you'll appreciate this marinated chicken variation. Perfect for a quick lunch or supper.

makes 4   each: 165 calories, 3 grams fat

1 whole chicken breast
  (1 pound), skinned, boned
  and sliced in thin
  ½-inch strips
½ teaspoon chili powder
¼ teaspoon onion powder
⅛ teaspoon garlic powder
1 tablespoon fresh lime
  juice

4 flour tortillas
2 tablespoons plain lowfat
  yogurt
2 tablespoons salsa, fresh
  or bottled
2 tablespoons chopped green
  onion
¼ cup chopped tomato
½ cup shredded lettuce

Place sliced chicken in a glass bowl and sprinkle with chili powder, onion powder, garlic powder and lime juice. Stir well to spread seasoning evenly. Cover and refrigerate for 30 minutes; this is not necessary if time is short, but adds some flavor.

Have all other ingredients ready before you continue. Warm tortillas either by quickly heating them in a wide skillet or by wrapping them in foil and warming in the oven about 10 minutes at 200 degrees.

Coat a large nonstick skillet with cooking spray and heat to medium-hot. Stir-fry the chicken until brown on all sides, about 3 minutes. While chicken is cooking, spread warm tortillas with yogurt, salsa, onion, tomato and lettuce. Top with hot chicken pieces, roll up tortilla and wrap in foil for tidy eating.

Remove the skin before cooking chicken. If you wait until after it's cooked, too much fat has soaked into the chicken. Besides, all your seasoning and browning flavor is on the skin which you then take off – doesn't make sense to us.

Fat-less Fettucine

A quick, gourmet delight – fettucine without too much fat! A steamed green vegetable is all that is needed to complete this meal, ready in less than 30 minutes.

serves 2　　　　　　　　　　　per serving: 425 calories, 5 grams fat

4 oz. fettucine

1 whole chicken breast (1 pound), skinned, boned and cut in 1-inch pieces

2 cups sliced mushrooms (about ⅓ pound)

1 clove garlic, minced

1 teaspoon olive oil

¼ cup dry white wine or regular strength chicken broth

½ cup plain lowfat yogurt

1 tablespoon Dijon mustard

1 teaspoon cornstarch

salt and pepper to taste

Bring a 4-quart pot of water to a boil. Cook fettucine according to package directions, about 10 minutes. Drain and keep warm.

Meanwhile, coat a large nonstick skillet (one with a cover) with cooking spray and heat to medium-hot. Brown the chicken on all sides, about 3 to 5 minutes. Add mushrooms and garlic and continue browning for 2 minutes. Add oil and "sizzle" for 1 minute.

Add white wine or chicken broth to skillet, cover and simmer for 5 to 7 minutes until chicken is tender and liquid just covers bottom of skillet.

In a small bowl, blend yogurt, Dijon mustard and cornstarch until smooth. Stir into chicken mixture and simmer for 1 minute until sauce is hot. Adjust for salt. Pour chicken into hot, drained fettucine and serve immediately.

Chicken Asparagus Stir-Fry

A fresh combination of flavors, with the added advantage of being very fast to prepare. Slightly crunchy, fresh asparagus gives this dish texture, so don't overcook it.

serves 2   per serving: 200 calories, 4 grams fat

1 whole chicken breast,
  (1 pound), skinned, boned
  and cut in 1-inch pieces
1 teaspoon olive oil
1 cup chopped asparagus, cut
  in 1-inch pieces
1 cup chopped onion

1 clove garlic, minced
¼ teaspoon Italian seasoning
½ cup regular strength
  chicken broth
1 tablespoon lemon juice
1 teaspoon cornstarch
  salt and pepper to taste

Coat a large nonstick skillet with cooking spray and heat to medium-hot. Brown chicken quickly on all sides, about 2 minutes. Add oil, asparagus, onion and garlic and cook until crisp-tender, about 3 minutes, stirring frequently. Sprinkle with Italian seasoning.

Combine broth, lemon juice and cornstarch in a small jar and shake well until completely blended. Pour over chicken, bring to a boil and cook 2 minutes or until thickened. Season to taste. Serve immediately.

The mild taste of chicken adapts well to many herbs. Experiment with dill, rosemary, savory or sage the next time you poach a chicken breast. Remember the rule of thumb that one teaspoon of dried herbs equals one tablespoon of fresh.

Country Captain

Here's a recipe where timing isn't critical. It can be reheated without problems, making it ideal for uncertain schedules. Makes lots of sauce, so serve it over noodles or rice.

serves 2	per serving: 385 calories, 10 grams fat

4 **chicken thighs (1¼ pounds total), skinned and trimmed of excess fat**
2 **cups chopped mushrooms (about ⅓ pound)**
½ **cup chopped onion**
2 **teaspoons curry powder**

1 **cup regular strength chicken broth**
1 **cup stewed tomatoes**
¼ **cup raisins**
1 **tablespoon** *each* **cornstarch and water, stirred smooth**

Heat a deep, nonstick skillet (one with a cover) to medium hot. Brown chicken on both sides, about 10 minutes. Remove chicken from pan, add mushrooms and onion and cook for 5 minutes, until soft. Stir in curry powder and cook 1 minute.

Return chicken to pan, add chicken broth, tomatoes and raisins. Bring liquid to a boil, reduce heat, cover and simmer for 15 minutes. Remove cover and continue to simmer an additional 5 to 10 minutes until chicken is cooked and sauce is slightly thickened.

Remove chicken to warm serving dish and increase heat under sauce. Stir in cornstarch and water mixture and boil sauce 1 to 2 minutes or until thick. Adjust seasoning.

Calories and fat are calculated based on two chicken thighs per serving, each weighing about 5 ounces raw. Close to half that amount is fat and bone. Check the weight of the ones you buy. Since even skinned thigh meat has about four times the fat of breast meat, be sure to trim all visible fat before cooking. To save fat, chicken breasts can be substituted in recipes but the final taste and texture may be different because of their lower fat content.

Oven-Baked Chicken Chunks

The paprika gives the chicken a rich, brown, "fried" look, making it hard to believe that there's no skin.

makes 4	each: 135 calories, 4½ grams fat

4 chicken thighs (1¼ pounds total), skinned and trimmed of excess fat
¼ cup skim milk
¼ cup flour

½ teaspoon paprika
¼ teaspoon poultry seasoning
¼ teaspoon onion powder
½ teaspoon salt

Preheat oven to 400 degrees. Coat a large baking sheet with cooking spray. Pat chicken dry. Pour milk into a wide bowl. Combine flour and seasonings in a second bowl. Dip chicken pieces first into milk, then into seasoned flour, coating well. Place on baking sheet and bake for 20 minutes. Turn chicken over and bake an additional 20 minutes or until golden brown. Serve hot or cold.

Lemon Chicken 'n Rice

A one-pot meal that takes just a few minutes to assemble, this dinner lets you do something else while it simmers on the stove.

serves 2	per serving: 310 calories, 3½ grams fat

1 whole chicken breast (1 pound), skinned, boned and cut in 1-inch pieces
⅛ teaspoon lemon pepper
⅛ teaspoon paprika
½ cup white rice, uncooked

¼ teaspoon dried oregano
¼ teaspoon grated lemon peel
2 tablespoons lemon juice
1½ cups regular strength chicken broth
fresh parsley, chopped

Sprinkle chicken with lemon pepper and paprika. Coat a large nonstick skillet (one with a cover) with cooking spray and heat to medium-hot. Brown chicken on all sides. Add rice and stir it around with chicken until lightly glistening; add oregano, lemon peel, lemon juice and chicken broth. Bring to a boil, reduce heat, cover and simmer for 25 minutes or until rice is tender. Sprinkle parsley over top when serving.

Picnic Chicken

A hit at any picnic, this oven-baked chicken offers the piquancy of Dijon mustard. No extra fat is needed; you'll be surprised at the amount of fat that sizzles out of the chicken itself, causing the coating to become crisp.

makes 4   each: 170 calories, 5½ grams fat

4 chicken thighs (1¼ pounds total), skinned and trimmed of excess fat	⅛ teaspoon Worcestershire sauce
¼ cup plain lowfat or nonfat yogurt	¼ cup dry bread crumbs
2 tablespoons Dijon mustard	1 tablespoon grated Parmesan cheese
	¼ teaspoon salt

Preheat oven to 400 degrees. Coat a large nonstick baking sheet with cooking spray. Pat chicken dry.

Combine yogurt, mustard and Worcestershire sauce in a small bowl. In a wide bowl, combine bread crumbs, Parmesan cheese and salt.

Spread yogurt mixture on each piece, covering both sides. Dip into crumb mixture and place on baking sheet. Bake 20 minutes. Turn over and bake an additional 20 minutes or until golden brown.

Note: This recipe also works well with chicken breasts. Skin and bone the chicken and flatten to about half an inch. Spread with coating as described. Bake at 400 degrees for about 25 minutes total, until chicken is cooked through but not over-cooked. Because of its lower fat content, white meat has a tendency to dry out; the coating will not become as crisp. Both this recipe and *Oven-Baked Chicken Chunks* are easily multiplied. Use the same proportions of coating for every four pieces of chicken.

Tub o' Lard Award

What is it about low fat chicken that makes people want to load it up with high fat sauces? This award goes to a Northwest restaurant, which shall remain nameless, for its rendition of **Stuffed Chicken Breasts.**

The recipe starts with 12 chicken breasts, then adds 12 ounces prosciutto ham, 12 ounces Bel Paese cheese and 12 ounces Parmesan cheese. The chicken is stuffed with these treats, then browned in oil. Mushrooms are cooked along with it and the whole dish is covered with 6 cups of whipping cream!

It's intended for only six people, so each happy diner gets his or her own cup of whipping cream. Each will consume over **1200 calories and 100 grams of fat** just in the cheese and whipping cream alone. This doesn't include figures for the chicken and ham, and we had no idea how much oil was used for browning, so the totals would be even higher.

Oh well, at least it started with skinned chicken. Conclusion: The common recommendation, *"When in doubt, choose chicken,"* doesn't always work.

Finger-Lickin' Bombay Chicken

This excellent company dish for 4 has a spicy flavor that appeals to everyone. Prepare the sauce ahead of time. Serve with chutney, lowfat yogurt and green pepper jelly, if desired.

serves 4   per serving: 310 calories, 11 grams fat

8 chicken thighs (2½ pounds total), skinned and trimmed of excess fat
2 slices bacon
1 cup chopped onion
4 teaspoons curry powder
1 cup regular strength chicken broth
1 cup unsweetened applesauce
¼ cup lemon juice
2 tablespoons chutney
1 tablespoon Worcestershire sauce
2 teaspoons sugar
1 teaspoon salt

Early in the day: Heat a large nonstick skillet (one with a cover) to medium-hot. Add bacon and cook until crisp. Remove bacon from pan, drain well and crumble. Keep one teaspoon of bacon fat in skillet, discard rest. Add onion and cook for 5 minutes. Stir in curry powder and cook for 1 minute. Add bacon and remaining ingredients, bring to a boil and stir until smooth. Boil sauce for 10 minutes or until moderately thick. Cover and refrigerate sauce until needed.

When ready to bake, preheat oven to 375 degrees. Coat a 7x11-inch baking dish with cooking spray. In a hot nonstick skillet, brown chicken 3 minutes on each side until golden. Remove chicken from pan and place in baking dish.

Spoon half the sauce over the chicken, bake 20 minutes; turn over chicken and spoon the rest of the sauce evenly over the pieces. Bake an additional 20 minutes until chicken is golden brown and sauce is almost gone; chicken should have a glazed, barbecued look. If not, a few minutes under a broiler just before serving will put the finishing touch on it.

Note: For an attractive presentation, serve on a bed of brown rice, surrounded by a ring of bright green peas.

Turkey Parmigiana

The most time-consuming part of this recipe is preheating the oven. The turkey will be ready to eat 15 minutes later.

serves 2   per serving: 280 calories, 6 grams of fat

½ **pound skinless raw turkey breast, sliced ¼-inch thick**
1 **egg white**
1 **tablespoon skim milk**

¼ **cup dry bread crumbs**
½ **cup bottled low fat spaghetti sauce**
2 **oz. part-skim Mozzarella cheese, very thinly sliced**

Preheat oven to 400 degrees. Coat a baking sheet with cooking spray. Cut turkey slices into 4-inch long cutlets.

Beat egg white and milk together. Dip turkey into egg mixture, then into bread crumbs. Place on baking sheet in single layer. Bake for 5 minutes; remove sheet from oven.

Spread spaghetti sauce evenly over cutlets. Top each cutlet with sliced cheese. Return to oven for an additional 5 to 7 minutes, until turkey is tender, sauce is hot and cheese is melted. Serve at once.

Note: Read labels carefully to find a spaghetti sauce that is low in fat. They do exist. We have found some brands that contain no fat at all.

It's hard to beat turkey when you want a meal that is filling, quick to cook, yet low in fat and cholesterol. A 3-ounce serving of cooked turkey breast has only 120 calories and 1 gram of fat. Don't wait for a holiday dinner to add it to your diet.

Turkey Scallopini

This recipe is a quickie. Double it for a fast company meal. See below for an elegant variation.

serves 2   per serving: 205 calories, 6 grams fat

½ **pound skinless raw turkey breast, sliced ¼-inch thick**
2 **tablespoons flour**
⅛ **teaspoon black pepper**
2 **cups sliced mushrooms (about ⅓ pound)**

¼ **cup minced onion**
1 **clove garlic, minced**
1 **teaspoon olive oil**
1 **teaspoon margarine**
¼ **cup regular strength chicken broth**
½ **lemon, cut into wedges**

Cut turkey into 4-inch long cutlets. Combine flour and pepper and coat turkey with flour mixture, shaking off excess. Set aside.

Coat a large nonstick skillet with cooking spray. Over medium heat, cook mushrooms, onion and garlic until lightly browned; add oil and stir-fry vegetables for 1 minute, until sizzling. Remove from pan.

After mushrooms have been removed from skillet, melt margarine over medium-high heat and brown turkey slices on both sides. This should take only 1 to 2 minutes per side, depending on thickness. Don't overcook.

Spread vegetables over turkey, add chicken broth, cover and simmer for 2 to 3 minutes, until hot. Squeeze some lemon over everything and serve at once with additional lemon wedges.

Recipe tip: For *"Fast 'n Fancy Scallopini,"* cook a pot of wild or brown rice ahead of time. When preparing the turkey, substitute 2 tablespoons dry sherry and 2 tablespoons water for the chicken broth. To serve, mound cooked rice on a platter, top with cooked turkey slices, scatter mushrooms over turkey and sprinkle chopped parsley on top. Arrange half slices of fresh tomatoes around the edge.

California Clucker Salad

Chicken or turkey, fresh plums and wild rice make a great combination for a warm summer evening. Can be made early in the day.

serves 2   per serving: 355 calories, 10 grams fat

¼ cup brown rice
¼ cup wild rice
1½ cups regular strength
    chicken broth
1 cup chopped cooked
    chicken or turkey
⅓ cup diced celery
⅓ cup diced red pepper

2 tablespoons diced red
    onion
2 fresh plums, thinly sliced
⅛ teaspoon dry mustard
2 tablespoons lemon juice
1 tablespoon salad oil
    salt and pepper to taste

Cook rice in chicken broth, covered, for 45 minutes or until tender and all liquid is absorbed; cool. Mix rice and chicken or turkey together with celery, red pepper, onion and plums.

For dressing, combine dry mustard, lemon juice and oil in a small jar. Shake vigorously to blend and pour dressing over rice mixture. Toss lightly. Season to taste, depending on saltiness of broth. Sprinkle with pepper. Chill until ready to serve.

Chutney Waldorf Salad

Use leftover chicken or turkey to make a crunchy Waldorf salad.

serves 2   per serving: 240 calories, 4 grams fat

1 **cup diced green apple***
1 **cup diced celery**
1 **cup chopped cooked**
   chicken or turkey
1 **orange**
2 **tablespoons plain lowfat**
   yogurt

1 **tablespoon light**
   mayonnaise
1 **tablespoon chutney**
1 **teaspoon honey**
   salt to taste
   lettuce leaves

*Leave peel on apple for color and fiber.

In a medium bowl, combine apple, celery and chicken or turkey. Cut the orange in half and squeeze out 2 tablespoons of juice from one half; place in small bowl. Cut the remaining half into thin, parallel slices. Set aside.

In a small bowl, combine squeezed orange juice, yogurt, mayonnaise, chutney and honey. Whisk together until smooth. Salt lightly to enhance the sweet taste of the dressing. Pour over salad and toss well.

Place lettuce leaves on each of two plates. Divide salad equally onto lettuce and place sliced oranges along one side.

> *Traditional Waldorf salads often include walnuts. If you're used to topping fruit salads with a handful of nuts, be aware that every tablespoon of chopped nuts will add about a teaspoon of fat (4 to 5 grams).*

Turkey Tetrazzini

Often leftover turkey is used for nothing more than hot and cold sandwiches. Try this classic for a change.

serves 2   per serving: 395 calories, 6 grams fat

3 oz. spaghetti
3/4 cup 1% milk
1/2 cup regular strength
   chicken broth
1 tablespoon cornstarch
1/4 cup grated part-skim
   Mozzarella cheese (1 oz.)
1/4 cup plain lowfat yogurt

1/4 teaspoon salt
   few grains cayenne pepper
1 small can (4 oz.) sliced
   mushrooms, drained
1 cup diced cooked turkey
1/2 cup frozen peas
   paprika

Break spaghetti in half and cook according to package directions until just tender; it will cook a little more in the oven. Drain and set aside.

Meanwhile, preheat oven to 425 degrees. Pour milk into small saucepan and heat slowly. In a small jar, shake together chicken broth and cornstarch until smooth. Add to milk and cook over medium heat, stirring constantly, until mixture thickens and boils. Boil 1 minute and remove from heat. Add cheese to sauce and stir until melted. Stir in yogurt, salt, cayenne, mushrooms, turkey and peas. Combine with spaghetti.

Coat a 1-quart baking dish with cooking spray. Pour mixture into dish and sprinkle with paprika. Bake casserole, uncovered, for 15 minutes or until hot.

Make-ahead instructions: Prepare casserole as described, cover and refrigerate until ready to cook. Preheat oven to 425 degrees and bake for about 25 to 30 minutes or until hot.

If your roast turkey recipe which was cut out of the paper 21 years ago says to baste with a cube of butter, that's probably just what you've been doing for 21 years. Put on your thinking cap and try chicken broth the next time.

Turkey Enchiladas

A family favorite, easily doubled for more mouths.

serves 2   per serving: 470 calories, 11 grams fat

4 corn tortillas	½ cup grated part-skim
1 can (10 oz.) enchilada	Mozzarella cheese (2 oz.)
sauce	2 cups shredded lettuce
1 teaspoon salad oil	¼ cup plain lowfat yogurt
⅓ cup chopped onion	or light sour cream
1½ cups ground or shredded	¼ cup salsa, fresh or
cooked turkey (about	bottled
½ pound)	1 cup chopped fresh tomato
¼ cup chopped green onion	

Preheat oven to 200 degrees. Wrap tortillas in foil and heat for 10 minutes until soft and pliable. Remove from oven and keep wrapped until ready to use. Increase oven temperature to 350 degrees. Meanwhile, coat a 1-quart baking dish with cooking spray and spread ¼ cup enchilada sauce over bottom.

In a small skillet, heat oil, add onion and cook until tender, about 5 minutes. In a small bowl, combine onion, turkey and ¼ cup enchilada sauce. Divide filling evenly among tortillas, sprinkle lightly with green onion, roll up and place in baking dish, seam side down. Pour remaining enchilada sauce over tortillas and sprinkle grated cheese on top. Bake for 20 minutes or until hot and bubbly.

Make bed of shredded lettuce on two plates; put two enchiladas on each and top with yogurt, salsa and chopped tomato.

Make-ahead instructions: Prepare enchiladas and cover with sauce as described above; do not add cheese. Cover and refrigerate until ready to cook. Preheat oven to 350 degrees. Sprinkle cheese on enchiladas and bake, uncovered, for 25 to 30 minutes, until hot. Serve as described.

Seafood

The fishy fats of life

Seafood has always been on the "good to eat" list because of its low calorie content. Now there is another reason to add more fish to your diet. Fish contains omega-3 fatty acids, a type of polyunsaturated fat which may actually protect us from heart problems. The primary dietary source of this good fat is seafood, whether it is salt water fish, fresh water fish or shellfish.

Studies on the beneficial aspects of omega-3 fatty acids have shown three effects. First, they have an ability to lower blood triglycerides. They also appear to lower the level of the low density lipoproteins (LDLs) which transport cholesterol to the artery walls. A third benefit is an apparent decreased "stickiness" of blood platelets, which are responsible for clotting. All of these properties may result in a decreased risk for coronary heart disease.

> Cold ocean fish, such as salmon, mackerel, tuna and sardines, have higher quantities of omega-3 fatty acids, but all fish contain it, so you should be able to find something you like. Taking fish oil capsules is not recommended by the medical community; as is usually the case with dietary recommendations, the best source is the food itself.

Try to eat fish two to three times a week. It's not hard to do; even the popular tuna sandwich can count as one meal. However, remember that frozen, breaded, fried fish is not exactly what the doctor ordered. Check the labels before you buy or you may get an unwelcome surprise.

To frustrate the heart-conscious fat-watchers, it appears that the fatter the fish, the more omega-3 fatty acids it contains. Mackerel, salmon and sardines are often shunned because of a perceived high fat content, yet they're the very ones which are richest in these fatty acids. Here we go again, trying to make a wise decision from apparently conflicting numbers.

A look at those numbers, however, will show that "high fat" is relative. Compare 3½ ounces of chinook salmon at 12 grams of fat with the same amount of beef, pork or lamb. The meats range from 6 grams, for very lean cuts, to over 30 grams of fat. Even the supposedly high fat salmon is at the lower end of this scale. Just be aware of the total amount you eat.

You can mix and match high and low fat fish to get enough omega-3s without too much fat. Fresh, canned or frozen is fine, as long as you don't fry your healthful fish in too much fat!

Don't overcook fish. When it is mushy and tends to fall apart, it's no wonder that no one likes it. Ten minutes per inch is usually enough, or just until the flesh begins to flake. Timing may vary, depending on temperature and whether the fish is covered with sauces or other ingredients as in the next recipe. Good fresh fish has little odor but frying it may sometimes result in a "fishy smell." Try a lower heat level or reconsider that type of cooking!

Baked Cod Marengo

*A juicy and colorful topping gives eye and taste appeal. The mild flavor will make this a winner even with non-fish-fans. We suggest serving it with **Barley Pilaf**.*

serves 2   per serving: 210 calories, 4 grams fat

¾ pound cod
2 tablespoons lemon juice
⅛ teaspoon onion powder
⅛ teaspoon lemon pepper
1 teaspoon olive oil
½ cup chopped onion
1 clove garlic, minced

¼ cup chopped green
   pepper
1 cup whole canned tomatoes,
   drained
¼ teaspoon dried oregano
¼ teaspoon salt

Preheat oven to 400 degrees. Coat a shallow baking dish (one with a cover) with cooking spray. Cut cod into two serving pieces, place in dish; sprinkle with lemon juice, onion powder and lemon pepper.

Heat oil in small skillet, add onion, garlic and green pepper and cook for 2 to 3 minutes, until softened. Remove from heat. Add tomatoes, oregano and salt to skillet. Spoon mixture evenly over cod.

Cover baking dish and bake 10 to 15 minutes or until cod flakes easily when tested with fork.

Sea-Breeze Stew

This is a breeze to make on a cold, rainy night. Add some French bread for great "dunking."

makes 4 cups   each: 150 calories, 1 gram fat

- 1 can (6½ oz.) chopped clams (save juice)
- 1 small can (8 oz.) stewed tomatoes
- ½ cup tomato sauce
- ½ cup regular strength chicken broth
- ½ cup chopped onion
- 1 clove garlic, minced
- ¼ teaspoon dried basil
- 1 medium potato, peeled and cut in ½-inch cubes (about 1 cup)
- ¼ cup dry white wine or chicken broth
- ½ pound cod, cut in 1-inch pieces

Drain clam juice into a large saucepan. Set clams aside. To clam juice, add tomatoes, tomato sauce, broth, onion, garlic, basil and potatoes. Bring to a boil, then reduce heat, cover and simmer until potatoes are tender, about 20 minutes.

Add reserved clams, wine and cod and simmer 5 minutes more, just until fish is cooked.

See also **The Shrimper, Hawaiian Tuna and Tuna Pockets** in **"Sandwiches,"** Clam and Corn Chowder in **"Soups."**

Shrimp Casserole

This easily assembled casserole is great for parties or unpredictable family meals; it is good hot or cold and can be prepared ahead. Since leftovers make a nice lunch, this recipe makes four servings.

serves 4	per serving: 325 calories, 3 grams fat

1 cup sliced mushrooms
1 cup finely chopped onion
1/4 cup regular strength chicken broth
2 cups cooked brown rice

2 cups cooked tiny shrimp (about 2/3 pound)
1 teaspoon dried dill weed
3 large egg whites
2 cups 1% cottage cheese

Preheat oven to 350 degrees. Coat a nonstick skillet with cooking spray and heat to medium-hot. Add mushrooms and brown for 5 minutes. Add chopped onion and brown lightly. Add chicken broth and cook vegetables 5 minutes or until onions are soft and liquid has been absorbed. Combine vegetables, rice, shrimp and dill in a large bowl.

In a separate bowl, beat egg whites lightly. Stir in cottage cheese and combine this with rice mixture. Coat a 2-quart baking dish with cooking spray and spoon in rice mixture. Bake, covered, for 30 minutes.

Remove from oven and let stand, uncovered, for 10 minutes. Casserole will be moist when it comes out of the oven but excess juices will be absorbed into the rice as it stands.

Make-ahead instructions: Prepare casserole as instructed and place in baking dish. Cover and refrigerate until ready to cook. Preheat oven to 350 degrees and bake, covered, for about 35 minutes or until heated through.

Scallop and Vegetable Fettuccine

Toss together this speedy meal when you have only half an hour to spare. Serve with good bread and a tossed salad or sliced ripe tomatoes.

serves 2	per serving: 460 calories, 10 grams fat

4 oz. fettuccine
1 stalk celery
2 green onions
¼ small red pepper
2 teaspoons olive oil
½ cup snow peas (in pods)

½ pound scallops, cut in
  ½-inch pieces
⅛ teaspoon garlic powder
¼ cup dry white wine
¼ cup grated Parmesan cheese
  lemon pepper to taste

In a large saucepan bring water to a boil and cook pasta according to package instructions. Drain and keep warm if done before sauce is finished.

Meanwhile, cut celery, onions and red pepper into thin strips. Heat olive oil in a large nonstick skillet. Add cut vegetables and snow peas and stir-fry about 10 minutes, until crisp but tender.

Add scallops and toss until opaque and lightly browned, about 2 minutes. Sprinkle with garlic powder, add wine and cook 1 minute. Pour over drained pasta. Add cheese and toss well. Sprinkle with lemon pepper to taste. Serve at once, with additional Parmesan if desired (1½ grams of fat per tablespoon).

What about shellfish and a heart-healthy lifestyle? People have been told for years that they shouldn't eat shellfish because of its high cholesterol levels. It turns out that older measurements were detecting "cholesterol-like" substances as well as cholesterol, contributing to readings that were too high. This is good news for those of us who like low fat, low calorie shellfish. Enjoy it, in moderation.

Salmon Loaf

Salmon loaf is great when hot and makes an excellent cold light lunch. Serve it with one of the sauces below.

makes 8 1-inch slices   per slice: 125 calories, 4½ grams fat

1 can (15½ oz.) pink salmon, drained and flaked
1 large egg
¼ cup 1% milk
1 tablespoon lemon juice

1 teaspoon Worcestershire sauce
¾ cup dry bread crumbs
½ teaspoon dried dill weed
¼ cup finely chopped celery

Preheat oven to 400 degrees. Combine all ingredients and pack into an 8x4-inch loaf pan. Bake 30 minutes. Serve hot or cold.

Cucumber-Caper Sauce

Cucumbers and salmon are made for each other; this sauce adds contrasting taste and texture without fat.

makes about ¾ cup   per tablespoon: 7 calories, almost no fat

½ cup plain lowfat yogurt
½ cup finely diced cucumber
¼ cup chopped green onion
1 tablespoon capers, drained

1 tablespoon lemon juice
1 teaspoon dried dill weed
½ teaspoon salt or to taste

Combine all ingredients and keep chilled.

Tasty Tartar Sauce

If you've got a member of the family who is dubious about fish, this zippy sauce will help. Make it ahead so flavors blend.

makes ¾ cup   per tablespoon: 25 calories, 2 grams fat

¼ cup light mayonnaise
¼ cup plain lowfat yogurt
1 tablespoon chopped parsley
1 tablespoon chopped green onion

2 tablespoons sweet pickle relish
2 teaspoons capers, drained
⅛ teaspoon dried tarragon

Combine all ingredients. Refrigerate for at least 2 hours.

Seafood Pasta Salad

Here's a refreshing, main dish salad which is best made ahead. Any cooked seafood can be used, such as tiny bay shrimp, crab, scallops, seaflakes, canned or cooked salmon or tuna.

makes 4 cups   per cup: 170 calories, 1½ grams fat

3 oz. rotelli or other
   small pasta
1 cup chopped broccoli
½ cup frozen peas, thawed
1 green onion, chopped
1 small tomato, chopped

1 cup cooked seafood
2 tablespoons reduced fat
   Italian dressing
¼ cup plain lowfat yogurt
2 tablespoons lemon juice
½ teaspoon dried dill weed

Cook pasta according to package instructions. Drain well and set aside. Cook broccoli until crisp-tender.

In a large bowl, mix together rotelli, broccoli, peas, onion, tomato and seafood. Combine Italian dressing, yogurt, lemon juice and dill and pour over salad. Toss lightly. Chill at least two hours to develop flavors. Serve on a bed of lettuce.

Tuna Rice Salad

Stretch a can of tuna by combining it with a grain, and save money and time as well as fat. This improves with age so plan on leftovers.

serves 4   per serving: 200 calories, 3 grams fat

2 cups cooked rice
1 can (6½ oz.) water-
   packed tuna, drained
¼ cup chopped green onion
½ cup chopped celery
1 jar (2 oz.) diced
   pimentos

2 tablespoons plain lowfat
   yogurt
2 tablespoons light
   mayonnaise
1 tablespoon lemon juice
½ teaspoon salt or to taste

Combine all ingredients and toss to mix. Adjust seasoning. Chill for at least 1 hour before serving.

Shrimp Fried Rice

When the day has been too busy or the weather too warm, you'll appreciate the quick preparation of this main dish. You do need to cook some rice ahead of time.

serves 2   per serving: 260 calories, 6 grams fat

1 cup sliced mushrooms	1 large egg white
1 teaspoon salad oil	1 cup cooked rice, chilled
2 green onions, sliced	$\frac{3}{4}$ cup cooked tiny shrimp,
$\frac{1}{2}$ teaspoon minced fresh	about $\frac{1}{4}$ pound
ginger (optional)	2 teaspoons soy sauce
1 large egg	

Coat a large nonstick skillet or wok with cooking spray. Brown mushrooms about 3 minutes, until juices start to cook out. Add oil, green onions and ginger and stir-fry for 1 minute. Push vegetables aside. Beat egg and egg white lightly together, pour into skillet and scramble until just set. Stir in rice, separating grains. Add shrimp and soy sauce; cook and stir until everything is thoroughly heated. Serve at once.

Tub o' Lard Award

Seafood may be heart-healthy, but once the inventive cook gets in the act, watch out. The addition of just a few ingredients can transform polyunsaturated seafood into a fat bullet swimming straight for your heart. **Barbecued Shrimp** sounds healthy, but take a closer look.

The recipe starts with a mixture of $\frac{1}{4}$ cup butter and $\frac{1}{4}$ cup olive oil, seasoned with Worcestershire and hot sauce. This is poured over 1 pound shrimp and heated. After cooking, the shrimp is served in soup bowls, with French bread for dipping. The sauce is almost 100% fat, with **460 calories and 51 grams of fat** per serving.

The shrimp and bread are not the problems in this dish!

Fish Fry

Add the snap of fresh vegetables to low fat fish to make a flavor-filled combination you can enjoy with a good conscience. Preparation takes a bit of advance work, but cooking takes only minutes.

serves 2   per serving: 260 calories, 4½ grams fat

½ pound fillet of snapper, cod, or other thick, firm white-fleshed fish
¼ pound scallops
1 teaspoon cornstarch
¼ cup white wine
¾ teaspoon salt-reduced soy sauce

⅓ cup orange juice
¼ teaspoon dried ginger
1 teaspoon salad oil
1 clove garlic, minced
½ cup snow peas (in pods)
1 cup thinly sliced red pepper
2 green onions, sliced

Cut fillets into 1-inch pieces. Cut scallops in half and set aside. Combine cornstarch, wine, soy sauce, orange juice and ginger. Add fish pieces only and marinate in refrigerator for 30 minutes.

Heat oil in nonstick skillet. Add garlic and cook for 1 minutes. Drain fish, reserving marinade. Add fish to skillet and stir-fry 4 minutes, or until medium-rare. Add scallops and vegetables; stir-fry 2 to 3 minutes more. Add reserved marinade and cook just until sauce thickens. Serve immediately.

Serving tip: Pour over fresh Oriental-style noodles or rice.

Noodle note: Beware the prepackaged, dried Oriental-type noodles. Although you'd expect plain noodles to be very low in fat, we found a brand that contains 17 grams of fat (and 1500 milligrams of salt) per serving. Read that label!

Foiled Fish

A main dish that is easily doubled for company, foil-baked fish makes an attractive, colorful presentation. You can prepare the packets ahead and refrigerate until time to bake.

serves 2   per serving: 240 calories, 5 grams fat

¾ **pound halibut**
1 **small zucchini, unpeeled**
1 **medium carrot**
2 **green onions**
1 **teaspoon olive oil**

1 **clove garlic, minced**
½ **teaspoon dried dill weed**
   lemon pepper
2 **tablespoons lemon juice**

Preheat oven to 400 degrees. Tear off two square sheets of aluminum foil and coat with cooking spray. Cut halibut into 1-inch pieces and divide equally onto foil; set aside. Slice zucchini and carrot into thin 2-inch strips, julienne style. Slice onion diagonally into ½-inch pieces.

Coat large nonstick skillet with cooking spray. Heat oil to medium-hot; add sliced vegetables and garlic. Stir-fry vegetables for 7 to 10 minutes, until just barely tender. Arrange vegetables evenly over the halibut and sprinkle with dill and lemon pepper. Pour 1 tablespoon of lemon juice into each packet. Fold foil over ingredients, folding edges over twice to make a tight double fold.

Place packets on baking sheet and bake about 15 minutes or until halibut is just cooked. To test, unwrap the top fold carefully to avoid steam and see if the fish flakes with a fork.

Make-ahead instructions: Prepare packets as outlined. Fold foil tightly and refrigerate until ready to cook. Preheat oven to 400 degrees; bake packets 20 minutes, or until fish flakes.

Serving tip: Open packets and "up-end" contents onto a bed of rice so juices soak into the rice, vegetables are next and fish is on top. Sprinkle with parsley and serve with lemon wedges.

Perfect Poached Fish

*Serve **Tasty Tartar Sauce** or **Cucumber Caper Sauce** alongside this basic fish presentation.*

serves 2   per serving: 145 calories, 1½ grams fat

2 cups water (or 1½ cups water plus ½ cup white wine)
1 teaspoon pickling spice
¾ teaspoon salt
2 whole peppercorns
2 tablespoons lemon juice
1 stalk celery, with leaves
¾ pound fresh fillets (sole, lingcod, snapper, perch)

Combine all ingredients except fish in deep skillet. Heat liquid to a full boil and boil for 10 minutes. Strain and discard spices and vegetables. Reheat poaching liquid to a simmer; add fish, cover and simmer 7 to 10 minutes for thick fillets, less for thinner fillets. Fish is done when it flakes easily when tested with fork. Carefully remove with slotted spoon.

Catfish, grouper, halibut, mahimahi, mackerel, monkfish, perch, pike, rockfish, sea bass, snapper, shark, swordfish, trout, turbot, orange roughy, sablefish...there's more to fish than cod and salmon. How many have you tried?

Meat

The merits of meat

Many people are confused about the merits of including meat in their low fat diets. Articles about its saturated fat content and concerns about cholesterol may cause them to think about giving it up altogether. Our lowfat lifestyle message of "everything in moderation" says that this is not necessary. The meat group is a superb source of complete protein, containing all the essential amino acids in the proper proportions necessary to build, maintain and repair body tissues.

> Cholesterol content of beef, pork or lamb is approximately 95 milligrams per 3½-ounce serving, only slightly more than chicken and turkey. Saturated fat ranges from 35% for pork and lamb to about 48% for beef (poultry is approximately 30%). Keep these percentages in perspective; in a portion of lean beef containing 9 grams of total fat, about 4 grams would be saturated.

In addition, meat is an excellent source of many vitamins and minerals. Beef and lamb contribute significant amounts of iron and zinc, and all three provide B-vitamins. If you enjoy meat, include it in your meal planning.

Recent surveys show that the average layer of fat on a piece of meat in the supermarket is now being trimmed to ⅛-inch, a big drop from the previous ½-inch layer. People are getting wiser about fat and are not willing to pay for what they don't plan to eat. Butchers have had to change how they trim because the steaks with too much fat don't sell. Similarly, breeders are adapting their herds to consumer choices; for example, today's hog is 50% leaner than it was 25 years ago.

There are two ways to cut the fat and keep the meat. First, switch to leaner cuts. Look for sirloin or round steak instead of prime rib. Use low fat ground beef in casseroles. Choose pork tenderloin instead of spareribs. Eat lean leg of lamb. (See *Choices: Meat* at the end of this chapter.) Visualize your meat choices as being on a sliding scale, ranging from high to low fat, and keep working your way gradually down that scale.

Second, learn to eat less meat. Many of us take in far more protein than we need. Dietary guidelines suggest that 10% to 15% of our daily calories should come from protein; that's only 200 to 300 calories in a 2000 calorie day. Since protein has 4 calories per gram, this equals 50 to 75 grams of protein per day. A 3½-ounce piece of sirloin steak contains 30 grams of protein. Since many people do not eat just 3½ ounces of sirloin steak, you can see that it is easy to reach and exceed your protein limit.

One easy way to cut the amount of meat is by replacing some of it with carbohydrates. Take a 12-ounce piece of lean steak. Cut it in half. Cut one half in half again and place a 3-ounce piece on a plate. Is that enough meat for your dinner? If you still consider protein as the prime feature of your meal, you'll probably say, *"No way!"*

But slice the other half into very thin strips and arrange flat on a plate. It immediately looks like more meat and is adequate in a stir-fried meal, such as *Oriental Pepper Steak*. Seeing is believing! It is not impossible for the man who used to eat a 12-ounce steak to eventually cut down to a 6-ounce steak and then be happy with 3 ounces in a stir-fried dinner.

This mental picture will help you make gradual changes in the amount of animal protein you eat. Going directly from a huge piece of meat to a tiny cube sitting on a plate usually results in feelings of hardship, but sliding down that scale, gradually making small changes, will do the trick.

Oriental Pepper Steak

Stretch a modest amount of lean beef with lots of rice and crunchy vegetables. When the rice is cooked ahead of time, the whole meal takes just 10 minutes to make.

serves 2	per serving: 350 calories, 10 grams fat

6 ounces lean flank steak
1 cup red pepper strips
1 cup green pepper strips
1 cup yellow onion strips
1 clove garlic, minced

¼ cup water
¼ cup chopped green onion
1½ cups cooked brown rice
1 tablespoon oyster sauce

Cut flank steak across the grain into thin strips and set aside. Coat two large nonstick skillets (one with a cover) with cooking spray. Heat the one with a cover to medium-hot and cook peppers, onions and garlic, stirring frequently until lightly browned, about 5 minutes.

When vegetables are browned, pour in water and cover skillet immediately. Steam for 5 minutes. Add green onion and cooked rice and stir to combine evenly. Cook until rice is heated through before cooking steak.

Heat second skillet to medium-hot. Add steak strips and cook for 1 to 2 minutes, tossing constantly. Combine with pepper-rice mixture and add oyster sauce. Serve at once.

Learn to use meat in combination with vegetables and grains and cut the pieces small. Meat chunks scattered throughout a mixture of other ingredients result in savings of both fat and money. When you cut down on animal protein you automatically cut down on total fat, saturated fat and cholesterol.

Chili Meatloaf

Adding grated vegetables stretches ground beef with no additional fat and almost no calories. As a bonus, the resulting loaf is very moist. Twelve ounces of meat turns into a large meatloaf which easily serves four (or makes great leftovers).

makes 1 loaf   per quarter: 260 calories, 11 grams fat

¾ **pound extra lean**
   ground beef
½ **cup grated carrot**
½ **cup grated potato**
½ **cup grated onion**
¼ **cup dry bread crumbs**
2 **large egg whites,**
   lightly beaten

½ **teaspoon salt**
¼ **teaspoon garlic powder**
1 **teaspoon Worcestershire**
   sauce
⅓ **cup chili sauce**
2 **tablespoons white vinegar**
1 **tablespoon brown sugar**
2 **teaspoons Dijon mustard**

Preheat oven to 350 degrees. Combine ground beef, carrot, potato, onion and bread crumbs and mix well with wooden spoon. Stir in egg whites, salt, garlic powder and Worcestershire sauce and mix well. Form meat into a round loaf about 3 inches high at the center and place in a flat baking dish.

Combine chili sauce, vinegar, brown sugar and mustard and spread half of the mixture over meatloaf. Bake for 25 minutes, then spread remaining sauce evenly over the loaf and bake an additional 20 minutes.

Note: Balance the fat in the meatloaf by serving with plain potatoes or pasta and steamed vegetables. If you want to cut the fat in the loaf itself, make it with ground turkey; fat then drops to about 8 grams per serving.

New Mexican Minestrone Stew

You don't need anything else with this filling, main dish stew except a salad and some crusty bread. Add more hot sauce if you like a zippier taste. Using canned pinto beans instead of dried saves time.

makes about 4 cups   per cup: 240 calories, 7 grams fat

1/2 **pound lean ground beef or raw ground turkey**

1/2 **teaspoon chili powder**

1/4 **teaspoon garlic powder**

1/4 **teaspoon salt**

1/2 **cup chopped onion**

1 **can (15 oz.) kidney or pinto beans, drained and rinsed**

1 **can (8 oz.) stewed tomatoes**

1/2 **cup regular strength beef broth**

1 **cup water**

1/2 **teaspoon hot pepper sauce**

1 **cup shredded raw cabbage**

1/2 **cup uncooked macaroni**

Combine meat, chili powder, garlic powder and salt. Form into small, 1-inch meatballs. Brown meatballs in large skillet. Remove from skillet and blot with paper towel to remove excess fat. Place meatballs in heavy 2-quart pot.

Pour off any fat remaining in skillet. Add onion to skillet and cook for 5 minutes. Add onion to pot along with all remaining ingredients **except** uncooked macaroni. Bring to a boil, reduce heat, cover and simmer for 30 minutes.

Add macaroni and cook for an additional 15 minutes or until tender.

Barbecue tip: So many marinades call for at least 1/2 cup of oil per 1 to 2 pounds of meat. While some may be needed to help the marinade stick to the meat, we find that 1 to 2 tablespoons is plenty. Why have a piece of meat dripping with external fat before you cook it?

Ever-Ready Meat Sauce

Cook once and eat for days! Prepare this energy-saving meat sauce on the weekend and pop it in the freezer for busy days ahead. Don't be alarmed at the fat content – a cup of meat sauce will feed two when combined with vegetables, pasta, beans, etc. With different ingredients, you can make casseroles, pizza, tacos, spaghetti and soups; see following pages for ideas.

makes about 6 cups	per cup: 340 calories, 16 grams fat

1 **pound lean ground beef**	**½ teaspoon dried basil**
1 **pound raw ground turkey**	**¼ teaspoon dried thyme**
2 **cups chopped onion**	**½ teaspoon chili powder**
2 **cloves garlic, crushed**	**1 teaspoon salt**
1 **can (14½ oz.) stewed tomatoes**	**1 tablespoon Worcestershire sauce**
1 **can (15 oz.) tomato sauce**	**¼ teaspoon hot pepper sauce**
½ **cup regular strength beef broth**	**salt to taste**

Brown beef and turkey in a nonstick skillet, breaking up into small chunks. Remove from pan after browning, drain in a colander and blot with paper towel. Place in a 4-quart pot. Pour off any fat remaining in skillet. Add onion and garlic to skillet and cook for five minutes, until soft, then add to meat.

Add all other ingredients and stir well. Bring to a boil, reduce heat, cover and simmer for 2 hours. Remove cover and simmer an additional 30 minutes to thicken. Cool and adjust seasoning. We recommend very light salt to start, leaving the final seasoning until you actually combine the meat sauce with other ingredients. Freeze in 1-cup batches.

Ever-Ready Tacos make a super-quick meal. Add half an envelope of taco seasoning to a cup of meat sauce and heat until bubbling. Fill commercial taco shells with ¼ cup meat mixture and one tablespoon each shredded part-skim Mozzarella and plain lowfat yogurt. Top with chopped lettuce, tomatoes and green onions.

Ever-Ready Italian Pasta Shells

*Here's a great family-pleaser, easy to fix using commercial spaghetti sauce. If you have your own low fat sauce, that's even better, e.g. **Secret Tomato Sauce**. You can make it ahead, then just heat it and serve with salad and garlic bread.*

serves 2 to 3	per shell: 75 calories, 2 grams fat

12 jumbo pasta shells (not manicotti tubes), about 3½ oz.

1 cup low fat spaghetti or marinara sauce

1 cup *Ever-Ready*, **p. 134**

⅛ teaspoon *each* garlic powder and dried oregano

2 tablespoons Parmesan cheese

Cook pasta shells according to package directions; drain, rinse and cool. Preheat oven to 350 degrees.

Spoon ¼ cup spaghetti sauce over bottom of an 8x8-inch baking dish (one with a cover or deep enough to cover with foil). Combine meat sauce, garlic and oregano. Stuff cooked shells and place in a single layer in baking dish. Spoon remaining spaghetti sauce over the top. Bake shells, covered, for 15 minutes. Remove cover and sprinkle Parmesan cheese over top; bake, covered, 10 more minutes or until steaming hot.

Make-ahead instructions: Prepare shells and place in baking dish as indicated. Cover and refrigerate until ready to cook. Preheat oven to 350 degrees and follow above instructions, increasing first baking time to 20 minutes.

Note: Take a close look at prepared spaghetti sauces. You'll see that they can range from 60 calories and no fat to 140 calories and 6 grams of fat per ½ cup.

Ever-Ready Double Corn Casserole

Here's a steaming hot, complete-meal casserole to warm you up on a cold winter night.

serves 2   per serving: 380 calories, 10 grams fat

¾ cup skim milk
¼ teaspoon salt
¼ cup cornmeal
2 large egg whites
½ cup chopped green pepper
1 cup creamed corn

1 cup *Ever-Ready*, p. 134
1 teaspoon hot chili powder
2 tablespoons shredded
  part-skim Mozzarella
  cheese (½ oz.)

Preheat oven to 350 degrees. Heat milk and salt in a small saucepan until almost boiling. Stir in cornmeal and cook, whisking frequently to avoid lumps, about 5 minutes or until thick and smooth. Mixture should be very thick. Remove from heat and let cool to lukewarm.

Beat egg whites lightly and add slowly to cornmeal, stirring constantly. Set aside.

While cornmeal is cooling, coat a small skillet with cooking spray, add green pepper and cook just until soft, about 5 minutes. Stir in corn, meat sauce and chili powder.

Coat a shallow 1-quart baking dish with cooking spray and add meat sauce mixture. Spread cornmeal evenly on top and bake for 20 to 25 minutes, until topping is firm. Sprinkle cheese on top and bake 5 minutes more.

---

*Make **Ever-Ready Pizza** with a jar of pizza sauce and a pot of **Ever-Ready Meat Sauce**. Buy an unbaked pizza crust, spread it with pizza sauce, then top with meat sauce. Sprinkle onions, chopped green pepper and mushrooms on top plus a small amount of grated part-skim Mozzarella cheese, about 1 ounce per person. Bake at 400 degrees for about 10 minutes.*

Barbecued Beef

Lean stew beef is often on sale and can provide many meals when combined with "stretchers" (see below for ideas). Make ahead and freeze until ready to use.

makes 4 cups   per cup: 315 calories, 10 grams fat

1½ pounds lean stew beef
  2 cups chopped onion
  2 cloves garlic, minced
  1 small can (8 oz.) stewed
    tomatoes
  1 cup regular strength
    beef broth
½ cup white vinegar

½ cup chili sauce
  1 tablespoon brown sugar
  1 tablespoon Worcestershire
    sauce
  1 teaspoon Dijon mustard
  2 teaspoons hot chili powder
¼ teaspoon dried thyme

Preheat oven to 300 degrees. Trim fat and cut meat into 1-inch pieces. Brown in a hot nonstick skillet. Add onion and garlic and cook 5 minutes, stirring frequently. Place meat and vegetables in a 2-quart casserole.

Add all other ingredients, stirring to mix well. Cover and bake for 2 to 2½ hours, or until meat is very tender and shreds with a fork. (Meat should be barely covered with liquid while cooking; if necessary, add some water.) Refrigerate beef or freeze in 1-cup portions.

BBQ Stretchers

Cut the fat by stretching the beef with starchy foods.

Barbecued Beef on a Bun: Shred beef, add tomato sauce to make it spreadable, serve on toasted hamburger rolls.

Instant Chili: Stir in kidney beans and extra chili powder.

Beefy Burritos: Season mashed pinto beans with garlic, chili powder and lime juice; fill a warm flour tortilla with beans, meat, shredded lettuce and salsa.

"Anything Goes" Meatloaf

The ultimate ingredients in this tasty loaf depend on what's left over in the refrigerator, so the name is appropriate! Delicious hot or cold. Try this one with ground turkey.

makes 8 slices   per slice: 160 calories, 6 grams fat

1½ **pounds raw ground turkey**
 ½ **cup cooked rice**
 ¼ **cup chopped onion**
 1 **large egg white,**
    lightly beaten
 ⅓ **cup buttermilk**
 ¼ **teaspoon mustard**

 1 **tablespoon Worcestershire**
    sauce
 ½ **teaspoon salt**
 ¼ **teaspoon** *each* **garlic**
    powder, sage and pepper
 ⅓ **cup ANYTHING***

*ANYTHING means any leftovers in the refrigerator, such as chopped raw spinach or cabbage, diced mushrooms, shredded carrots, mashed pinto or kidney beans.

Preheat oven to 350 degrees. Coat an 8x4-inch loaf pan with cooking spray. Combine all ingredients and pat into pan. Bake 1 hour, uncovered. Serve hot or cold.

Tub o' Lard Award

There is no end to creative ways of adding fat to our food, even to simple things like hamburgers. While lean ground veal is an excellent starting point in this **Super-Burger**, take a close look at the rest of it.

For 1 serving, ¼ pound of lean ground veal is mixed with 3 tablespoons of heavy cream, fried in 1 tablespoon of oil and topped with 1 tablespoon of melted butter. Total: **580 calories and 54 grams of fat.** That's a whole day's supply of fat for many of us – and all you've got on your plate is one miserable little meat patty!

This is a classic example of wasting your fat. Will adding cream to a hamburger make a big difference in the taste?

Sausage and Sauerkraut

Here's a generous, one-pot meal that's perfect for a rainy day.

serves 2   per serving: 315 calories, 7 grams fat

6 ounces turkey Polish
  sausage
1 cup diced onion
1 clove garlic, minced
1 large potato, about
  8 oz.

1 small apple
1½ cups sauerkraut, drained
½ cup regular strength
  beef broth
½ cup water
2 teaspoons Dijon mustard

Coat a large, deep skillet (one with a cover) with cooking spray
and heat to medium-hot. Cut sausage into ¼-inch slices, then
cut these in half. Brown lightly on both sides. Add onion and
garlic to skillet and cook for 5 minutes, or until lightly browned.

Meanwhile, scrub the potato and apple well, leaving skin on for
added color and fiber. Dice both into ¼-inch cubes and add to
skillet. Spread sauerkraut over the top. Stir together broth,
water and mustard and pour into skillet. Bring to a boil, reduce
heat, cover and simmer for 25 minutes or until potatoes are
tender.

The best of the wurst

We use turkey Polish sausage in the above recipe. A look at
other alternatives will show you the reason for that choice.

3 oz. serving	Calories	Grams of Fat
"Real" Polish sausage	275	24
Beef or pork frankfurter	270	24
Knockwurst	260	24
Bratwurst	255	22
Turkey frankfurter	190	15
Turkey Polish sausage	120	6

Sweet and Spicy Pork Medallions

Pork has often been avoided by those trying to cut fat and calories. However, new, leaner cuts have been developed which fit easily into a low fat diet, as shown by this very fast recipe.

serves 2   per serving: 245 calories, 5 grams fat

½ pound pork tenderloin | 2 teaspoons cornstarch
¼ cup water | 2 teaspoons sugar
¼ cup white vinegar | 2 teaspoons dry sherry
2 tablespoons apricot | 2 teaspoons soy sauce
preserves | 1 clove garlic, minced

Cut pork tenderloin crosswise into 6 pieces, each approximately 1-inch thick. Flatten each piece with a mallet to ¼-inch thickness. Meanwhile combine water, vinegar, preserves, cornstarch, sugar, sherry, soy sauce and garlic in small bowl; set aside.

Heat a large nonstick frying pan to medium-hot. Brown pork 2 to 3 minutes on each side. Remove to platter and keep warm. Add preserves mixture to frying pan and cook for 3 to 5 minutes or until thickened, scraping up browned bits from pan. Add pork, turning over to coat. Serve at once.

---

*Here's another quick recipe, **French Tenderloin**, using the same technique. Flatten half a pound of sliced tenderloin, as above, sprinkle with garlic salt and brown on each side. Remove from pan and keep warm. Shake together ½ cup regular strength chicken broth and 1 teaspoon cornstarch. Pour into pan and boil until thick. Reduce heat, stir in 2 teaspoons Dijon mustard, ¼ teaspoon dried dill weed and ¼ cup plain lowfat yogurt. Return pork to pan and simmer just until heated through. Serves 2. Per serving: 190 calories, 5½ grams fat.*

Jambalaya

Jambalaya is an easy, spicy way of using up leftover ham. With pre-cooked rice, the whole dinner can be ready in half an hour.

serves 2   per serving: 310 calories, 5½ grams fat

1 teaspoon salad oil
½ cup diced green pepper
½ cup diced onion
1½ cups cooked white rice
¼ pound lean ham, cut in
   small cubes (about 1 cup)
½ cup tomato sauce

½ cup regular strength
   chicken broth
½ teaspoon chili powder
¼ teaspoon garlic powder
½ teaspoon hot pepper sauce
½ teaspoon salt or to taste

Coat a large nonstick skillet with cooking spray. Heat oil, add green pepper and onion and cook for 5 minutes or until soft. Stir in rice, add ham and mix well.

Blend together tomato sauce, broth and seasonings. Stir sauce into rice mixture and simmer until liquid is absorbed. Stir frequently to avoid sticking. Jambalaya should be almost dry when it is served.

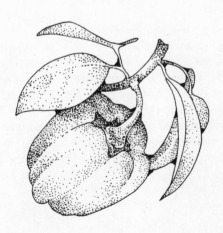

Ham 'n Yam

You can assemble this dinner in 5 minutes then throw it in the oven and go away for a while. Good with barley or potatoes to soak up the sweet juices.

serves 2   per serving: 335 calories, 6 grams fat

½ **pound lean ham or turkey ham, sliced ¼-inch thick**	2 **tablespoons maple syrup**
1 **fresh yam, about 8 oz., peeled and sliced ¼-inch thick**	2 **tablespoons orange juice**
	1 **teaspoon Dijon mustard**
	2 **teaspoons cider vinegar**

Preheat oven to 350 degrees. Use a baking dish large enough so that everything can be arranged in one layer. Coat the dish with cooking spray and place the ham slices down the center. Place the yam slices along either side, laying them flat so they will steam in the basting mixture.

Combine remaining ingredients. Spoon half the syrup mixture over the ham and yams and bake for 20 minutes. Turn everything over and baste with remaining liquid. Bake an additional 10 to 15 minutes or until yams are fork-tender.

> *For those of us who can't imagine a holiday dinner without baked ham, the good news is that leaner hams are now in the marketplace. Look for a maximum of 5% fat, or, as they say, "95% fat free." A 3½ ounce serving of lean ham will have approximately 120 calories and 4 to 5 grams of fat. Hams that are less well-trimmed and combine lean and marbled meat could have almost three times as much fat.*

Dilly Tomato-Lamb Stew

*The following recipe is a family favorite from **"The Lowfat Life-style."** We have served it to many guests, some of whom would have claimed they didn't like lamb before they had this! We encourage you to try it – the flavor is light and the texture is creamy. Excellent over pasta.*

---

serves 2   per serving: 265 calories, 6½ grams fat

½ **pound lean boneless lamb**
½ **cup chopped onion**
1 **small can (8 oz.) stewed tomatoes**
¼ **cup white wine or regular strength chicken broth**
½ **teaspoon dried dill weed**

½ **teaspoon salt**
2 **teaspoons** *each* **cornstarch and water, stirred together**
2 **tablespoons plain lowfat yogurt**

Coat a large skillet (one with a cover) with cooking spray and heat to medium hot. Cut lamb into 1-inch pieces and brown 4 to 5 minutes. Add onion, cook 5 minutes or until soft. Add tomatoes, wine or broth, dill weed and salt. Bring liquid to a boil, reduce heat, cover and simmer for 20 to 25 minutes, until lamb is tender.

Add cornstarch mixture to skillet and boil until thick, stirring constantly. Reduce heat to a simmer, stir in yogurt and cook gently for 1 to 2 minutes until heated through.

Choices: Meat

Although many processed meats are high in fat, meat in general doesn't have to be off-limits. While there will always be high fat ways to eat meat, there are also choices that are relatively low in fat and calories. If not otherwise mentioned, values listed here are for meat that has been trimmed of separable fat. Note, also, the serving size is 3½ ounces, unless otherwise listed. If you normally eat twice this much, double the values shown below and read the start of this chapter again!

Meat	Calories	Grams of fat
Prime rib, lean and fat	360	30
Regular ground beef	290	21
Corned beef	250	19
Extra lean ground beef	255	16
Flank steak	240	15
Prime rib, lean only	245	14
Bottom round	225	10
Sirloin steak	210	9
Top round	195	6
Spareribs	400	30
Canned ham, regular	190	13
Pork tenderloin	165	5
Canned ham, lean	120	5
Bacon, 3 pieces broiled	110	9
Canadian bacon, 2 slices	90	4
Lamb shoulder chop	210	11
Lamb leg, roasted	180	7
Veal loin chop	215	8
Veal cutlet	180	5

Pasta, Legumes & Grains

Learn to stretch

Adding pasta, legumes (beans, peas, lentils) and grains (rice, barley, wheat) to your meals will help stretch your fat, your money and your time. They add variety and good nutrition to your diet, supplying carbohydrates, protein, vitamins and fiber, all for minimum cost and effort.

Although some people think of them as fattening, these "stretchers" contain almost no fat. By combining them with meat products, which are often accompanied by too much fat, you can cut the total fat content of your meal easily. In addition to combining them with meat, you should plan a meatless meal occasionally. Don't think that "meatless" means "no protein" or "not filling"; legumes in particular are very high in protein. The table on the next page shows the amount of protein from different plant sources.

> If this is a new way of eating for your family, steaming a big pot of vegetables and announcing that this is dinner may not impress them. Instead, start out with a hearty recipe such as *Lentil Chili*. It will satisfy and surprise the most skeptical eaters.

One caution about meatless meals: A common mistake is to remove red meat and then substitute excessive amounts of eggs and high fat cheese to make up for it. We have seen many meatless recipes that are loaded with fat. Not exactly an improvement over the original!

Pasta, legumes and grains make your money go further. Since they are available for just pennies per serving, they can bring down the average cost of your meals. One filling cup of cooked barley, brown rice, split peas, lentils, or beans generally costs less than 20 cents. Of course, you can always buy a small bag of pre-mixed beans tied with a pretty bow and pay a dollar per serving!

A beef stew stretched with barley or pasta can feed twice as many people for almost no additional cost. With a bit of meat, several pounds of pasta and a sack of beans, you could feed a crowd inexpensively for several days. A few cups of lentils and a ham bone makes a huge pot of nourishing, low cost soup.

Although these foods often take a few hours to cook, most take only a short time to prepare; once they're put together, your time's your own. Separate the two tasks. Prepare the slow cookers ahead of time and refrigerate or freeze until needed. That way dinner can be on the table half an hour after walking in the door, with almost no extra effort.

Protein sources

Here's a brief list of some plant sources of protein. Fat is not listed since it is almost non-existent in all of them. For reference, recommended daily protein intake is 10% to 15% of total calories, about 50 to 75 grams.

1 cup (cooked)	Calories	Protein (grams)
Pinto beans	330	22
Lentils	210	16
Navy beans	225	15
Kidney beans	220	14
Noodles	200	7
Bulgur	200	6
Brown rice	230	5
Pearl barley	200	5

Pasta pointers

It's difficult to find anyone who doesn't like pasta. In fact, according to the National Pasta Association, by the late 1980s Americans were eating about fourteen pounds per person per year. Are you getting your share, or do you pass up nutritious, delicious pasta because "it's fattening!"?

In reality, pasta fits current dietary guidelines of avoiding too much fat and cholesterol, eating adequate starch and fiber and avoiding too much sodium. It is a complex carbohydrate providing energy, vitamins and minerals, with less than half the calories of fat. (Remember that carbohydrates and proteins provide 4 calories per gram, fat provides 9 calories per gram.)

> Pasta is considered "nutrient dense," meaning that it provides good food value for the number of calories per serving. As well as being a source of complex carbohydrates, it provides protein, vitamins (such as thiamine and riboflavin) and several minerals (such as iron and zinc) and is almost salt-free.

The word "pasta" covers two different products, macaroni and noodles. Macaroni products are made from enriched flour and water. Noodles are made from the same dough with the addition of eggs. A standard serving, two ounces uncooked, contains 210 calories and only 1 to 2 grams of fat. Remember, it's not the pasta that's the problem! Just ignore the suggestions to toss it with butter and cream before serving.

Secret Tomato Sauce

Keep this easy, flavor-filled tomato sauce on hand for quick meals. The "secret" is the large amount of basil. Excellent over plain pasta or with vegetables, see next page. It freezes well, so this recipe makes 8 cups.

makes 8 cups   per cup: 145 calories, 2 grams fat

4 cans (14½ oz. each) whole tomatoes	2 cloves garlic, crushed
1 can (6 oz.) tomato paste	1 tablespoon olive oil
2 large onions, chopped (about 3 cups)	2 tablespoons honey
	4 tablespoons dried basil
	1-3 teaspoons salt, to taste

Combine all ingredients in a heavy 4-quart pot. Bring to a boil, reduce heat, cover and simmer for 30 minutes. Remove cover and simmer an additional 30 minutes. Cool and refrigerate or freeze until needed.

How to cook pasta

The National Pasta Association offers some tips on how to make sure your meals are pasta perfect. First, always cook pasta uncovered at a fast boil, using plenty of water – at least a quart for every four ounces of dry pasta. This circulates the pasta for uniform results.

Stir frequently to prevent sticking. The NPA says that, contrary to popular belief, the addition of oil to the pot does nothing to prevent sticking. Oil floats. While the water boils beneath it, the oil sits on the top in a corner. When the pasta is drained, the oil is the first thing lost.

If pasta is to be used as part of a dish requiring further cooking, undercook slightly. Follow the package directions. For the degree of tenderness desired, from tender to fairly firm, the cooking time varies from 5 to 20 minutes. Drain pasta to stop the cooking action. Do not rinse unless the recipe specifically says to do so.

Refrigerator Pasta

Use this quick dish as an excuse to clean out your refrigerator! For a different variation another time, use mushrooms, onions and green pepper strips in this fast meal.

serves 2   per serving: 390 calories, 8 grams fat

4 oz. linguine, uncooked
1½ cups *Secret Tomato Sauce,*
**   p. 148**
1 teaspoon olive oil
1 cup chopped raw broccoli
1 celery stalk, sliced

1 small zucchini, unpeeled,
**   sliced ¼-inch thick**
2 oz. lean ham or turkey
**   ham, diced (about ½ cup)**
2 tablespoons grated
**   Parmesan cheese**

Cook linguine in a large pot of boiling water, according to package directions. Drain and keep warm until vegetable mixture is ready. Meanwhile, heat tomato sauce to a simmer.

Coat a large skillet with cooking spray. Heat oil to medium-hot, add vegetables and stir-fry for 5 to 7 minutes, until barely tender. Add diced ham and cook until lightly browned.

Add vegetable mixture to drained pasta and toss well. Divide into two portions and top each with tomato sauce. Sprinkle Parmesan cheese over top and serve at once.

Be a "starch starter." Learn to combine larger quantities of pasta, rice, legumes and vegetables with smaller amounts of lean meat, fish or poultry.

Veggie Linguine

Quite different from the previous recipe, this quick pasta meal does not have the typical tomato sauce but concentrates on the wonderful flavor of fresh vegetables alone.

serves 2   per serving: 270 calories, 6 grams fat

4 oz. linguine, uncooked
2 teaspoons olive oil
1 clove garlic, minced
1 cup unpeeled zucchini,
  cut in 1-inch slices
½ cup sliced celery
½ cup chopped onion

¼ teaspoon dried basil
¼ teaspoon salt
⅛ teaspoon pepper
½ cup sliced mushrooms
½ cup cherry tomatoes,
  cut in half

Cook linguine in a large pot of boiling water, according to package directions. Drain and keep warm.

Coat a large nonstick skillet with cooking spray. Heat oil to medium-hot and add garlic, zucchini, celery and onion to skillet. Stir-fry about 6 minutes or until vegetables are crisp-tender. Sprinkle with basil, salt and pepper. Add mushrooms and tomatoes and stir-fry 4 more minutes or until heated through. Toss with linguine.

Note: If you want to add some protein, cut a skinned chicken breast into small cubes and stir-fry for 3 to 4 minutes before you add the vegetables.

*See also **Turkey Tetrazzini** in "Poultry," **Scallop and Vegetable Fettucine** in "Seafood," **Italian Pasta Shells** in "Meats."*

Spaghetti Cake

No, it's not a weird dessert but a tasty quick meal, just 15 minutes from start to finish and a great use for some leftover ham.

serves 2   per serving: 245 calories, 5 grams fat

3 oz. spaghetti, uncooked	**1 large whole egg**
2 oz. lean ham, diced	**1 large egg white**
(about ½ cup)	**1 tablespoon water**
1 green onion, chopped	**salt to taste**
¼ teaspoon dried dill weed	

Cook the spaghetti, following package directions, until just tender. It will cook more in the skillet, so don't overdo it.

Meanwhile, coat a large skillet with cooking spray and heat to medium-hot. Brown ham and green onion. Drain spaghetti and add to skillet. Sprinkle with dill. Cook the spaghetti mixture 3 to 4 minutes, until it starts to turn golden.

Beat whole egg, egg white and water together until foamy. Pour this over the spaghetti mixture, stir to coat and flatten into a pancake. Continue cooking just until eggs are set. Salt to taste.

Italian, anyone?

If you're bored with the same old plate of noodles, try something different. Too many of us think only of spaghetti when we want some pasta, but "muffs" and "mustaches," "butterflies" and "little hats" are all yours for the cooking. The labels will say Manicotti and Mostaccioli, Farfalle and Capelletti.

Fusilli (long, corkscrew-shaped spaghetti), rotini (spirals) or ziti (small tubes) will make your favorite sauce appear just a bit more exotic. Even though these fancy words simply describe different shapes and sizes of macaroni, they somehow seem to be more fun to eat.

Creamy Clam Pasta

While the preceding recipe makes a quick lunch, you might choose to serve this meal as an elegant dinner...one that the cook can enjoy too since it's so easy and very fast! Excellent with French bread and spinach salad.

serves 2   per serving: 350 calories, 7 grams fat

4 oz. noodles, uncooked	1 tablespoon chopped fresh
1 clove garlic, mashed	parsley
1 cup sliced mushrooms	salt and pepper to taste
1 teaspoon olive oil	1 teaspoon *each* cornstarch
1 can (6½ oz.) chopped	and water, stirred
clams, drained well	together
⅓ cup plain lowfat yogurt	2 tablespoons grated
½ teaspoon dried basil	Parmesan cheese

Cook noodles in a large pot of boiling water, according to package directions. Drain and keep warm.

Meanwhile, coat a large nonstick skillet with cooking spray and heat to medium-hot. Brown garlic and mushrooms for 5 minutes. Add oil and sizzle for 1 minute. Add drained clams, yogurt, basil and parsley and simmer gently for 5 minutes. Season to taste.

Add cornstarch mixture to sauce and boil 1 minute or until thickened. Pour clam sauce over drained noodles, toss and serve immediately. Sprinkle with Parmesan cheese.

Pineapple Ham Pasta Salad

Here's an easy and colorful main dish salad, best when made a few hours ahead to let the flavors blend.

makes 4 cups   per cup: 185 calories, 3 grams fat

½ cup elbow or shell macaroni, uncooked	¾ cup pineapple chunks, juice-packed, drained
½ cup tiny frozen peas, thawed but not cooked	½ cup chopped celery
	1 tablespoon capers, drained
½ pound lean ham or turkey ham, cut in ½-inch cubes	⅓ cup apple cider vinegar
	2 tablespoons sugar

Cook macaroni according to package directions. Drain and rinse. Place in a large bowl. Add peas, ham, pineapple, celery and capers; set aside.

Over low heat, warm vinegar and sugar in a small saucepan just until sugar dissolves; cool. Pour over ham mixture and toss. Cover and refrigerate salad until ready to serve.

Tub o' Lard Award

While pasta by itself is very low in fat, gourmet cookbooks seem to outdo themselves in trying to pile more and more fat onto that simple plateful of carbohydrates. Our vote for "the most fat in a forkful" has to go to **Four-Cheese Pasta**.

The recipe calls for 1½ cups of whipping cream, ¼ cup of butter and 8 cups of cheese (Gruyere, Gorgonzola, Mozzarella and Parmesan). Even though it serves eight, this artery-clogging grease totals **600 calories and 53 grams of fat** per serving. And this is a first course!

It is hard to believe that these happy eaters don't realize, or care about, how much fat they are eating. We hope you do.

Pea 'n Pasta Salad

This salad makes a colorful addition to a picnic table. Make it ahead of time so flavors blend.

makes 4 cups	per cup: 230 calories, 7½ grams fat

½ cup dried green split peas
2 cups water
2 cups cooked orzo or other small pasta, rinsed and drained
⅔ cup diced red pepper
⅔ cup chopped green onion
1 tablespoon lemon juice

3 tablespoons white wine vinegar
2 tablespoons olive oil
1 clove garlic, minced
1½ teaspoons Dijon mustard
¼ teaspoon salt
⅛ teaspoon black pepper
⅛ teaspoon cayenne pepper

Combine peas and water in small saucepan. Bring to a boil, reduce heat, cover and simmer 20 to 25 minutes, or until peas are just tender. Drain and put peas in large bowl. Add cooked pasta, red pepper and green onion.

In a separate small jar, combine lemon juice, vinegar, olive oil, garlic, mustard, salt, black pepper and cayenne pepper. Cover and shake to blend well. Pour over salad ingredients and toss to coat evenly. Chill for 2 or more hours.

Split peas and lentils have the added advantage of cooking quickly, without overnight soaking.

Personalized pasta

Need some quick meal ideas for hot summer days? You don't need more recipes – just pick and choose from the following lists and build your own pasta salad. Toss together any combination of ingredients, one from each section, and you've got it made!

Note that using the amounts given will make a salad large enough to serve six, another bonus if you want to cook once and eat for a couple of days. Add up the calories for each item that you use to get the total calories per serving. Calories are approximate, depending on the combination of ingredients used.

Cooked pasta (8 oz., uncooked; 140 calories per serving): rotini, mostaccioli, salad macaroni, rotelle, shell macaroni, rigatoni, tricolor pasta, cut fusilli, elbow macaroni, cut ziti.

Cubed or sliced cooked meat (2½ to 3 cups, unless specified; 140 calories per serving): chicken, turkey, lean beef, lean pork, shrimp, crab, tofu (12 oz. cubed, delete 10 calories per serving), egg (add 20 calories per serving), tuna, chick peas (add 70 calories per serving).

Chopped or sliced raw vegetables (2 to 3 cups; 25 calories per serving): carrots, celery, broccoli, tomatoes, cauliflower, cucumber, mushrooms, zucchini, green pepper, radishes.

Reduced calorie salad dressing (1 cup, or to taste; 60 calories per serving): Creamy Cucumber, Blue Cheese, Italian, Creamy Dijon, French, Ranch, Tomato and Bacon, Creamy Italian, Thousand Island.

General instructions: Cook pasta according to package directions; drain. Rinse with cold water to cool quickly; drain well. In large bowl, combine meat, vegetables and cooked pasta. Add dressing and toss lightly. Chill.

Look at legumes

Legumes include beans, split peas, lentils. They can be used, often interchangeably, in soups, stews, chili and casseroles. Because legumes vary in nutritional content, your best bet is to eat a wide variety.

The **common bean** originated in Mexico and came under cultivation about 6000 B.C. It has been developed into hundreds of varieties, including the following:

Kidney (red) beans – oval, medium-sized, great for soups, chili, red beans and rice.

Pinto (pink) beans – oval, small, beige, brown-red or speckled; a favorite for real southern chili, minestrone and tamale pie.

White (Great Northern, navy, pea) beans – small to large; we know them best in New England baked beans and famous Senate bean soup.

Black beans – popular in Caribbean and Latin American cooking; also a great soup bean.

Garbanzo (chickpea) beans – round and firm, often served cold in salads.

The **pea** spread from the Middle East to the Mediterranean, India and China. It also was domesticated about 6000 B.C. Split peas (green or yellow) are flat disks which cook quickly to soft texture, no soaking needed; excellent in soups.

The **lentil** is considered the oldest cultivated legume, originating in Southwest Asia about 7000 B.C. Small disks, brown, green or red, cook quickly, no soaking required; a very versatile legume found in soups, curries, chili, stews and loaves.

Lentil Chili

This chili will convince any skeptic about the merits of meatless, low fat eating. Leftovers freeze well.

makes about 4 cups   per cup: 290 calories, 2 grams fat

1 cup dried lentils
3 cups water
1 teaspoon olive oil
2 cloves garlic, minced
2 cups chopped onion
2 tablespoons chili powder

2 cans (14½ oz. each) stewed tomatoes
1 small can (8 oz.) tomato sauce
1 teaspoon salt or to taste

Wash and pick over lentils to discard any debris. In a large saucepan, cover lentils with water and bring to a boil. Reduce heat, cover and simmer for 30 minutes or until tender and water is absorbed.

Coat large nonstick skillet with cooking spray. Heat oil to medium-hot and brown garlic and onion for 5 minutes. Add to lentils, along with all other ingredients. Simmer for an additional 45 minutes or until flavors are well blended. Thin out with water if too thick. Serve hot.

Note: We like to use hot chili powder; adjust amount to taste. For added zip, use Mexican-style stewed tomatoes.

The humble legume has existed for centuries, offering its inexpensive package of protein, vitamins and minerals, without cholesterol and almost no fat. It fits right into our low fat, high fiber recommendations.

Bar-B-Q'd Lentils

A very easy variation on traditional baked beans.

makes about 3 cups   per ½ cup: 175 calories, ½ gram fat

1 cup dried lentils	1 tablespoon brown sugar
3 cups water	1 tablespoon vinegar
1 can (8 oz.) tomato	½ teaspoon dry mustard
sauce	½ teaspoon Worcestershire
¼ cup molasses	sauce
¼ cup catsup	⅛ teaspoon liquid smoke
1 tablespoon minced onion	salt to taste

Wash and pick over lentils to discard any debris. Cover lentils with water and bring to a boil. Reduce heat, cover and simmer 30 minutes or until tender and water is absorbed.

Preheat oven to 350 degrees. Place cooked lentils and all remaining ingredients in a large pot and bake for 45 minutes.

Rice and Lentil Salad

Add a whole wheat roll and a glass of milk for a complete lunch. Make ahead for maximum flavor.

makes 2 cups   per cup: 235 calories, 7½ grams fat

¾ cup cooked lentils	2 tablespoons lemon juice
¾ cup cooked brown rice	½ teaspoon dried marjoram
¼ cup chopped tomato	⅛ teaspoon salt
¼ cup chopped green onion	1 tablespoon minced parsley
1 tablespoon olive oil	

Combine lentils, rice, tomato and green onion. In a small jar combine oil, lemon juice, marjoram, salt and parsley. Cover and shake well, then pour over lentil mixture, tossing lightly to mix. Cover and chill for several hours or overnight to blend flavors.

Lentil Pepper Pot

Serve this one-pot meal with crusty bread and a salad. Very fast to prepare, it makes a tummy-warming meal for a cool evening and great leftovers for a hot lunch.

makes 4 cups · per cup: 220 calories, 2 grams fat

1 teaspoon olive oil	2 tablespoons tomato paste
1 medium onion, chopped (about 1 cup)	1 teaspoon brown sugar
1 small red pepper, cut in lengthwise strips (about 1 cup)	¼ teaspoon hot pepper sauce
	½ cup dried lentils
2 cups regular strength beef broth	1 can (15 oz.) Great Northern beans (white), drained and rinsed
	1 small red onion, chopped

Coat a large pot with cooking spray. Add oil, heat to medium-hot and add onion and red pepper; stir-fry for 5 minutes. Wash and pick over lentils to discard any debris; add to pot, along with all other ingredients except red onion. Bring to a boil, reduce heat, cover and simmer for 30 to 35 minutes, or until lentils are tender.

Serve with condiment of chopped red onion.

Note: Can be made ahead and refrigerated overnight or frozen for later use.

Legumes: *Flowering plants which produce seeds in pods; they include lentils, peas and beans.* **Grains**: *Grasses which produce separate small kernels or grains; they include wheat, oats, barley, rice and corn. When cooked, legumes double or triple in volume, grains triple in volume. For example, 1 cup of dried peas makes 2 to 3 cups cooked; 1 cup of uncooked rice makes 3 cups cooked.*

Bean tips

You can't go wrong by adding more beans to your diet. Low cost, low fat and cholesterol free, they've got protein, iron, calcium, B-vitamins, fiber and more. They add texture, bulk and taste, as well as food value, to many meals.

You've probably noticed that most recipes using dried beans start by telling you to soak them for several hours or to boil them briefly and set them aside for an hour or two. After years of doing this automatically, assuming we were just saving cooking time, we finally learned the real explanation.

How many of you have made a casserole with beans and meat in tomato sauce and had the beans remain slightly crunchy even after hours of cooking? Harold McGee, the author of *"On Food and Cooking, The Science and Lore of the Kitchen,"* states that the cell walls of beans will not soften in acidic conditions, so if they're added to something like tomatoes **before they're soft** they'll never get any softer, no matter how long you simmer them. Conclusion: Don't rush the soaking step.

In addition, one of the consequences of eating legumes is the production of excess gas, or flatulence, in some people. Some cooks find that soaking legumes in very large amounts of water, to be discarded before cooking, will also decrease gas production. Not all are affected by this and even those who are may find that it decreases over time as the body's digestive system appears to adapt to the challenge. If you're not used to eating many legumes, we recommend starting with small portions at occasional meals.

Smoky Beans

The addition of liquid smoke adds a flavor dimension to this super-simple pot of beans. Plan ahead for soaking and baking.

makes 4 cups   per ½ cup: 140 calories, ½ gram fat

1½ cups dried pinto or kidney beans	1 cup chopped onion
4 cups water	½ teaspoon liquid smoke
1 clove garlic, minced	1 teaspoon salt or to taste

Rinse and pick over beans, discarding any debris. Soak the beans overnight in enough water to cover. The next day, drain beans and place in a 4-quart pot. Add the 4 cups of water and all other ingredients. Bring to a boil, reduce heat, cover and simmer until beans are tender and liquid is absorbed (about 2 hours). Add additional small amounts of water, if necessary. Salt to taste.

Four Fiber Casserole

This recipe combines barley, bulgur and beans with carrots. It is easy to throw together and makes a different lunch. Green pepper and celery can be added for extra crunch and color.

makes 2 servings   per serving: 205 calories, 5½ grams fat

1 cup regular strength chicken broth	½ small onion, chopped
¼ cup pearl barley	2 tablespoons snipped fresh parsley
2 tablespoons bulgur	⅛ teaspoon garlic powder
½ cup canned kidney beans, drained and rinsed	⅛ teaspoon black pepper
1 medium carrot, thinly sliced	2 tablespoons shredded Cheddar cheese (1 oz.)
	salt and pepper to taste

Preheat oven to 350 degrees. Coat a 1-quart casserole with cooking spray. Combine everything in casserole except cheese. Bake, covered, for 50 minutes. Sprinkle cheese over top and bake a few minutes more or just until cheese melts.

Summer-Easy Baked Beans

A pot of richly-flavored baked beans is a popular addition to a picnic. These are very easy to prepare.

makes 2 cups   per ½ cup: 140 calories, almost no fat

1 can (15 oz.) pinto beans, drained and rinsed	2 tablespoons cider vinegar
½ cup chopped onion	1 teaspoon Dijon mustard
2 tablespoons molasses	2 tablespoons chili sauce
1 teaspoon Worcestershire sauce	⅛ teaspoon garlic powder
	½ cup tomato sauce

Preheat oven to 350 degrees. Combine all ingredients in a 1-quart casserole, cover and bake 1 hour. Serve warm.

Barley Pilaf

Combine mushrooms and barley for a hearty side dish. You can also turn it into a light meal by stirring in bits of slivered, cooked chicken before adding the chicken broth.

serves 2   per serving: 120 calories, 2 grams fat

1 cup sliced mushrooms	1 cup regular strength chicken broth
½ teaspoon olive oil	
¼ cup finely chopped onion	⅛ teaspoon Italian seasoning
1 clove garlic, minced	⅛ teaspoon salt or to taste
⅓ cup pearl barley	

Coat a large nonstick skillet with cooking spray. Heat to medium-hot and add mushrooms. Cook and stir mushrooms for 2 to 3 minutes until lightly browned; add oil, onion, garlic and barley. Cook for 2 to 3 minutes until vegetables are soft and barley is lightly toasted. Place mixture in a small saucepan.

Add chicken broth, Italian seasoning and salt, bring to a boil, reduce heat, cover and simmer for about 45 minutes or until barley is tender and liquid is absorbed.

Vegetable Rice Pancakes

*These pancakes-with-a-twist make a different meat accompaniment. Serve with a meal that contains a sauce (e.g. **Country Captain**), or spread with yogurt.*

makes 6 pancakes   each: 60 calories, almost no fat

1 cup cooked brown rice
1 tablespoon minced parsley
⅓ cup grated carrot
¼ cup finely chopped red onion
¼ teaspoon salt

⅛ teaspoon pepper
2 large egg whites, lightly beaten
¼ cup flour
lemon wedges

Thoroughly mix all ingredients (except lemon wedges!). Coat a nonstick skillet with cooking spray and heat to medium-hot. Drop spoonfuls of batter onto skillet and press flat with a spoon. Cook until brown, turn and cook other side, about 2 minutes per side. Remove to a warm plate and keep warm in the oven until all pancakes are cooked.

Squeeze fresh lemon juice over pancakes and serve at once.

Rice is a complex carbohydrate which is very low in fat. There are the same number of calories in one 3-pound can of lard as there are in about 50 cups of cooked brown rice. Seems to us there's a lot more good eating in the rice! We enjoy brown rice and tend to substitute it in most rice recipes. With its bran layer still intact, brown rice has more flavor, a chewy texture and extra nutrients. Its only possible disadvantage is that it does take longer to cook, but just learning to put the rice on first will take care of that.

Baked Rice Casserole

If you think the only way to serve rice in a low fat kitchen is plain and boiled, you will be surprised and pleased with this version. The casserole can be prepared ahead and makes a good accompaniment to a light dinner of cold turkey and salad.

serves 2   per serving: 190 calories, 4 grams fat

1 **cup regular strength chicken broth**
⅓ **cup brown rice, uncooked**
1 **cup chopped mushrooms**
¼ **cup chopped green onion**
2 **tablespoons light cream cheese**

2 **tablespoons 1% cottage cheese**
¼ **teaspoon dried thyme**
⅛ **teaspoon garlic powder**
  salt and pepper to taste

In a small saucepan, bring chicken broth to a boil, add rice, reduce heat, cover and simmer 40 to 45 minutes, until rice is tender and liquid is gone. Set aside.

After rice is cooked, preheat oven to 325 degrees. Meanwhile, coat a large skillet with cooking spray, add mushrooms and cook over medium-high heat until they begin to brown. Remove from heat and stir in green onion.

Blend cream cheese and cottage cheese until smooth. Combine cooked rice, mushrooms and onion and stir in blended cheese, thyme and garlic. Season to taste. Coat a shallow 1-quart casserole dish with cooking spray and pat rice mixture into a 1-inch-thick layer. Bake casserole, covered, for 15 minutes or until warm.

Make-ahead instructions: Prepare mixture as described and pat into casserole dish. Cover and refrigerate until ready to cook. Preheat oven to 325 degrees and bake casserole, covered, for 25 minutes or until heated through.

*See also: **Lemon Chicken 'n Rice** in "Poultry," **Jambalaya** in "Meats," **Shrimp Fried Rice, Tuna Rice Salad** in "Seafood."*

Vegetables and Salads

More is better

Studies suggest that consumers are trying to change their eating habits to include more fresh produce. However, a recent national health and nutrition survey found that on the day questioned close to 50% had eaten no vegetables other than potatoes, beans or salad, and 40% had eaten no fruit at all.

Dietary guidelines state that we should be eating at least four servings of fruits and vegetables daily. They add vitamins and satisfaction without excess calories and rarely any fat. Unfortunately, too many of these power-packed foods are ignored.

Most of us have long-held ideas about what tastes good and are downright unadventurous about trying new foods. How many different vegetables do you eat? The next time you go shopping, count all the fresh vegetables in your favorite store, then check how many you eat regularly, occasionally, rarely or never. If you're like most people, you'll probably find quite a few in the last two categories. It's not hard to list fifty different vegetables, without including every kind of lettuce, yet many of us eat only a few of them. Resolve to do better.

The easiest way to add more fresh fruits and vegetables to your daily diet is to have them ready to eat. Prepare small, covered bowls of broccoli, jicama, cauliflower, carrots, sprouts, radishes, cherry tomatoes, red pepper, cucumber or zucchini. Similarly, keep fruit washed and ready to eat. When we put a bowl of grapes out on the counter, they're gone within hours. Left in the bottom of the refrigerator, they're forgotten.

Try a new piece of fruit with your lunch, add an extra, unusual vegetable at dinner. Add slices of green pepper or tomato to every sandwich. Blend up a quick, chilled soup with almost any green vegetable which has been quickly cooked in some chicken broth plus buttermilk or lowfat milk. Toss together a stir-fry with whatever you find in the refrigerator. Appealing, inexpensive and abundant, low calorie fruits and vegetables should be part of every meal.

Not a fan of cooked vegetables? You may be overcooking them. Once you try lightly steamed, still crunchy broccoli, you'll agree that it tastes much better than those gray-green, limp stalks that lie on too many plates. Frankly, we like most of our vegetables simply prepared – barely cooked and served with just a squeeze of lemon juice, a sprinkle of herbs and some artificial butter flavoring. See *Do yourself a flavor* later in this chapter for use of herbs.

Quick Italian Zucchini

When zucchini beds are overflowing you need lots of ideas for fast ways to get rid of it, particularly those large ones!

serves 2   per serving: 50 calories, 2½ grams fat

1 teaspoon olive oil	few sprinkles of Italian
1 medium zucchini,	seasoning, salt and pepper
unpeeled and cut in	½ cup regular strength
¼-inch thick slices	chicken broth
½ cup minced red onion	

Coat a large nonstick skillet with cooking spray. Heat oil and place zucchini in a flat layer. Sprinkle with onion and cook about 4 minutes, until zucchini is browned on one side.

Turn zucchini over, sprinkle with Italian seasoning, salt and pepper. Increase heat, add chicken broth and boil down liquid 2 to 3 minutes, until it is almost gone and zucchini is soft. Serve at once.

166

Zucchini Provencal

Thinly sliced vegetables cook quickly.

serves 2   per serving: 50 calories, 2½ grams fat

1 teaspoon olive oil
½ cup thinly sliced red
  or yellow onion
1 medium zucchini,
  unpeeled, thinly sliced
¼ cup water

½ cup diced fresh tomato
  or canned whole tomatoes,
  drained
¼ teaspoon dried basil
  lemon pepper

Heat oil in a large nonstick skillet (one with a cover). Add onion and cook for 2 to 3 minutes or until golden. Add zucchini and stir-fry 2 to 3 minutes. Add water, reduce heat, cover and steam for 2 minutes.

Remove cover, stir in tomato and basil and sprinkle lightly with lemon pepper. Cover and simmer 2 minutes until everything is hot. Adjust for salt.

Gingered Carrots

Great looks, great taste and good for you – the perfect vegetable.

serves 2   per serving: 60 calories, 2 grams fat

1 cup baby carrots, or
  regular carrots cut in
  small chunks (about
  ⅓ pound)
1 teaspoon margarine

1 teaspoon brown sugar
1 teaspoon grated orange
  rind
½ teaspoon dried ginger

Steam carrots for 15 minutes, or until barely tender.

In a separate small pan, melt margarine and add brown sugar and orange rind. Add steamed carrots and toss. Sprinkle with ginger, toss lightly to coat carrots and continue cooking 1 to 2 minutes until carrots are lightly glazed.

Confetti Corn Cakes

A colorful adaptation of a favorite corn fritter recipe.

makes about 6 cakes   each: 40 calories, 1 gram fat

1 teaspoon olive oil	1 large egg white
¼ cup diced green onion	⅓ cup flour
¼ cup diced red pepper	½ teaspoon baking powder
1 cup canned creamed corn	¼ teaspoon salt
1 large whole egg	

Heat oil in large nonstick skillet. Cook onion and red pepper until soft, about 5 minutes. Remove skillet from heat and combine vegetables and corn in a small bowl. Lightly beat whole egg and egg white; add to corn. Add flour, baking powder and salt, blending well.

Coat cool skillet with cooking spray and heat to medium-hot. Drop large spoonfuls of batter into skillet and cook on both sides until golden. Keep cooked cakes warm while the rest are being prepared. Serve at once.

Pepper Fry

Low fat food doesn't have to be dull in taste or looks. This colorful presentation will attract attention even before the first bite.

serves 2   per serving: 40 calories, 2½ grams fat

½ cup sliced* red pepper	1 teaspoon olive oil
½ cup sliced* yellow pepper	garlic salt
½ cup sliced* onion	

*Slice all vegetables lengthwise into long thin strips, julienne style.

Coat a large nonstick skillet with cooking spray. Heat pan to medium-hot and add peppers and onion; stir-fry for 2 to 3 minutes until vegetables start to brown. Add olive oil and stir to coat all pieces. Sprinkle with garlic salt and continue to stir-fry for 2 to 3 more minutes, until vegetables are crisp-tender. Serve at once.

Baked Orange Squash

A good accompaniment to a holiday dinner, this colorful vegetable dish can be prepared early in the day. To serve more, just multiply ingredients.

serves 2	per serving: 85 calories, almost no fat

1 small acorn squash (about 1¼ pounds)

1 tablespoon frozen orange juice concentrate

1 tablespoon brown sugar

¼ teaspoon salt

pinch of nutmeg

few shakes of artificial butter buds or sprinkles

Cut squash into quarters and steam over boiling water until tender (about 20 minutes). Remove pieces from water and cool.

Preheat oven to 350 degrees. Scoop out squash into large bowl and mash with fork until smooth. Add orange juice, brown sugar, salt, nutmeg and a few shakes of artificial butter sprinkles. Mix well until smooth. Coat a small baking dish with cooking spray, pour in squash mixture and bake, uncovered, for 20 minutes or until hot.

Make-ahead instructions: Prepare squash mixture as described, place in baking dish, cover and refrigerate until ready to cook. Preheat oven to 350 degrees and bake for about 30 minutes or until heated through.

Do yourself a flavor

The flavor of fresh vegetables can be varied and enhanced by the use of herbs. Consider the following combinations: cauliflower with caraway, marjoram or nutmeg; green beans with basil, dill or savory; peas with curry, mint or rosemary; potatoes with basil, chives or dill; tomatoes with celery seed, oregano or thyme; tossed green salads with basil, celery seed, paprika or tarragon.

The US National Arboretum herb garden offers several suggestions for using herbs as creative and tasteful additions to your recipes and as alternatives to salt. They suggest that to become familiar with the specific flavor of an herb try mixing it with light cream cheese, let it sit for an hour, and spread on a plain cracker.

The following herbs have medium flavors and a moderate amount is recommended – one to two teaspoons for six servings: basil, celery seed and leaves, cumin, dill, fennel, French tarragon, garlic, marjoram, mint, oregano, summer and winter savory, thyme and turmeric.

The following should be used with care since their flavors are strong – one teaspoon for six servings: bay, cardamom, curry, ginger, hot peppers, mustard, black pepper, rosemary and sage.

If you like the taste of fresh herbs, remember that they are less concentrated than the dried ones you may be used to. You will need two to three times more fresh herbs if the recipe calls for dried. (Note: Our recipes generally use dried herbs for year-round convenience.)

In praise of the potato

Pity the poor potato, a victim of bad press. As soon as people decide to lose a few pounds, they cut out this healthful, high carbohydrate food. Too bad. If instead they added potatoes to their daily diet, they'd probably find it easier to lose those pounds. The potato itself is relatively low in calories and fills you up so that you can't eat too much more of anything else. Every time you can work in some potatoes, you have an opportunity to cut fat. For example, adding shredded potatoes to beef in a meatloaf recipe stretches the higher-fat animal protein and cuts the total fat per serving.

Unfortunately, the potato suffers from the same problem as pasta; it's the preparation that adds the fat. The sour cream, oil, cheese and mayonnaise that cover and flavor so many innocent potatoes are responsible for its "fattening" reputation.

When you add potatoes to your meal, please start with fresh or plain frozen ones; the highly processed potato often bears little resemblance to the real thing. In fact, it's amazing what you can do to a potato. Values given below, except potato chips, are for 4-ounce servings.

Potato	Calories	Grams of fat
Fast food fries	360	19
Baked with "everything"*	270	18
Frozen fries	250	10
Potato salad	180	10
Potato chips, 1 oz. (12!)	150	10
Scalloped potatoes	140	5
Plain baked potato	90	0

*1 tbsp. butter, 2 tbsp. sour cream, 1 tbsp. bacon bits

The Stuffed Potato

Guaranteed to be a family-pleaser, this twice-baked potato has the flavor of a "baked with everything" potato, but not the fat. It can be prepared ahead, with only last-minute reheating required. An excellent company dish, the recipe can be easily multiplied.

makes 2 servings   per serving: 165 calories, 1 gram fat

1 **large potato (about**	¼ **cup chopped green onion**
12 oz.)	¼ **teaspoon salt**
¼ **cup plain lowfat yogurt**	**paprika**
2-3 **tablespoons 1% milk**	

Preheat oven to 400 degrees. Scrub potato clean and bake about 1 hour, or until soft. Cut in half lengthwise and carefully scoop out pulp, leaving the two shells intact.

Mash pulp with fork; stir in yogurt and milk and mix until potato is smooth and fluffy, like mashed potatoes. Stir in green onion and salt. Pile potato mixture back into shells. Sprinkle with paprika. Place on baking sheet and bake for 20 minutes or until hot.

Make-ahead instructions: Prepare potatoes as described, place in baking dish, cover and refrigerate until ready to cook. Preheat oven to 400 degrees and bake for about 30 minutes or until hot.

According to The Potato Museum in Washington, DC, a family of four throws away more than 100 pounds of potato peelings a year. In so doing, they lose the equivalent of the iron in 500 eggs, the protein from 60 steaks and the vitamins from nearly 200 glasses of orange juice. A potato offers complex carbohydrates, protein, vitamins (especially C and B), minerals (notably iron) and almost no fat. Be sure to eat your share of the national average of 120 pounds per person each year, roughly one small potato a day.

Oven Fries

Nothing could be easier than these delicious substitutes for French fries. Even at the end of a busy day, only five minutes of work gets them ready, then the oven does the rest while you put up your feet.

serves 2   per serving: 300 calories, 5 grams fat

2 large baking potatoes   **onion powder**
      (about 10 oz. *each*)*   **salt**
2 teaspoons salad oil   **malt vinegar**
      garlic powder

*The size of the potatoes isn't a misprint; these are so good that you will want to eat every bite. They're worth it.

Preheat oven to 400 degrees. Cut potatoes into long French fry shapes, ¼-inch to ½-inch thick: Cut in several lengthwise slices, then lay the flat side down and cut into long strips. If you like very crisp potatoes, cut them narrow. Place cut potatoes in a large bowl and blot dry with a paper towel.

Add oil to potatoes and toss until well coated. Sprinkle with garlic powder, onion powder and salt; toss again. Coat a 10x15-inch nonstick baking sheet with cooking spray and spread out potatoes in a single layer.

Bake for 20 minutes. Remove cookie sheet from oven, turn potatoes over and bake another 10 to 15 minutes or until crisp. Thicker slices will take the longer time.

Serve potatoes with malt vinegar sprinkled over them for the British "chips" flavor.

To add creaminess to mashed potatoes without adding butter and cream, stir in some blended cottage cheese after the potatoes have been mashed. Season to taste and beat briefly with a wooden spoon until fluffy.

Tub o' Lard Award

This award goes to a Sunday brunch potato dish featured at a popular Northwest restaurant. **Fat-Potato Casserole** proves that there's no limit to the fat that can be added to a nonfat starter like the potato.

> The recipe starts out innocently enough with 2 pounds of potatoes, but then combines them with (are you ready?) 4 eggs, 1 pound of cheese, 1½ cubes of butter, 2 cups of sour cream and 1½ cups of whipping cream! Since all this fat serves only 12 people, each person gets **510 calories and 44 grams of fat**.

Many menu choices that list cheese and cream should have red flags beside them. If you're going to indulge in these treats now and then, at least do it at home where you have some control over the amount you use.

Salad smarts

When you consider all the possible combinations of salad ingredients, it's surprising that we don't eat them every single day. Unfortunately, too many people think of salads as "rabbit-food" to be eaten only when on a diet. If your idea of salad is a bowl of chopped lettuce topped with vinegar, we agree that that's for the bunnies, not for people! Let your creative talents run and consider the endless combinations that could be made from these ingredients.

Greens: Iceberg, Bibb, romaine, red or green leafy lettuce, spinach, red or green cabbage.

Vegetables: asparagus, avocados, sprouts, green beans, marinated mixed bean salad, cooked beets, pickled beets, broccoli, Brussels sprouts, carrots, cauliflower, celery, corn, cucumber, garbanzo beans, kidney beans, mushrooms, onions (white, yellow, red or green), peas, pea pods, peppers (red, yellow or green), potatoes, sprouts, tomatoes, zucchini.

Fruits: apple, banana, berries, cantaloupe, cherries, dates, figs, grapes, grapefruit wedges, honeydew melon, mandarin orange segments, nectarine, fresh orange segments, papaya, peach, pear, pineapple (fresh or canned), plum, prune, raisins.

Protein: roast beef, lamb, pork, crisp bacon bits, lean ham, tiny cooked meatballs, cooked chicken or turkey, salmon, tuna, crabmeat, shrimp, pickled herring, sardines, anchovies, smoked oysters, hard-cooked egg wedges, lowfat cheese cubes or strips, grated Parmesan or Feta, lowfat cottage cheese.

Garnishes: chives, parsley, radishes, watercress, green onions, croutons.

Now don't say you can't think of anything to put in a salad!

Put it together

The preceding list of salad ideas shows that "having a salad" can mean much more than tossing together some lettuce and tomatoes. The California Iceberg Lettuce Commission offers some interesting combinations:

Salad: lettuce, mushrooms, green onions, tomato wedges and shredded cooked chicken (skin removed). **Dressing**: oil, orange juice and soy sauce, with a bit of dried ginger powder and garlic juice.

Salad: lettuce, roast beef strips, sliced mushrooms, thin onion slices, cooked cauliflower florets and cherry tomatoes. **Dressing**: oil and vinegar, chopped parsley, dry mustard and a pinch of sugar.

Salad: lettuce topped with cold poached salmon, hardcooked egg chunks, tomato wedge, bell pepper strips and thinly sliced red onion. **Dressing**: oil and tarragon vinegar blended with salt, pepper and dill weed.

Be creative with flavors and textures and you'll find salads will become an enjoyable addition to your diet.

See ***"Dressings and Sauces"*** *for salad dressing recipes:* ***Dijon Vinaigrette, Lowfat Ranch Style, Creamy Cucumber, Blue Cheese, Lemon Herb****.*

Dress it down

There are three distinct advantages to making your own oil and vinegar dressing for salads. First, you can use the best, extra virgin, monounsaturated olive oil. Research suggests that we should increase our consumption of monounsaturated fat as we lower saturated fat.

Second, you know exactly what's in your own dressing. It may be even more satisfying to know what's not in it; the back label of a prepared dressing sometimes lists a lot of strange-sounding ingredients.

Finally, making your own allows you to decrease the total fat. Although classic vinaigrettes are usually three parts oil to one part vinegar, we suggest a one to one mixture, equal parts of oil and vinegar. You still get the rich flavor of olive oil and your taste buds will learn to "like it light."

Salad savvy

Spin or towel dry the greens well after washing; a small amount of oil goes a long way on dry leaves.

Don't sabotage your salad with too much high fat dressing. It's too easy to add several hundred calories with just a "tip of the wrist."

Salad seasonings/herb toppings: Salt has 2300 milligrams (mg) of sodium per teaspoon. Garlic salt has 2050 mg, onion salt 1500 mg. Despite their names, seasoned peppers, such as Lemon Pepper, often have salt as the first ingredient and sodium content varies widely (from 400 to 800 mg).

Coool Cucumber Salad

An excellent complement to any salmon dish. Make ahead for maximum flavor.

makes 2 cups   per ½ cup: 30 calories, almost no fat

2 **cups thinly sliced, unpeeled cucumber***

¼ **cup finely chopped red onion**

½ **cup plain lowfat yogurt**

¼ **cup white or red wine vinegar**

½ **teaspoon dried dill weed**

¼ **teaspoon salt or to taste**

*Before slicing, score the cucumber skin by running the tines of a fork along it in parallel rows. When sliced cross-wise, the cucumber will have a scalloped edge. Slice it as thin as possible. Place it in a wide serving bowl and sprinkle onion on top.

In a small jar shake together yogurt, vinegar, dill and salt and pour over vegetables. Marinate in refrigerator for at least 2 hours.

Crunchy Cheese Salad

A cool and colorful salad combines crunchy fresh vegetables with the protein of cottage cheese to make a refreshing lunch.

makes 2 cups   per cup: 100 calories, 1 gram fat

1 **cup 1% cottage cheese, small curd**

½ **cup finely diced, peeled cucumber**

¼ **cup finely chopped green onion**

¼ **cup finely chopped red pepper**

¼ **cup grated carrot**

¼ **teaspoon dried dill weed**

¼ **teaspoon salt or to taste paprika**

Combine all ingredients in a mixing bowl. Stir until evenly mixed. Serve immediately, sprinkled with paprika, or cover and refrigerate until ready to eat.

Cracked Wheat and Cabbage Salad

This crunchy salad makes a great lunch to eat at home, take to work or bring on a picnic. It improves with age so plan to make it ahead.

makes 4 cups · per cup: 150 calories, 6 grams fat.

½ cup cracked wheat (bulgur)
1 cup water
½ teaspoon salt
¼ cup light mayonnaise
¼ cup plain lowfat yogurt
3 tablespoons cider vinegar
2 tablespoons sugar
¼ teaspoon dried dill weed
¼ teaspoon hot pepper sauce
¼ teaspoon Dijon mustard
¼ cup finely chopped onion
2 cups finely shredded cabbage
½ cup sliced celery
½ cup shredded carrot

In small saucepan combine cracked wheat, water and salt. Bring to a boil, stir, reduce heat, cover and simmer 15 minutes or until water is absorbed. Remove from heat.

Combine mayonnaise, yogurt, vinegar, sugar, dill, hot pepper sauce and mustard. Blend this dressing into cooked wheat. Add onion, cabbage, celery and carrot. Toss to blend well, adjust seasoning to taste, cover and chill at least several hours or overnight.

Gazpacho Salad

This is primarily a vegetable salad with bright red tomatoes as the focal point; the barley adds protein, fiber and a pleasant chewy contrast. An excellent accompaniment to cold meats.

serves 2   per serving: 170 calories, 7½ grams fat

⅔ cup cooked barley
½ cup sliced mushrooms
1 medium tomato, cut in wedges
¼ cup green or yellow pepper, cut in strips
1 green onion, sliced

1 tablespoon olive oil
1 tablespoon vinegar
1 small clove garlic, minced
¼ teaspoon minced fresh basil leaves
¼ teaspoon salt
⅛ teaspoon pepper

Combine barley, mushrooms, tomato wedges, pepper strips and green onion.

In a small jar, mix together oil, vinegar, garlic, basil, salt and pepper; cover, shake well and pour over vegetables, tossing lightly. Chill at least an hour before serving.

Super Slaw

Creamy dressing and crunchy, colorful vegetables give this easy coleslaw taste and texture appeal. Chilling improves flavor.

makes about 2½ cups   per ½ cup: 70 calories, 4 grams fat

2 cups shredded cabbage
1 cup shredded carrot
¼ cup chopped green onion
¼ cup chopped red pepper
¼ cup light mayonnaise

¼ cup plain lowfat yogurt
1 tablespoon white vinegar
½ teaspoon dried tarragon
½ teaspoon sugar
¼ teaspoon salt

Combine vegetables in a large bowl. In a separate bowl, mix mayonnaise, yogurt, vinegar, tarragon, sugar and salt. Blend well and pour over vegetables. Refrigerate for 2 to 24 hours.

Basil Potato Salad

When the weather forecast says it's going to be hot, make this in the morning to serve with sliced tomatoes and cold meat or poultry from the deli. Use fresh basil, if available, for a delicate color and taste. This recipe makes four servings so you can have leftovers to enjoy.

serves 4   per serving: 175 calories, 6 grams fat

1 **pound small red potatoes, scrubbed, unpeeled**	¼ **cup light mayonnaise**
½ **cup frozen peas, thawed but not cooked**	1 **tablespoon minced fresh basil or 1 teaspoon dried**
½ **cup chopped red pepper**	1 **green onion, sliced**
½ **cup plain lowfat yogurt**	½ **teaspoon salt**
	¼ **teaspoon pepper**

Cook potatoes in boiling, salted water for 20 to 30 minutes, until just tender; drain and cool. Cut in ¾-inch cubes and place in large bowl. Add peas and red pepper.

In a small bowl combine yogurt, mayonnaise, basil, green onion, salt and pepper. Pour over vegetables and stir lightly to coat. Cover salad and chill for several hours before serving.

---

*Consider having a salad buffet. Many salads improve with age and benefit from being made in the cool morning hours or even the night before, so it's not hard to make several (see **Index** for more ideas in other chapters). Serve with a variety of breads and rolls and some sliced low fat meat for a summer salad party ready to go.*

Choices: Fresh fare

A heaping plate from the salad bar can make a healthful meal. However, before you load up your plate, remember that even with salads it is not hard to overdo it. "A bit of everything" can add up fast.

Food	Calories	Grams of fat
The basics		
Cabbage, 1 c.	15	0
Tomato, ¼ c.	12	0
Lettuce, 1 c.	10	0
Carrot, 2 tbsp.	6	0
Cucumber, 5 slices	4	0
Sprouts, 2 tbsp.	2	0
The extras		
Macaroni salad, ¼ c.	100	6
Potato salad, ¼ c.	90	5
Coleslaw, ¼ c.	60	5
Cottage cheese, ¼ c.	60	2
Three bean salad, ¼ c.	60	1
Kidney beans, ¼ c.	55	0
The toppings		
Sunflower seeds, 2 tbsp.	160	14
Bacon bits, 2 tbsp.	60	3
Croutons, 2 tbsp.	60	3
Parmesan, 2 tbsp.	45	3
The dressing		
Blue cheese, 1 tbsp.	75	8
Oil and vinegar, 1 tbsp.	70	8
French, 1 tbsp.	70	6
Thousand Island, 1 tbsp.	60	6

Sandwiches

The lunch bunch

A daily chore that faces many of us is making healthful lunches. Although there are many possibilities for lunch, let's be realistic. Sandwiches are the first, and sometimes only, choice of most people. Everybody loves a sandwich. Seemingly endless combinations of breads and fillings offer variety and good nutrition if prepared sensibly.

However, while they can be lean and filling, sandwiches often pack excess calories. The big culprits include high fat meats, mayonnaise-loaded fillings and too much spread. Note that bread is not included on our list of high fat culprits. On the contrary, you can cut calories and fat by increasing the bread (carbohydrate) and decreasing the filling (fat and protein).

Ever see anyone at a "make your own" sandwich bar loudly and righteously pass up the second piece of bread while piling his one piece high with salami, cheese and mayo? One thin slice of lunch meat doesn't look like much, so it's natural to want to pile those skinny little slices fairly high. The result is that it is very easy to end up with more than 20 grams of fat in a sandwich (see *Choices: Sandwich fixings* at the end of the chapter).

An extra piece of bread will fill that empty stomach better than an extra ounce of meat or cheese, so enjoy it instead of passing it up. Sandwiches made with two pieces of whole grain bread add fiber and filler to your lunch, without a lot of extra calories or fat.

Look for variety in breads. French, Italian, sourdough, rye, pumpernickel, whole grain, bagel, English muffins, pita...the list is long and the fat is low in most cases. Read the package labels for fat content and you'll be pleasantly surprised.

Learn where the fat comes from in a sandwich. Compare a bologna sandwich with Cheddar cheese, white bread, margarine and regular mayonnaise to a lean ham sandwich with part-skim Mozzarella, whole grain bread, Dijon mustard and light mayonnaise. In both cases, you have meat, cheese, bread and spread, but in the second sandwich you have dropped from 500 calories to 300 and from 34 grams of fat to 14.

Obviously, there are more choices for lunch than sandwiches. A good-for-you lunch should be a combination of meat or meat alternatives, fruit and/or vegetable, milk or a milk product and a grain product. Sound familiar? Yes, those are the same, boring old food groups we learned all those years ago when we went to school. Note that fat is not included in these four food groups! Yet many lunches have more calories contributed from fat than from any other source.

The trick is to put all the good nutrients into your bag without too much added fat. If you choose a low fat item from each category as you make up your lunch, you'll find you have so much food that there's no room for high fat extras. This way, your brown bag lunch becomes another opportunity to cut some fat out of your diet. On the next page we have some examples of how to include the different food groups in your lunch.

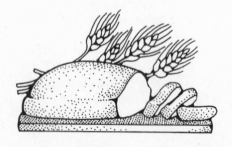

Lunch time fat-fighters

Below we have listed some brown bag ideas which may add a little variety to your lunch life. Words in italics indicate the food group each item comes from.

Lean meats – read the package labels *(meat)*

Thinly sliced cold meatloaf *(meat)*

Raisin-bran bread and light cream cheese *(grain, milk)*

Three bean salad *(vegetable)*

Chunks of part-skim Mozzarella cheese and apple *(milk, fruit)*

Sliced turkey, plain or smoked *(meat)*

Cottage cheese with fruit salad and muffin *(milk, fruit, grain)*

Hearty soups *(meat, meat alternative and/or vegetable)*

Hot lentil or all-bean chili *(meat alternative)*

Any leftover low fat casserole *(meat or meat alternative)*

Bagels, whole wheat rolls, bread sticks *(grain)*

Carrot and celery sticks *(vegetable)*

Oven-baked skinless chicken pieces *(meat)*

Your own fruit yogurt, made with less sugar *(fruit, milk)*

Water-packed tuna or canned salmon *(meat)*

Whole fresh fruit (both fiber and filler) *(fruit)*

Commercial spreads

Standard spreads are all high in fat, even though the fat may be different (saturated, polyunsaturated, hydrogenated, etc.). You can cut out the butter and replace it with margarine, but doing so will change only the type of fat, not the total amount of fat. Cutting out both butter and margarine and slathering on mayonnaise instead does not change total fat content either.

Each tablespoon of butter, margarine or mayonnaise has approximately 100 calories and 11 grams of fat. For reference, each tablespoon of catsup or mustard has 15 calories and almost no fat. One tablespoon of pickle relish has about 20 calories, no fat. One tablespoon of sandwich spread, on the other hand, has 60 calories and 5 grams of fat.

No one likes dry sandwiches and we're not suggesting that you should eat your bread with nothing spread on it. You need substitutes. Make a pot of each of these on the weekend and you'll have something to reach for instead of the fat.

Whipped Cream Cheese

makes about ¾ cup   per tablespoon: 20 calories, 1 gram fat

½ **cup 1% cottage cheese**   ¼ **cup light cream cheese**

Rinse cottage cheese in a strainer and press out excess moisture; blend together with light cream cheese until smooth.

Mustard-Yogurt Spread

makes ¾ cup   per tablespoon: 8 calories, almost no fat

¼ **cup Dijon mustard**   ½ **cup plain lowfat yogurt**

Stir together and refrigerate.

Bombay Sandwiches

Here's a sandwich spread with a subtle taste. Use it on plain or toasted whole grain bread and serve either open-faced, with some chopped parsley on top, or between two slices of bread, with shredded lettuce added.

makes about 1½ cups filling   per ½ cup: 75 calories, 2½ grams fat

1 cup diced cooked chicken or turkey (4 oz.)
½ cup chopped celery
1 green onion, chopped
1 teaspoon curry powder
½ teaspoon salt

1 tablespoon light mayonnaise
1 tablespoon plain lowfat yogurt
1 teaspoon lemon juice

Combine all ingredients; spread on choice of bread.

Tuna tips

If you are a frequent dieter, you may think that the only way you can eat tuna is plain...out of the can...with a squeeze of lemon...sigh. We suggest a tuna salad sandwich instead. Made with small changes that will cut the fat considerably, it makes a simple meal that is much more satisfying than plain tuna.

Use water-packed tuna. One can of water-packed tuna contains 230 calories and 3 grams, or less than 1 teaspoon, of fat. One can of oil-packed tuna, even drained, can contain 300 calories and 10 to 12 grams of fat, close to 3 teaspoons. That's quite a difference.

A tuna salad sandwich made with water-packed tuna can exceed 20 grams of fat, however, if it is held together with a big glob of regular mayonnaise. Mix the tuna with light mayo instead, cutting calories and fat almost in half. Go a step further and mix equal amounts of light mayo and lowfat yogurt. This cuts the calories and fat in half again. One day you may even decide to make it with straight yogurt – and like it!

Hawaiian Tuna Sandwich

A slightly sweet variation on a tuna sandwich, this can also be made with 1 cup of chopped, cooked chicken or turkey instead. Spread on cracked wheat or whole grain bread and top with a handful of sprouts.

makes about 2 cups filling   per ½ cup: 100 calories, 2 grams fat

- 1 can (6½ oz.) water-packed tuna, drained
- ½ cup crushed pineapple, drained
- ¼ cup shredded carrot
- ½ cup diced water chestnuts
- 2 teaspoons fresh lime juice
- ⅛ teaspoon dried ginger
- ¼ teaspoon salt
- ¼ cup *Whipped Cream Cheese*, p. 186

Combine all ingredients; spread on choice of bread.

Tuna Pockets

To pack this for lunch, put tuna filling, lettuce, tomato and cucumber dressing in separate containers. Stuff the pita just before you're ready to eat.

makes 4 half pockets   each: 150 calories, 3 grams fat

- 1 can (6½ oz.) water-packed tuna, drained
- 1 green onion, chopped
- 2 tablespoons chopped red pepper
- ¼ cup diced celery
- ¼ cup reduced fat Italian dressing
- 1 tablespoon lemon juice
- ¼ cup crumbled feta cheese (1 oz.)
- 2 large pita pockets
- 1 cup shredded lettuce
- 1 cup diced tomato
- ½ cup plain lowfat yogurt
- ½ cup peeled, seeded, shredded cucumber

Combine tuna, onion, red pepper, celery, Italian dressing and lemon juice. Stir in feta cheese gently. Cut pita in half and stuff with lettuce. Fill pockets with tuna mixture, top with tomato.

Combine yogurt and cucumber. Spoon 1 to 2 tablespoons into each pocket. Serve immediately.

Salmon Rolls

Make these ahead of time for a picnic outing or a long drive. This leaves nothing to do at lunch but unwrap and eat. Salmon is high in those good omega-3 fatty acids.

serves 2	per serving: 195 calories, 5 grams fat

2 **flour tortillas**
¼ **cup** *Dill Cream Sauce*, **below**
½ **cup canned pink salmon, drained**

1 **medium tomato**
¼ **small cucumber**
shredded lettuce
salt to taste

Spread each tortilla evenly with *Dill Cream Sauce*. Spread salmon over the surface of each tortilla, dividing equally.

Cut tomato in half, squeeze out seeds, slice thinly and cut slices into ½-inch strips. Peel and seed cucumber and cut into thin strips. Scatter tomato and cucumber strips evenly over each tortilla. Top with a handful of lettuce. Sprinkle with salt, if desired.

Roll up into a tight cylinder and wrap securely with plastic wrap. Refrigerate until ready to eat. Cut in half to serve.

Dill Cream Sauce

Light cottage cheese keeps total fat content very low.

makes ½ cup	per ¼ cup: 40 calories, ½ gram fat

½ **cup 1% cottage cheese**
1 **tablespoon chopped green onion**

2 **teaspoons lemon juice**
¼ **teaspoon dried dill weed**
salt to taste

Using a blender or food processor, blend all ingredients thoroughly until smooth. Chill for 2 hours to develop flavors.

Note: This sauce is also good as a celery stuffer or cracker spread.

The Shrimper

Here's a fast sandwich that's ready in just a few minutes.

serves 2   per serving: 260 calories, 6 grams fat

1 tablespoon light
  mayonnaise
1 teaspoon light cream
  cheese
1 teaspoon lemon juice
1 cup cooked tiny shrimp
  (about 1/3 pound)

2 tablespoons chopped
  green onion
1/4 teaspoon dried dill weed
1/8 teaspoon salt
2 English muffins, split
  and toasted

Combine mayonnaise, cream cheese and lemon juice; beat until smooth. Stir in shrimp, green onion, dill and salt. Put equal amounts of shrimp filling on each toasted muffin half. Serve immediately.

Tub o' Lard Award

The quest for variety in sandwiches can result in some not-so-healthy combinations, like **Croissant Nicoise**, a name that gives one clue to its fat content right away. Any time you see sandwich filling tucked into a croissant instead of bread, your "fat alert bell" should start ringing.

> This filling combines tuna fish (good), hard-cooked eggs (too many, six for four servings) and olives (100% fat). They're all dumped into a creamy dressing of oil, vinegar and sour cream and stuffed into a fat-laden croissant. Result: **500 calories and 40 grams of fat**.

Described by the creators as an "upscale" treat, this sandwich will certainly up your scale!

Muffin Melt

Quick, simple and satisfying. You can substitute turkey ham for lean ham, if you wish.

serves 2   per serving: 240 calories, 6 grams fat

- **2 English muffins**
- **¼ cup *Mustard-Yogurt Spread*, p. 186**
- **3 oz. lean ham, diced (about ¾ cup)**
- **½ cup chopped ripe tomato**
- **¼ cup shredded part-skim Mozzarella cheese (1 oz.)**
- **⅛ teaspoon dried basil**
- **⅛ teaspoon salt**

Preheat broiler. Split muffins, toast lightly and spread with *Mustard-Yogurt Spread*. In a small bowl, mix together remaining ingredients. Place muffins close together on broiler pan and top with equal amounts of filling. Broil 2 to 3 minutes, or just until cheese is melted.

Mini Pizza

An extra ounce of cheese makes this special and is nothing to worry about since there is no other significant source of fat.

serves 2   per serving: 240 calories, 6 grams fat

- **2 English muffins, split**
- **¼ cup bottled pizza sauce (check label for low fat)**
- **¼ cup thinly sliced onion**
- **¾ cup sliced mushrooms**
- **¼ cup diced red pepper**
- **½ cup shredded part-skim Mozzarella cheese (2 oz.)**

Preheat broiler. Split muffins, toast lightly and spread with pizza sauce. Layer a few pieces of onion on each half. (We like the sweet red onions best, sliced paper-thin.)

Top with mushrooms and red pepper. Sprinkle cheese over each half. Broil 2 to 3 minutes, or just until cheese is bubbly.

Scandinavian sandwiches

Years ago we went to a restaurant in Denmark famous for its huge selection of 178 sandwiches. We were so impressed that we brought back a menu for ideas. A recent look at the menu showed an astonishing number of very high fat selections, something we hadn't noticed then.

> Think there are no new ideas for sandwiches? Look, but don't touch: Bacon, tomato and liverpaste; Steak, parboiled egg and onions on toast; Ham with fried calves' kidney; Hot fried eel; Parboiled egg with cheese mayonnaise; Macaroni, chicken and giblets in mayonnaise with egg and smoked salmon; Smoked cheese with raw egg yolk and chives; Salami with spiced lard (!).

More than 30 sandwiches mentioned the word "fried," 62 had an egg in them. #178 was one slice of bread with butter or drippings! The only thing that probably saved us was that servings were small – and we were young.

Ever indulge in a "Healthy Vegetarian" sandwich? It's been a longtime favorite among people who think they know how to eat properly. It usually features good things such as tomatoes, cucumbers, onions, peppers, lettuce, sprouts and.......about a quarter inch of cream cheese and half an oil-filled avocado. Figure on eating over 30 grams of fat with this little gem.

Crunchy Ham Pockets

Mixing ham with cabbage and carrots extends the protein so you get fewer calories per sandwich.

serves 2   per serving: 225 calories, 8 grams fat

- 3 oz. lean ham, diced (about ¾ cup)
- ½ cup shredded cabbage
- 1 small carrot, shredded
- 2 tablespoons light mayonnaise
- 1-2 teaspoons creamed horseradish
- salt and pepper
- 2 pita pockets
- lowfat yogurt (optional)

Combine ham, cabbage, carrot, mayonnaise and horseradish (add to taste, depending on "heat"). Sprinkle with salt and pepper. Cut pita in half. Spread each half with a small amount of yogurt, if desired, and divide filling equally.

Spicy Rollups

An easy, nourishing, at-home lunch.

makes 2   each: 190 calories, 4 grams fat

- ½ cup kidney beans, drained and rinsed
  small pinch *each* chili powder and onion powder
- 3 tablespoons salsa, fresh or bottled
- 2 corn tortillas
- 2 tablespoons plain lowfat yogurt
- ¼ cup shredded part-skim Mozzarella cheese (1 oz.)

Mash kidney beans, add chili powder and onion powder; add 1 tablespoon salsa to thin to spreading consistency. Heat briefly in small saucepan.

Heat a large nonstick skillet to medium-hot. Heat tortillas, one at a time, for about 1 minute on each side until warm and soft. Spread each with ¼ cup mashed beans. Spread remaining salsa and yogurt over beans and sprinkle with cheese. Roll up and eat immediately.

Choices: Sandwich fixings

Fat lurks everywhere, even in your brown bag lunch. You may be startled at how quickly it piles up when you look at the hidden fat in some common lunch choices. Unless otherwise listed, values shown for meat are for 2 ounces (a typical sandwich). Check your scale to see how much you really use.

Food	Calories	Grams of fat
Dry salami	235	19
Deviled ham spread	195	18
Pastrami	200	17
Beef bologna	175	16
Canned corned beef	145	9
Turkey bologna	120	9
Regular ham	110	7
Roast beef	100	4
Turkey pastrami	80	3
Turkey ham	75	3
Lean ham	75	3
Turkey breast	65	1
Peanut butter, 1 oz. (2 tbsp.)	190	16
Cream cheese, 1 oz. (2 tbsp.)	100	10
Swiss cheese, 1 oz.	105	8
Part-skim Mozzarella, 1 oz.	70	5
Butter, 1 tbsp.	110	12
Margarine, 1 tbsp.	100	11
Mayonnaise, 1 tbsp.	100	11
Sandwich spread, 1 tbsp.	60	5
Mustard, 1 tbsp.	5	0
Onion roll, 1	190	2
Whole grain bread, 2 slices	140	2
Pita pocket, 1	105	1

Dressings and Sauces

Dress it up

A tasty sauce can make the difference between "diet food" and "real food." If you think following a lowfat lifestyle means facing a plateful of plain, unadorned meat or vegetables all the time, you are mistaken. Just because many of the classic versions are heavy in oil or enriched with butter and cream doesn't mean that you have to give up sauces and dressings entirely. With simple changes you can cut out a lot of fat and still retain flavor and texture.

Alter the proportion of oil to vinegar in dressings. Most "oil and something" salad dressing recipes suggest three to four tablespoons of oil for every tablespoon of vinegar or lemon juice. Make the mixture no more than one to one and you'll cut the fat dramatically.

Use cornstarch instead of butter and flour to thicken a sauce. It makes a thick, smooth sauce without excess fat, creating rich finishing touch to many meals.

As your taste buds adapt to lower fat foods in general, you will find that many of the traditional sauces and dressings are too rich. (See our *Tub o' Lard Award* in this chapter for an example.) Once you learn to make some low fat alternatives, they will be much preferred, delicious additions to many otherwise plain meals.

As an added bonus, most dressings and sauces benefit by being prepared ahead of time.

Dijon Vinaigrette ·

This zesty dressing also makes a good sauce for cold roast chicken or beef.

makes ¾ cup   per tablespoon: 25 calories, 2½ grams fat

2 tablespoons olive oil	2 tablespoons Dijon mustard
2 tablespoons red wine vinegar	⅓ cup plain lowfat yogurt
2 tablespoons white wine or lemon juice	¼ teaspoon salt
	¼ teaspoon garlic powder
	⅛ teaspoon pepper

Combine all ingredients in a blender or beat with a wire whisk until completely smooth. Place in a small jar, cover and refrigerate at least 2 hours. Shake well before serving.

Lemon-Herb Dressing

This dressing has more lemon juice than oil, much different from a typical recipe. It is slightly sweet.

makes 1 cup   per tablespoon: 45 calories, 5 grams fat

⅔ cup lemon juice	1 teaspoon chopped parsley
⅓ cup olive oil	¼ teaspoon dried tarragon
1 tablespoon sugar	¼ teaspoon seasoned salt
½ teaspoon dried basil	¼ teaspoon minced garlic
½ teaspoon paprika	⅛ teaspoon pepper

Combine all ingredients in a small jar. Cover and shake well to blend. Refrigerate. Shake again just before serving.

For an easy, creamy dressing, blend your favorite ranch or buttermilk dry dressing with 1 cup of yogurt, ½ cup milk, 1 tablespoon lemon juice and 1 to 2 teaspoons Dijon mustard.

Creamy Cucumber Dressing

Instead of using the bottled, preserved variety, make your own variation with fresh cucumbers. Good as a dip, also.

makes ¾ cup   per tablespoon: 20 calories, 2 grams fat

¼ cup light mayonnaise
¼ cup plain lowfat yogurt
2 teaspoons lemon juice
¾ cup chopped cucumber, peeled and seeded

2 tablespoons chopped green onion
¼ teaspoon salt
⅛ teaspoon garlic powder

Combine all ingredients in blender or food processor and blend until smooth. Place in a small jar, cover and refrigerate.

Lowfat Ranch Style Dressing

Here's a low fat, low sodium variation of a popular taste. Also good as a dip or as a topping for baked potatoes.

makes 1 cup   per tablespoon: 15 calories, 1 gram fat

2 tablespoons light mayonnaise
⅓ cup plain lowfat yogurt
½ cup buttermilk
2 teaspoons minced onion

⅛ teaspoon dried basil
⅛ teaspoon dried sage
⅛ teaspoon dried thyme
⅛ teaspoon garlic powder
2 teaspoons minced parsley

Combine all ingredients in blender or food processor. Place in a small jar, cover and refrigerate.

It's no secret to fat-watchers that salad dressings are the main problem with salads. Compare our recipes to typical creamy dressings which have about 80 calories and 8 grams fat per tablespoon.

Tub o' Lard Award

People beginning to change to a lowfat lifestyle often worry that they will never be able to adjust their taste buds to lower fat, that they will always feel deprived. To prove that your tastes can change, the following **Gourmet Sauce** recipe comes from my own "pre-lowfat" files.

> For 2 servings, I browned 2 cups of mushrooms in ¼ cup of butter, then added ¼ cup of whipping cream and two egg yolks to thicken it. This recipe had gobs of fat, much of it highly saturated, plus a huge dose of cholesterol. The terrible total: **385 calories and 40 grams of fat** per serving. (And this is only a sauce, not the main course!)

Although I can't remember the last time I made it, fortunately, this bowl of grease must have been a favorite at one time because it had a place of honor in my "company" section. The fact that someone who used to cook this way now thinks a mustard-yogurt sauce is better proves that tastes do change.

Burgundy Mushroom Sauce

Try this substitute for the "Gourmet Grease" on the previous page. It's a savory sauce, good with beef, lamb or pork, that transforms any plain meat into something special.

makes 1 cup   per ½ cup: 80 calories, almost no fat

- ½ **pound mushrooms**
- 1 **clove garlic, minced**
- ¼ **cup regular strength beef broth**

- ¼ **cup water**
- ¼ **cup red wine**
- 2 **teaspoons cornstarch**

Slice mushrooms. Coat a large skillet with cooking spray and heat to medium-hot. Brown mushrooms and garlic until juices have been cooked out and mushrooms turn golden brown, about 5 minutes.

In a medium jar, combine broth, water, wine and cornstarch; cover and shake well until completely smooth. Pour over sizzling mushrooms and cook for 2 minutes until clear and smooth. Spoon sauce over meat.

Red Hoss Sauce

Mix together this super-simple, all-purpose sauce for use on hamburgers or as a zesty topping for shrimp cocktails.

makes 1 cup   per tablespoon: 15 calories, almost no fat

- ⅔ **cup bottled chili sauce**
- 3 **tablespoons lemon juice**

- 3 **tablespoons prepared horseradish sauce**

Mix together and chill to blend flavors. That's it!

---

*See also **Mustard-Yogurt Sauce** and **Dill-Cream Sauce** in "Sandwiches," **Cucumber-Caper Sauce** and **Tartar Sauce** in "Seafood."*

Cheese Sauce

Here's an easy, rich and elegant sauce that's sure to please. Use it as a topping for poached fish or pour it over rice, pasta or vegetables for a special treat. You can make it ahead, then simply re-heat when ready.

makes 1 cup   per ¼ cup: 55 calories, 3 grams fat

¾ **cup 1% milk**
 2 **teaspoons cornstarch**
½ **cup shredded low fat**
    Swiss or Mozzarella
    cheese (2 oz.)

¼ **cup chopped green onion**
 1 **tablespoon lemon juice**
½ **teaspoon salt or to taste**

Combine milk and cornstarch in a small jar; cover and shake until smooth. Pour mixture into a small saucepan and heat gently until it begins to boil. Increase heat and boil, stirring constantly, until thick. Reduce heat, add cheese and green onion and stir until melted. Remove from heat, add lemon juice and salt. Serve hot.

Make-ahead instructions: Make as indicated above, cover and refrigerate until ready to use. Reheat slowly over low heat, stirring frequently, until hot and bubbling.

Note: To turn this into a fancy *Seafood Sauce*, simply stir in 1½ cups of cooked tiny shrimp, crab or seaflakes after the cheese has melted.

Cornstarch is a must-have for lowfat cooks. The trick is to blend equal amounts of cornstarch and water until you have a smooth paste. Then just pour this into hot liquid and boil for one to two minutes until desired thickness has been reached.

Bread and Breakfast

Doughs and batters

Flour and liquid are the basic ingredients of breads, muffins and pancakes. So simple yet so versatile, these two components can result in many delicious, low fat products. For people wanting to live a lowfat lifestyle, these foods can make easy, satisfying, filling and economical additions to everyday meals.

A mix of flour and liquid is either a dough or a batter, depending on the proportions. Doughs are heavier, having less liquid, and can be shaped and handled, as in breads, pasta, cookies. Batters are thin and pourable, as in crepes and pound cake. In each category there is wide variation in fat and calorie content.

> Consider the dough for bagels – water and flour only, no added fat or sugar; the batter for angel food cake – flour, no added fat but lots of sugar; and the batter for pound cake – flour, lots of fat, lots of sugar.

French bread, bagels and pita are great choices in the "no added fat or sugar" category, adding very few calories to a meal. Minimal fat foods include tortillas, whole grain breads, crepes and pancakes. Also containing few calories, they can change plain meals into something special. The end products of low fat doughs and batters can be covered, stuffed, enhanced and just plain enjoyed, so don't pass them up.

Note: Many weight-watchers use lower calorie, reduced fat margarine as a spread. Because they contain water, they don't work well in baking; regular margarine is preferable.

Super Easy Soda Bread

Don't miss this one even if you're not a bread baker! Soda bread requires no yeast and no kneading. Just stir it together and press it into a pan. In one hour you'll have a warm, fragrant, fresh loaf, just right with a bowl of soup. Thinly sliced, it makes great sandwich bread.

makes 16 slices   each: 95 calories, 1 gram fat

1½ cups whole wheat flour
1½ cups white flour
¼ cup grated Parmesan
   cheese
1 tablespoon sugar

1 teaspoon baking powder
½ teaspoon baking soda
½ teaspoon salt
¼ teaspoon Italian seasoning
1¾ cups buttermilk

Preheat oven to 350 degrees. Coat an 8x4-inch loaf pan with cooking spray and set aside.

In a large bowl, stir together flours, cheese, sugar, baking powder, baking soda, salt and Italian seasoning. Add buttermilk and mix well with a heavy wooden spoon, electric mixer or food processor. Dough will be very stiff; mix it until it is smooth and sticky.

Press dough into loaf pan, smoothing top with hands. Bake for 45 minutes or until top is dark brown. Remove from pan and cool on wire rack for at least 10 minutes before slicing.

Are you really sure how much spread you put on your toast? Test yourself. Fill one level teaspoon with your favorite spread and dip into that to butter your next piece. Were you pleasantly surprised to find that you had some left over? Or did it cover only half the bread? Train your eye to know exactly what you're putting into your mouth!

Dakota Bread

This bread uses ingredients produced in North and South Dakota and is a tasty way to increase your consumption of complex carbohydrates and fiber while getting protein, iron and vitamins.

makes 16 slices   each: 130 calories, 2½ grams fat

1 package active dry yeast
½ cup warm water
    (about 105 degrees)
1 teaspoon sugar
2 tablespoons sunflower oil
¼ cup honey
1 large egg, lightly beaten
½ cup 1% cottage cheese
1 teaspoon salt

2¼ cups white bread flour
½ cup whole wheat flour
¼ cup wheat germ
¼ cup rye flour
¼ cup rolled oats
    cornmeal
1 large egg white
2 tablespoons rolled oats

Sprinkle yeast in warm water; stir to dissolve, add sugar and set aside. In a large bowl, mix sunflower oil, honey, egg, cottage cheese and salt. Add dissolved yeast and 2¼ cups white flour, beating until flour is moistened. Gradually stir in whole wheat flour, wheat germ, rye flour and ¼ cup rolled oats, plus enough additional white flour, perhaps ¼ cup, to make a soft dough.

On a floured surface, knead dough about 10 minutes or until it is smooth and elastic, adding more flour if needed. Place dough in greased bowl; cover with a clean towel. Let rise in warm place until doubled in size, about 1 hour.

Punch down dough. Shape into one round loaf. Coat bottom and sides of a 10-inch pie pan with cooking spray and sprinkle with cornmeal. Place dough in center of pie pan and cover. Let rise until doubled in size, about 30 minutes.

Preheat oven to 350 degrees. Beat egg white lightly and brush top and upper sides of loaf with it; sprinkle with remaining rolled oats. Bake 30 minutes, then cover top loosely with foil and bake an additional 15 minutes until dark brown. Remove from pie pan and cool on a wire rack.

Apricot-Orange Quick Bread

Makes a lovely gift and can be frozen. Start by marinating dried apricots in orange juice for 2 hours.

makes 18 slices   each: 110 calories, 2 grams fat

½ cup dried apricots
2 tablespoons orange juice
½ cup raisins
1 tablespoon grated
  orange rind
2 tablespoons melted
  margarine
1 cup orange juice

1 large egg
1 teaspoon vanilla
2 cups flour
2 teaspoons baking powder
1 teaspoon baking soda
½ teaspoon salt
½ cup sugar

Pack apricots firmly into measuring cup to the ½ cup mark. After measuring, dice apricots and place in large bowl. Add 2 tablespoons orange juice and soak for 2 hours; do not drain.

Preheat oven to 350 degrees. Coat a 9x5-inch loaf pan with cooking spray. Add raisins and orange rind to marinated apricots.

In a medium bowl, combine margarine, 1 cup orange juice, egg and vanilla. Sift dry ingredients and stir into juice mixture just until blended. Fold in apricots and raisins and spoon mixture into baking pan.

Bake for 45 to 50 minutes or until cooked through when tested with a thin skewer. Cool in pan. When cool, remove and wrap tightly in foil or plastic wrap.

In recipes for quick breads such as pumpkin, banana, fruit, etc., leave out the nuts and substitute raisins or currants. One cup of nuts can add more than 70 grams, or 18 teaspoons, of unnecessary fat! Without nuts, quick breads are often quite low in fat.

Pumpkin Bread

Enjoy the flavor of Thanksgiving all year long with this low fat quick bread. It freezes well.

makes 18 slices   each: 115 calories, 3 grams fat

1/4 cup margarine
3/4 cup brown sugar
1/2 teaspoon vanilla
1 large whole egg
1 large egg white
1 cup plain canned
   pumpkin
1 2/3 cups flour

1/4 teaspoon salt
1/4 teaspoon baking powder
1 teaspoon baking soda
1/2 teaspoon nutmeg
1/2 teaspoon cinnamon
1/3 cup skim milk
1/2 cup currants

Preheat oven to 350 degrees. Coat a 9x5-inch loaf pan with cooking spray.

Beat margarine and brown sugar until smooth. Add vanilla, whole egg and egg white and beat well. Stir in pumpkin. Combine dry ingredients and add to dough alternately with milk (two additions of each). Beat lightly after each addition. Stir in currants.

Bake for 45 to 50 minutes or until cooked through when tested with a thin skewer. Cool in pan. When cool, remove and wrap tightly in foil or plastic wrap.

When you cut the fat in breads and muffins, you need to substitute something for the missing volume. Try additional buttermilk or egg whites. A little experimentation may be necessary.

Honey Oatmeal Muffins

Basic oat muffins sweetened lightly with honey make an excellent breakfast along with a piece of fruit.

makes 12 medium muffins	each: 90 calories, 3 grams fat

¾ **cup rolled oats**
½ **cup flour**
 2 **tablespoons brown sugar**
1½ **teaspoons baking powder**
⅓ **cup skim milk**

2 **tablespoons salad oil**
2 **tablespoons honey**
2 **large egg whites, lightly beaten**
¼ **cup currants**

Preheat oven to 400 degrees. Coat shallow, 2-inch muffin cups with cooking spray.

In a medium bowl, combine oats, flour, brown sugar and baking powder. In a separate bowl, blend milk, oil, honey and egg whites. Add to dry ingredients, stirring just until blended. Stir in currants. Batter will look very moist; don't worry about it, the rolled oats soak it up.

Fill muffin cups to the rim. Bake 15 to 18 minutes until golden brown and firm. Remove from baking pan to cool.

A note to muffin makers

It is possible to pack quite a few calories into "just one muffin." **Standard** muffin cups are 2½ inches across, hold about 4 to 5 tablespoons of batter. **Medium** muffin cups are 2 inches across, slightly shallower and hold 2 to 2½ tablespoons. **Mini** muffin cups are about 1¾ inches across at the top, hold 1½ tablespoons of batter. (Then there are Texas-Size muffin cups which we won't even discuss!)

All our recipes make medium muffins since we treat muffins as snacks, to be eaten instead of a cookie or piece of cake. (If you want larger muffins, the recipes will make half as many and calories and fat will double.) We suggest that you treat yourself to a medium muffin pan with a nonstick coating.

Blueberry Bran Muffins

A variation on refrigerator muffins, these have added molasses for rich flavor and blueberries for juiciness. Batter keeps well in refrigerator.

makes 20 medium muffins   each: 70 calories, 2 grams fat

1½ cups 100% bran cereal
1¼ cups buttermilk
  2 large egg whites
  2 tablespoons salad oil
  3 tablespoons molasses

  2 tablespoons brown sugar
1¼ cups flour
1½ teaspoons baking soda
 ¾ cup blueberries, fresh or
     frozen (no need to thaw)

Preheat oven to 400 degrees. Coat shallow, 2-inch muffin cups with cooking spray.

In a small bowl, soften cereal in buttermilk for a few minutes. In a separate small bowl, blend egg whites, oil, molasses and brown sugar and add to cereal.

Combine flour and baking soda and stir into moist ingredients just until blended. Stir in blueberries.

Fill muffin cups to the rim. Bake 15 to 18 minutes until brown and firm. Remove from baking pan to cool.

Use skim milk or buttermilk instead of whole milk in muffins and cakes. Save your fat calories for those times when you can taste the difference.

Oat notes

A member of the grass family, oats provide complex carbohydrates, fiber and high quality protein. They contain both water-soluble fiber, potentially helpful in lowering blood cholesterol levels, and water-insoluble fiber, important in maintaining regularity.

To begin processing, the inedible hulls are removed from the harvested oat kernels, leaving the "groat." The groats, which still contain the oat bran, are processed into a variety of products.

Oatmeal: Steel-cut oats are very crunchy, since the groats have only been cut, rather than rolled out. Regular, or old-fashioned, rolled oats are flattened whole groats. Quick-cooking rolled oats are cut first, then flattened. Instant oatmeal is precooked and rolled. One serving (⅓ cup dry) of regular rolled oats contains 110 calories and 2 grams of fat. Rolled oats make an excellent addition to hearty breads and pancakes.

Oat bran: The bran is the outer covering of the oat kernel; it is high in soluble fiber. Oat bran, the product, is a cereal especially milled to concentrate the protein, vitamins and minerals found naturally in whole grain oats. One serving (⅓ cup dry) contains 110 calories and 2 to 3 grams of fat.

Add oat bran to muffins, pancakes and breads, by replacing up to ⅓ of the flour with it. Because oat bran lacks the gluten of wheat flour, you won't get light baked goods if you replace all the flour with oat bran. You can also sprinkle a little on cold cereal, stir it into yogurt, add it to meatloaf or use it as a breading for oven-fried chicken.

Fiber Fillers

We've packed high fiber cereal, rolled oats and oat bran into these morsels – great for a satisfying breakfast, lunch or mid-day snack.

makes 15 medium muffins   each: 80 calories, 2½ grams fat

½ cup high-fiber cereal
  (your choice)
¼ cup rolled oats
¼ cup hot water
  2 large egg whites,
    lightly beaten
  2 tablespoons salad oil
  2 tablespoons molasses
  2 tablespoons honey

½ cup buttermilk
½ teaspoon vanilla
⅓ cup oat bran hot cereal,
    uncooked
⅔ cup flour
½ teaspoon baking soda
½ teaspoon baking powder
¼ cup raisins

Preheat oven to 400 degrees. Coat shallow, 2-inch muffin cups with cooking spray.

In a large mixing bowl, combine high-fiber cereal, rolled oats and hot water; stir to moisten and set aside.

In a separate small bowl, blend egg whites, oil, molasses, honey, buttermilk and vanilla. Add to cereal mixture and stir to blend. Combine oat bran, flour, baking soda and baking powder. Add to moist ingredients and stir just until blended. Stir in raisins.

Fill muffin cups to the rim. Bake 15 to 18 minutes until brown and firm. Remove from baking pan to cool.

No time for breakfast? Then you'll probably be starving when coffee break comes along – and your resistance to a doughnut or some other piece of "sweet grease" will be very low. Get into the habit of putting at least a little something in your stomach. Watch out for commercial breakfast bars (up to 200 calories and 11 grams of fat each), unless you're looking for a fast way to get your daily fat!

Branana Muffins

Add these moist little morsels to your brown bag lunch; they're just as tasty as cake and much better for you.

makes 12 medium muffins   each: 85 calories, 2½ grams fat

⅔ cup 100% bran cereal	¼ cup brown sugar
⅓ cup skim milk	½ cup flour
2 large egg whites, lightly beaten	1 teaspoon baking powder
2 tablespoons salad oil	¼ teaspoon salt
½ cup mashed ripe banana	¼ cup raisins

Preheat oven to 400 degrees. Coat shallow, 2-inch muffin cups with cooking spray.

Combine bran cereal and milk in a large bowl and let stand a few minutes until softened. Beat in egg whites and oil; stir in mashed banana and brown sugar.

In a separate small bowl, combine flour, baking powder and salt. Add dry ingredients to banana mixture, stirring just until blended. Add raisins.

Fill muffin cups to the rim. Bake 15 to 18 minutes or until golden brown and firm. Remove from baking pan to cool.

Muffin madness

Beware of those huge, "healthy" bran muffins sold in bakeries, the ones that are chock full of whole grains, nuts, etc. They are often a popular item gobbled down by people who think they're eating well. But are they really a healthy choice? One super muffin can easily hide 3 to 4 teaspoons of fat and over 300 calories. The muffin may be a better snack than a croissant because of its whole grain contents, but don't fool yourself that you're getting away from fat or calories. Buyer Beware!

Pineapple Carrot Muffins

These delightful, moist little muffins are handy to have around for visitors and make a tasty addition to any meal. It's an easy way to add the soluble fiber of carrots and oat bran to your diet.

makes 12 medium muffins   each: 65 calories, 2½ grams fat

½ cup grated carrot
½ cup crushed pineapple, with juice
2 tablespoons salad oil
2 large egg whites, lightly beaten
2 tablespoons honey
¼ cup white flour

¼ cup whole wheat flour
¼ cup oat bran hot cereal, uncooked
½ teaspoon baking powder
½ teaspoon baking soda
¼ teaspoon nutmeg
¼ teaspoon salt

Preheat oven to 400 degrees. Coat shallow, 2-inch muffin cups with cooking spray.

Mix carrot, pineapple, oil, egg whites and honey together in a small bowl.

In a separate bowl, combine flours, oat bran, baking powder, baking soda, nutmeg and salt. Add dry ingredients to moist ingredients and stir just until blended.

Fill muffin cups to the rim. Bake 15 to 18 minutes or until golden brown and firm. Remove from baking pan to cool.

Craving a sweet treat but no time to make muffins? Toast a piece of French bread, spread with a thin scraping of light cream cheese and top with spiced fruit butter or a drizzle of honey. Reminiscent of a sweet cheese Danish with only a fraction of the calories and fat.

Double Corn Muffins

Savory instead of sweet, these muffins are extra-moist because of the addition of canned creamed corn. Serve them with bean soup or lentil chili for a tasty combination.

makes 10 medium muffins   each: 70 calories, 2½ grams fat

½ cup yellow cornmeal
½ cup flour
1 teaspoon baking powder
½ teaspoon baking soda
¼ teaspoon salt

1 large egg white, lightly beaten
1 tablespoon salad oil
⅓ cup buttermilk
½ cup creamed corn

Preheat oven to 400 degrees. Coat shallow, 2-inch muffin cups with cooking spray.

In a medium bowl, combine cornmeal, flour, baking powder, baking soda and salt; stir well to mix. In a separate small bowl, combine egg white, oil, buttermilk and corn. Pour into flour mixture and stir gently just until blended.

Fill muffin cups to the rim. Bake for 15 to 18 minutes until golden brown and firm. Remove from baking pan and serve warm.

Breakfast breaks

Many people who used to eat eggs for breakfast every day now eat hot cereal every day and wonder if that's what breakfast is going to be for the rest of their lives. Others avoid the problem by avoiding breakfast altogether. Unfortunately, they then make up for it later with a mid-morning sweet roll or a high fat lunch because they're "starving." Not too smart.

If either of the above describes you, maybe you're stuck in a breakfast rut. Many choices are available to the creative, hungry person who wants to follow a low fat, high carbohydrate diet. Here, collected from a variety of health educators, are some ideas that might get you started in new directions:

Apple, reduced fat cheese and low fat crackers
Banana muffin, milk and apple juice
Boiled egg, cornmeal muffin and melon
Bran muffin, nectarine and milk
Broiled English muffin topped with turkey and part-skim Mozzarella cheese, plus a glass of juice
Cantaloupe, cottage cheese and whole grain muffin
Date bread, berries and milk
Fruit bowl with small scoop of low fat ice milk or frozen yogurt
Fruit milkshake with strawberries, orange juice and milk ...or banana, pineapple and buttermilk (or see *Peach Cooler* recipe in this chapter)
Plain lowfat yogurt mixed with fresh pineapple and toasted wheat germ or a tablespoon of granola
Raisin toast with cottage cheese and cinnamon, plus half a grapefruit
Ready-to-eat cereal, milk and cantaloupe
Rye bread, lean ham and vegetable juice cocktail
Shredded wheat, banana slices, milk and orange juice
Whole grain toast spread with lowfat ricotta cheese, plus sliced peaches
Whole wheat bagel, light cream cheese, jam and orange
Whole wheat pancakes spread with applesauce

Ranch Pancakes

We were served these delicious pancakes in a cozy ranch nestled at the foot of a snow-capped mountain. The chef didn't add any sugar because the pancakes were served with homemade wild huckleberry sauce. You'll have to make do with your favorite topping, sorry.

makes 8 pancakes   each: 75 calories, 2 grams fat

¾ cup flour

¼ cup rolled oats

½ teaspoon baking soda

1 teaspoon baking powder

1 large egg

1 teaspoon salad oil

1 cup buttermilk

Coat a nonstick griddle with cooking spray and heat to medium-hot. Combine dry ingredients in a bowl and mix well. In a separate bowl, lightly beat egg, oil and buttermilk. Stir moist ingredients into dry and blend until batter is smooth.

For each pancake drop about ¼ cup of batter onto griddle. Cook until lightly browned on both sides. Serve at once.

Pancake patter: It's always hard to gauge the appetite of pancake eaters, but don't throw out leftover batter. The ranch chef heats up the waffle iron and make waffles from it, then freezes them for a ready-to-toast treat. Be creative with toppings. Try different fruit butters, cut up peaches with nutmeg or sliced strawberries mixed with yogurt and orange juice.

Farmer's Breakfast

This hearty weekend breakfast can double as a lunch or light supper. Serve with chili sauce or salsa.

serves 2   per serving: 190 calories, 6½ grams fat

½ pound potatoes, boiled and cut in ¼-inch cubes (about 1½ cups)*	1 teaspoon salad oil
	garlic powder
½ cup diced lean ham (about 2 oz.)	1 large whole egg
	1 large egg white
¼ cup chopped green onion	1 tablespoon water
	salt and pepper to taste

*Potatoes can be cooked ahead of time. Coat a medium nonstick skillet with cooking spray and heat. Add potatoes, cook for 10 minutes, stirring occasionally, until lightly browned. Add ham, onion and oil, stir well and cook until potatoes turn slightly crisp and ham is heated through, about 3 minutes. Sprinkle with garlic powder.

Beat together whole egg, egg white and water. Pour evenly over potato mixture and cook until eggs are almost set. Cut potato cake into wedges and flip over to finish cooking eggs. Serve at once.

Muffin on the Run

Even if time is short, this quick breakfast is ready in just 5 minutes and you can take it with you.

makes 1   each: 245 calories, 7 grams fat

1 whole wheat English muffin, split	1 slice part-skim Mozzarella cheese (1 oz.)
1 slice lean ham (1 oz.)	

Preheat broiler. Toast muffin halves lightly. Top one half with ham, the other with cheese, broil until ham is hot and cheese is melted. Put them together, wrap in foil and rush out the door. (Remember to turn off the broiler!)

Holiday Life-Saver

We adapted this from a high fat recipe named a Wife-Saver. Our version may save a life and a wife! Must be made a day ahead.

serves 4   per serving: 245 calories, 7 grams fat

6-8 large slices French bread
  3 oz. turkey pastrami,
    thinly sliced
  ¼ cup shredded sharp
    Cheddar cheese (1 oz.)
  ¼ cup shredded part-skim
    Mozzarella cheese (1 oz.)

1 cup egg substitute*
1 cup 1% milk
1 teaspoon Dijon mustard
1 teaspoon artificial butter
  sprinkles
¼ teaspoon salt

*Look for an egg substitute with no fat; some contain more than 10 grams of fat per cup.

Coat an 8x8-inch baking dish with cooking spray. Trim crusts from bread and cover bottom of dish with half the bread. Layer turkey pastrami over bread. Sprinkle cheese over pastrami. Layer remaining bread on top.

Combine egg substitute, milk, mustard, butter sprinkles and salt. Pour over other ingredients. Cover and refrigerate overnight.

When ready to bake, preheat oven to 350 degrees. Bake the casserole, uncovered, 35 to 40 minutes or until knife inserted in center comes out clean. Let stand for a few minutes before cutting. (It may collapse slightly in the center; don't be alarmed.)

Peach Cooler

For a quick breakfast snack, blend together 1 cup sliced peaches (fresh or canned in juice), 1 cup buttermilk, 1 tablespoon sugar and a few drops of vanilla flavoring. Makes 2 cups, about 100 calories and 1 gram of fat each. Experiment with other fruits.

Desserts

The strawberry shortcake saga

When people think of a lowfat lifestyle, they often believe that there is no place in it for desserts, especially sweet, rich ones. While desserts, other than fresh fruit, do not have to be an every day or twice a day occurrence, we firmly believe that there are times when we deserve more than fruit.

For those occasions, we have included a selection of sweet treats, from shortcake and brownies to cookies and pie. Even though the fat and calorie content has been reduced, we think you'll agree that they still taste like something special.

The strawberry shortcake recipe is a good example of how we modify recipes. Quite possibly everybody's favorite dessert, the traditional recipes have usually been high in fat. Follow our experiences in modifying this treat over time.

Mom's original: The version I grew up with included real short-cake, split in two, with masses of sweetened whipped cream and berries between the layers and on top. Real shortcake is made from a buttery-rich biscuit dough, and contains about 6 grams of fat in a small piece. Because the biscuit dough always seemed a bit dry, we topped it with at least ½ cup of whipped cream per serving, for another 22 grams of fat. Total, about **28 grams of fat** - not unusual for a dessert.

Early lowfat version: In my "dieting" days but before my true "fat-awareness" days, I felt guilty about eating rich desserts and decided that substituting a small sponge cake for the shortcake would save this one. After all, sponge cake is made without added fat, so it seemed like a good substitute.

Saving all that fat meant that I could continue with the whipped cream, right? I did try to cut down the amount to ¼ cup (whipped) but would often have more because, again, the cake seemed rather dry. So what did I end up with? From 3 to 11 grams of fat removed, depending on the amount of cream, but still **14 to 25 grams of fat** left. Obviously the wrong focus.

The right stuff: Once I knew where the fat really was, two simple changes produced a great result. I kept the sponge cake, but moistened it with a bit of milk so it wouldn't be dry. The sliced, lightly sweetened berries were then topped with softened frozen yogurt or ice milk instead of whipped cream. This final modification resulted in only **7 grams of fat** per serving (see below). Quite a change from the starting point!

Strawberry Shortcake Supreme

This two-minute dessert will become a favorite treat. Frozen yogurt or ice milk is a lifesaver for those who want something creamy, with only 4 grams of fat in 4 ounces, about ½ cup.

serves 2   per serving: 280 calories, 7 grams fat

1 cup vanilla frozen yogurt or ice milk, softened	**1 teaspoon sugar or to taste**
	2 small sponge cakes
1 cup sliced strawberries	**2-4 tablespoons 1% milk**

Soften frozen dairy product until consistency desired. Sweeten berries with sugar to taste. Place cakes on individual serving plates. Drizzle 1 to 2 tablespoons milk over each, add berries and top with frozen yogurt or ice milk.

The result is an overflowing plate of strawberries 'n cream which will please everyone, we guarantee.

Fruit Cobbler

Summer fruits make wonderful desserts, either by themselves or cooked in a cobbler like this.

serves 2   per serving: 220 calories, 6½ grams fat

1½ cups raspberries, chopped
   peaches, blueberries or
   any favorite summer fruit
  1 teaspoon cornstarch
  1 tablespoon sugar
 ¼ cup flour

1 tablespoon sugar
½ teaspoon baking powder
1 tablespoon margarine
1 large egg white, lightly
  beaten
1 tablespoon 1% milk

Preheat oven to 375 degrees.

Place fruit in a medium saucepan. Combine cornstarch and 1 tablespoon of sugar, stir into fruit, heat slowly and simmer over low heat for 5 minutes or until thick. Pour fruit into a 1-quart baking dish.

Blend together flour, 1 tablespoon of sugar and baking powder. Cut in margarine with a fork until mixture looks like very small pebbles. Stir together egg white and milk and add to flour mixture, stirring until a soft, slightly lumpy dough is formed.

Drop spoonfuls of dough over the fruit. Bake for 20 minutes or until dough is lightly browned and crusty when tapped. Cool for 10 minutes; be careful, the fruit gets very hot. Best served warm.

Many people like a small dollop of whipped cream on their dessert, but what's a "dollop"? Let's call it 2 tablespoons (not much). If it's genuine whipped cream, 2 tablespoons contain about 50 calories and 6 grams of fat. If it's frozen or pressurized non-dairy topping, 2 tablespoons have about 25 calories and 2 grams of fat.

Strawberry de Lite

Make this early in the day and serve as a frozen sherbet or pour into a pre-cooked crumb crust and serve as pie. You can afford the crust since the filling is so low in fat.

serves 4   per serving: 110 calories, ½ gram fat

  2 **cups strawberries**   1½ **teaspoons lemon juice**
     (one pint)   ½ **teaspoon vanilla**
  ¼ **cup sugar**   ½ **cup lowfat strawberry**
  2 **large egg whites**   **yogurt (not frozen)**

Crush strawberries until you have one full cup. This will take about 1½ cups of whole berries. Set aside rest for garnish.

Combine crushed berries, sugar, egg whites, lemon juice and vanilla in a large, deep mixing bowl. Using electric beater, beat mixture on low speed to blend. Scrape down sides of bowl with spatula to be sure sugar has dissolved. Then increase speed to high and beat for 5 to 7 minutes or until mixture has doubled in size and has firm peaks.

With a rubber spatula, fold in yogurt and pour mixture into a 1-quart container or individual serving dishes. Freeze until firm, about 6 hours. Let soften at room temperature for about 10 minutes to get a creamy texture. Garnish each serving with sliced berries.

Cut the amount of sugar in a favorite recipe by at least one quarter. As your sweet tooth becomes used to less sugar, later on you can cut it again.

Fresh Berry Sauce

Any berries will work in this make-ahead recipe. Serve sauce over fat-free angel food cake for a delightful low calorie dessert.

makes 1½ cups   per ¼ cup: 50 calories, no fat

  2 cups berries (cut in half   ¼ cup sugar
    if strawberries)   1 teaspoon cornstarch
¼ cup water

Combine half the berries, water and sugar in saucepan. Bring to a boil and simmer 4 minutes. Pour mixture into strainer over a bowl. Press berries through strainer until a thick sauce is in the bowl, leaving seeds in strainer.

Mix 1 tablespoon of sauce with cornstarch until smooth. Add to rest of sauce. Pour sauce back into saucepan and reheat, stirring to prevent lumps. Cook for 3 to 4 minutes or until sauce is thick. Remove from heat, add remaining strawberries, cover and refrigerate for at least 3 hours.

Apple-Baked Apple

Use apple juice as a natural sweetener for this homey dessert that appeals to all ages.

serves 2   per serving: 145 calories, 3 grams fat

  2 tart apples, unpeeled   2 tablespoons currants
1½ tablespoons chopped   ¼ teaspoon cinnamon
    walnuts   ¼ cup apple juice

Preheat oven to 375 degrees. Remove cores from apples, leaving a 1-inch wide cavity (avoid cutting all the way through). Mix walnuts, currants and cinnamon and fill each cavity with half the mixture. Place apples in a small baking pan. Baste with apple juice and bake, uncovered, for 15 minutes. Carefully spoon out or pour off juices and baste again. Bake another 15 to 20 minutes, until apple is soft but not mushy. Serve warm.

Punkin-Orange Chiffon Pie

Do your friends a favor and end a heavy meal with a sweet but light pumpkin pie. Make it early in the day so it has time to set.

serves 8   per serving: 160 calories, 5 grams fat

1 cup crushed graham
  cracker crumbs
3 tablespoons melted
  margarine
1 tablespoon plain gelatin
¼ cup water
1¼ cups plain canned pumpkin
¼ cup brown sugar

⅓ cup orange juice
¼ teaspoon *each* cinnamon,
  nutmeg and ginger
¼ teaspoon salt
1 teaspoon grated orange
  peel
3 large egg whites
¼ cup sugar

Preheat oven to 350 degrees. Combine crushed graham cracker crumbs and melted margarine. Press mixture into bottom and sides of a 9-inch pie pan. Bake for 10 minutes. Remove from oven and cool.

Meanwhile, mix gelatin and water and let stand until gelatin is softened. In a small saucepan combine pumpkin, brown sugar, orange juice, spices, salt and orange peel. Beat smooth and place over low heat. Add softened gelatin and simmer gently until gelatin is dissolved, about 5 minutes. Remove pumpkin from heat and cool in refrigerator until mixture begins to hold its shape, about 30 minutes.

Once pumpkin begins to set, beat egg whites until stiff peaks form, adding sugar gradually. Fold whites gently into cooled pumpkin until no trace of dark orange remains. Pour filling into cooled pie shell. Refrigerate for 2 hours or until set.

Pie can fit into a lowfat lifestyle occasionally, as long as you recognize that most of the calories and fat are in the crust. A good low fat pie crust is difficult to make, since it's the fat that gives it the traditional texture. Solution: Make pies with top crust only – the bottom is usually soggy anyway and why eat soggy fat?

Cinnamon Pear

Satisfy your sweet tooth with this popular dessert and get a fiber boost as well. Good topped with a small spoonful of low fat frozen ice milk.

serves 2 generously   per serving: 245 calories, 7 grams fat

2 **tablespoons brown sugar**	2 **pears, about 1 pound total**
2 **tablespoons flour**	¼ **teaspoon cinnamon**
2 **tablespoons regular rolled oats**	**pinch of nutmeg**
1 **tablespoon margarine**	2 **teaspoons lemon juice**
	¼ **cup water**

Preheat oven to 350 degrees. To make topping, combine brown sugar, flour and rolled oats. Cut margarine into small pieces and work into dry ingredients with fork until mixture is crumbly and looks like small pebbles. Set aside.

Wash pears; do not peel. Cut in quarters and remove core. Cut pears crosswise into ½-inch thick slices. Coat a 1-quart baking dish with cooking spray and add pears. Sprinkle with cinnamon and a pinch of nutmeg. Combine lemon juice and water and pour evenly over pears. Toss with fork to spread spices evenly.

Crumble topping over pears. Bake, uncovered, for 30 minutes, or until pears are soft and topping is crisp. Serve warm or cold.

> *If you haven't tried ice milk in a long time, you're missing a real treat. Not at all like the frosty blends of the past, these are "milk" in name only. Some of them have very creamy textures and give gourmet ice creams a real run for their money.*

Tub o' Lard Award

The battle over the craving for high fat, high sugar treats is a hard one to win because of all the temptations. Our tubbie award goes to the food editors who print outrageous recipes, suggesting that they either don't know or don't care about even moderately sensible eating. This amazing gourmet treat is a chocolate peanut butter pie, which we've named **Killer Pie.**

> Imagine one 9-inch pie containing 10 tablespoons of butter, an 8-ounce brick of cream cheese, 1 cup of peanut butter, 2½ cups of whipping cream and 12 ounces of chocolate, plus a cup of sugar. Even we could hardly believe this one!

> This totals close to 8000 calories and 700 grams of fat. If the pie is cut into 12 small pieces each piece still delivers about **650 calories and nearly 60 grams of fat.**

The note at the bottom of the recipe suggested garnishing with whipped cream and peanuts! We didn't add those in. Please, food editors, do your readers a favor and exercise a little judgment in what you print.

If you have trouble imagining 700 grams of fat, pile up 4 cups, or 8 sticks, of margarine in the center of a pie plate. That's how much fat is in this recipe. Then serve yourself two-thirds of a stick. Care for a treat, anyone? Remember, that fat-packed mouthful may be with you for years to come!

Chocolate Mint Mousse

Chocolate is not off-limits in a low fat diet, as long as you don't overdo it. Make this elegant dessert for a special occasion. It is easily doubled for company and must be made ahead, another plus!

serves 2   per serving: 175 calories, 9 grams fat

1 tablespoon water	1 large egg white
¼ cup mint chocolate chips	1 tablespoon sugar
1 large whole egg	

Heat water and chocolate over very low heat until just melted. Set aside to cool slightly. Separate the whole egg and place yolk in one bowl, both egg whites in another bowl. With an electric mixer, beat egg whites until stiff and set aside.

Beat egg yolk until thick and lemon-colored, add sugar and beat until dissolved. Gradually stir in chocolate, beating until smooth. Add chocolate mixture to beaten egg whites and fold in gently until thoroughly blended. Pour into small dessert cups or stemmed glasses and refrigerate until firm, about 2 hours.

Cookie confession

Occasionally I get an urge for some homemade shortbread cookies, made with pure butter. In an attempt to deflect me from this hazardous path, one day my husband brought home some "healthy" oatmeal cookies from the store. Unfortunately, he didn't read the label first.

A close look showed that the fat was listed as "Vegetable and/or animal Shortening; Contains One or More of the Following Partially Hydrogenated Oils: Soybean *(OK)*, Cottonseed *(Uh-huh)*, Palm *(Boo)* and/or Beef Fat *(Whoops)*, Lard *(Yuk)*."

Most of the fat choices were over 40% saturated and two of them, beef and lard, contained cholesterol, too. Not such a great substitute for homemade shortbread, was it? Read the label before you buy, Dad!

Fudgy Brownies

With rich chocolate flavor and not too much fat, this treat will win you lots of friends. By making these brownies with margarine and cocoa, which is chocolate without most of the fat, you have very little saturated fat, unlike the typical butter and chocolate versions. We include a few nuts since brownies aren't the same without them. Cut small – these are very rich.

makes 32 bars	each: 95 calories, 4 grams fat

½ cup margarine
⅔ cup white sugar
⅔ cup brown sugar
1 cup flour
¼ cup unsweetened cocoa*

1 large whole egg
1 large egg white
2 teaspoons vanilla
½ cup chopped walnuts

*Be sure to use **unsweetened** cocoa, not premixed cocoa drink.

Preheat oven to 350 degrees. Coat an 8x8-inch baking pan with cooking spray.

Melt margarine and combine in a large bowl with sugars, flour, cocoa, whole egg, egg white and vanilla. Beat well until blended. Stir in walnuts.

Spread batter evenly in pan. Bake for 30 minutes or until firm when touched. Cool and cut into bars.

Note: To make these cholesterol-free, use ½ cup egg substitute instead of the egg and egg white.

When a recipe calls for 2 whole eggs, substitute 1 whole egg plus 1 to 2 egg whites, depending on size of eggs. Or replace with egg substitute.

Fresh Apple Snacking Cake

This delicious cake comes from a good friend's private collection. It's so moist and sweet that it doesn't need a frosting and keeps very well.

makes 24 pieces   each: 65 calories, 2 grams fat

¼ cup margarine
⅔ cup brown sugar
2 large egg whites
1 teaspoon vanilla
1 cup flour
1 teaspoon baking soda

1 teaspoon cinnamon
1 teaspoon nutmeg
¼ teaspoon salt
2½ cups peeled, diced, green
   apples (about ¾ pound)

Preheat oven to 375 degrees. Coat an 8x8-inch baking pan with cooking spray.

In a mixer, blend margarine until soft. Add brown sugar and cream until light. Beat in egg whites and vanilla until smooth.

In a separate bowl, combine flour, baking soda, cinnamon, nutmeg and salt. Add to moist ingredients and stir until well mixed. Add apples and beat batter for 1 to 2 minutes until well blended. Batter will be very thick and apple will still be in small chunks; batter will look somewhat like lumpy oatmeal.

Spread batter evenly in pan and bake for 30 minutes or until cake is lightly browned on top and springs back to the touch. Cool in pan before cutting.

One pecan half contains one gram of fat! Keep nuts out of desserts or cut them way down.

Grandma's Applesauce Cake

A low fat diet doesn't mean you have to give up sweet treats. Here's the kind of cake that Grandma used to make, after she made the applesauce that went into it! Don't worry, store-bought, unsweetened applesauce will also make a moist and delicious cake that kids from two to ninety will enjoy.

makes 24 pieces   each: 75 calories, 2 grams fat

¼ cup margarine	½ teaspoon cinnamon
¾ cup brown sugar	¼ teaspoon cloves
2 large egg whites	¼ teaspoon nutmeg
1¼ cups flour	1 cup unsweetened applesauce
¼ teaspoon baking powder	½ cup raisins
¾ teaspoon baking soda	powdered sugar (optional)

Preheat oven to 350 degrees. Coat an 8x8-inch baking pan with cooking spray.

Blend together margarine and brown sugar. Add egg whites and beat until fluffy. In a separate bowl stir together flour, baking powder, baking soda, cinnamon, cloves and nutmeg.

Add flour mixture alternately with applesauce, making two additions of each. Beat lightly after each addition. Stir in raisins.

Spread batter evenly in pan and bake for about 35 minutes, or until top is light brown and firm when gently pressed.

When cake is cool, sift 1 or 2 teaspoons of powdered sugar over the top, if desired.

If you must have frosting on cake, spread the cooled top with a thin layer of light cream cheese, thinned out and slightly sweetened by blending with fruit juice.

Cookie monsters?

There are many special occasions that just wouldn't be complete without cookies. I have to confess that our family tradition absolutely requires that I make shortbread every December. And every experienced cookie baker knows that shortbread is only flour, sugar and butter, so there's not much that can be changed. What can we do to get around these temptations? The answer is probably what you want to hear – enjoy them, knowing it isn't something you have all the time, and try to make a few changes wherever possible.

If you're the baker, go ahead and make your favorite cookies, but only occasionally. Perhaps you can make them smaller so the same fat goes further. A recipe that calls for a cup of butter and makes eight dozen cookies is better than a recipe that calls for a cup of fat but makes only four dozen cookies.

If you're the recipient of your friend's best cookies, you have a different problem. Full of butter, nuts and chocolate, they're hard to pass up. At least try to pick one that doesn't obviously have all three. Your first line of defense is to take only one at a time. You can always go back for another, but if you impulsively put three on your plate at once, you know you'll eat them; after all, it would be impolite to do otherwise!

Just remember that every time you eat a regular cookie you're eating at least one teaspoon of fat – 4 to 5 grams. Some have considerably more. So, please don't pick the biggest one; you're only fooling yourself.

Oat Chewies

*Every good lunch deserves a small treat. We predict these will be-
come favorite brown bag cookies – slightly crisp outside, soft inside, filled with nourishing oatmeal and raisins. You need a food
processor to make them.*

makes about 40   each: 55 calories, 2½ grams fat

½ cup margarine	½ teaspoon baking soda
⅔ cup brown sugar	¼ teaspoon salt
1 large egg	¼ teaspoon cinnamon
1 teaspoon vanilla	⅔ cup regular rolled oats
1 cup flour	½ cup raisins or currants
½ teaspoon baking powder	

Preheat oven to 350 degrees. Use steel cutting blade in food
processor. Place margarine, brown sugar, egg and vanilla in
bowl of food processor and blend until smooth and creamy.
Combine flour, baking powder, baking soda, salt and cinnamon
and add to batter. Blend until smooth.

Add rolled oats and blend with about half a dozen on-and-off
bursts until oats are finely chopped. You will still see small
pieces but not the original large flakes. Dough should be fairly
uniform in consistency. Turn dough out into mixing bowl and
stir in raisins or currants, distributing evenly.

Coat a baking sheet with cooking spray and drop dough onto it,
using about one round teaspoon for each cookie. Bake for 10
minutes or until golden brown. Remove and cool on wire rack.

---

*Caution: This cookie dough is delicious uncooked, so if you're
a secret "dough-snatcher," be forewarned. If your favorite
dough never seems to make as many cookies as stated in the
recipe, the reason may be the cookie-baker!*

Cranberry Cookie Bars

Try this pretty treat when the holiday season rolls around. You can use frozen cranberries if you make this in a food processor.

makes 24 bars   each: 55 calories, 2 grams fat

¼ cup margarine
¼ cup white sugar
¼ cup brown sugar
1 large egg
½ teaspoon vanilla
¾ cup flour

½ teaspoon baking powder
¼ teaspoon salt
¼ teaspoon cinnamon
½ cup cranberries
¼ cup currants

Preheat oven to 350 degrees. Coat an 8x8-inch baking dish with cooking spray.

Blend together margarine and both sugars. Beat in egg and vanilla. Add dry ingredients and blend until thoroughly combined. If using fresh cranberries, chop coarsely and blend into batter. If using frozen cranberries and a food processor, just drop them into batter and process until they are chopped in pieces. Stir in currants.

Spread batter evenly in pan. Bake 30 minutes. Cool, remove from pan and wrap tightly in foil or plastic wrap.

As a general rule, fruit breads and bars are often relatively low in fat; see **"Bread and Breakfast"** *chapter for more recipes.*

Choices: Desserts

These dessert values represent average numbers for rather plain fare. Your friend's company special will probably have much more fat in it! Note that desserts with "only" 15 grams of fat still represent 25% of the day's fat total for many people.

Dessert	Calories	Grams of fat
Cake, 1 small piece		
Carrot	260	11
Devils Food	250	11
Plain white	260	9
Sponge	190	3
Angel food	140	0
Pie, 1/8		
Pecan	430	24
Coconut cream	260	16
Lemon meringue	350	13
Pumpkin, baked	240	13
Apple	250	11
Frozen dessert, 1/2 cup		
Rich butter pecan	310	24
Rich vanilla	270	17
Ice milk, frozen yogurt	130	4
Fruit sorbet	120	0
Miscellaneous		
Apple snack pie	390	20
Cream puff	300	18
Chocolate brownie	150	8
Granola bar	150	6
Small snack cake	160	5

Why Bother?

Danger, curves ahead

In this century our eating patterns have changed dramatically, from a diet based on plant foods (e.g. grains, legumes, potatoes) to one based on animal foods. Along with that shift has come an increase in fat consumption, both too much of it and the wrong kind. These dietary changes have had a major impact on our health and our understanding of the relationship between diet and disease gets stronger with time.

Concentrating on fat is not just another health fad. There is no question that there is a relationship between fat and chronic disease. We hear the same message from US government departments and national health organizations: Excess fat is associated with many different health problems, including heart disease, cancer, stroke and diabetes. Not only is fat implicated directly in certain diseases, but excess fat can result in obesity which in turn is a factor in medical problems. The *Surgeon General's Report on Nutrition and Health* addresses fat specifically, with the recommendation, *"Reduce consumption of fat (especially saturated fat) and cholesterol. Choose foods relatively low in these substances."*

Decreasing the amount of fat you eat may be one of the most important dietary changes you can make – and this book has the tips and techniques to help you do it. Our basic message is simple: Minimize unnecessary fat consumption, of any kind, period. Or, to put it as clearly as we can, cut that fat!

Fat and heart disease

The American Heart Association states that excess body fat is clearly related to an increase in the prevalence of high blood pressure, elevated blood cholesterol levels and diabetes. High blood pressure, in turn, is a risk factor for heart attacks and strokes.

How does diet affect your heart? Both saturated fat and cholesterol can raise the level of blood cholesterol; too much cholesterol in the blood may lead to clogged arteries and increase the risk of coronary heart disease. It is generally accepted that there is a 2% decrease in the risk of coronary disease for every 1% drop in blood cholesterol levels. See the chapter on *"Fat and Cholesterol"* for more information.

A recent survey from the Food and Drug Administration showed a marked change, since the previous survey in 1983, in the average consumer's awareness of cholesterol and fat. The percentage of adults who had their blood cholesterol checked rose from 35% to 59%. The number of adults who knew their cholesterol level rose from 3% to 17%. The number of adults who were aware that dietary cholesterol and fat were risk factors nearly doubled, from 29% to 55%.

However, this increase in awareness was not accompanied by a gain in knowledge. They were asked, *"Where is cholesterol found? (a) vegetables and vegetable oils (b) animal products like meat and dairy (c) all foods containing fat or oil."* Only 33% answered correctly, (b). Did you get it right?

What can you do about the diet-disease relationship? Learn how to cut the fat. Surveys indicate that people are making changes in their diets. Fat consumption is now about 37% of our daily calories instead of the 40% (plus) of past years. A small change, but it's in the right direction.

Fat and cancer

In addition to the known risk of heart disease, fat is also closely linked to increased incidence of certain kinds of cancer. While it is not known how the link works, or whether one kind of fat is more harmful than another, the total amount of fat appears to be a key factor.

The National Cancer Institute has issued simple guidelines for a healthy diet, which include avoiding too much fat, saturated fat and cholesterol. They make a clear statement: *"A diet low in total fat may reduce risk for cancers of the breast, uterus, prostate, colon and rectum. Such a diet will probably be low in saturated fat and cholesterol and may also reduce risk of heart disease."* (From *"Diet, Nutrition and Cancer Prevention."*)

The NCI also agrees that obesity is a risk factor for many diseases, including heart disease, high blood pressure, diabetes and some cancers.

Fat and weight control

A problem shared by a great number of people is that of too much body fat. What causes this excess weight? Too many calories and not enough exercise. What's an easy way to eat too many calories? Eating too much fat. Fat plays a key role in weight control. Although all foods have calories, it can't be overlooked that cutting down on fat is probably the easiest and best way to lose excess pounds. Conversely, eating a diet high in fat is probably the easiest way to gain pounds. See the next chapter, *"Weight Control,"* for more information.

Does fat have any redeeming value? Of course; it is a concentrated source of energy, provides essential fatty acids needed by the body, and adds flavor and texture to our food. We're not against fat in itself, just fat consumed in excess.

Get shifty

To reduce the risk of excess weight, heart disorders, cancer and other diseases, we are encouraged to reduce dietary fat. Along with this change, we should increase the whole grains, fruits and vegetables in our diet. When we cut the fat and replace fat calories with carbohydrate calories, we can cut a risk factor and add a protective factor all at the same time.

The shift away from fat and toward carbohydrate is easy to accomplish by making small changes. The key is to follow a "choose more often" approach. This doesn't mean giving up your favorite foods, just shifting your choices; you can still have steak if you choose a leaner cut and trim off excess fat, you can still have pizza if you choose one with more vegetables than pepperoni.

Throughout the book, we have shown you how to shift your fat-filled shopping, cooking and eating habits. Remember to choose more often the foods that may help reduce your risks of certain diseases, less often those that might increase your risks. There are no guarantees, but common sense suggests this is a wise course of action. Choose:

More often: Whole grain products, fruits and vegetables
Less often: Bakery products, white bread, desserts

More often: Skinless chicken, fish, lean meat
Less often: Poultry with skin, marbled meats, luncheon meats

More often: Peas, beans and legumes
Less often: Nuts and seeds

More often: Mozzarella cheese, skim milk, frozen yogurt
Less often: Cheddar cheese, sweet or sour cream, gourmet ice cream

Weight Control

Don't be a yo-yo

Although this book has been written for those who want to watch how much fat they eat, it is not designed specifically for weight loss. On the other hand, there is no question that cutting the fat can result in weight loss for those who have excess fat on their bodies. Because of this, a few words about dieting are in order.

Every weekend millions of people decide to go on a diet...on Monday. In an attempt to try to lose some weight, one more time, many reach for the latest, highly advertised "quickie" diet and start following it blindly. If this describes you, recognize that this kind of unsupervised, crash dieting is probably the worst thing you can do. It can be unhealthy, defeating, miserable and do just the opposite of what you want. Note that we are not talking about medically supervised diets, but about those fad diets that sweep the country, appearing in heavily publicized books and magazines.

The typical "magic-answer" diet usually requires instant changes in your eating style. You are faced with a big list of foods you can't eat and a new list of foods you must eat, all accompanied with a promise for instant change. The approach sets up an immediate feeling of deprivation or a *"Well, I can do it for 2 weeks"* syndrome.

But what are you really saying? *"I'll go on this diet for 2 weeks and then I can go back to the way I really like to eat."* Anything you "go on" implies that some day soon you'll "go off" it! It's a recipe for failure.

237

"Magic-answer" diets have another problem. There is strong evidence now that repetitive crash dieting doesn't work. The fad diets work briefly, while your body pours out water, breaks down muscle protein and gives up some fat. But then your smart body simply slows down to conserve calories. Once you quit the diet, the body continues plugging along at this slower pace, making it inevitable that weight will increase once you get back to your normal way of eating.

In fact, research shows that your weight may even rebound higher after very low calorie diets. That's worse than the familiar "yo-yo" description implies, since a yo-yo only goes back up to where it started, it doesn't go higher! After the crash diet is over, you may end up with not only more pounds, but more body fat, than you had before you started. Since fat tissue can get by on fewer calories than muscle tissue, the next time you try to lose weight it will be even more difficult.

Although a sudden drop of several pounds may be pleasing, the results will be less satisfying when you realize that you will likely regain what you've lost and that your weight control problem will be more difficult in the future.

Too many changes, made too quickly, will not lead to new habits. Although it may be tempting to dream of losing those extra pounds in just ten days, isn't it more tempting to think that you can learn to modify some habits so that crash diets won't be necessary ever again? Instead of making another short-term decision that results in a feeling of failure, choose a path that will add to your self-esteem.

Resolve to control your weight for overall health reasons, not just because you want to fit into some new clothes. Don't go overboard. What you should be looking for is a lifestyle change. Choosing foods with an eye to balance, variety and moderation will establish or reinforce good lifelong habits. By learning how to make small, permanent changes in the way you eat, you can control your weight for life.

Getting started

The best way to control your weight is to take a balanced approach, choosing foods from the four food groups: meat, milk, grains and fruits and vegetables (see *"Good Food Guidelines"* chapter). Selections can be made to fill any calorie allotment; this way the whole family can participate in healthful eating, even if not all are trying to lose weight. The ideal mix is high carbohydrate, moderate protein, low fat. Choosing foods from these four groups will give you enough variety to continue, one of the keys to sticking with a new eating plan.

We remind you that all foods don't have the same number of calories. Ounce for ounce or gram for gram, a mouthful of fat has more than twice the calories of protein or carbohydrate: 9 calories per gram of fat, 4 calories per gram of protein, 4 calories per gram of carbohydrate. Don't forget this fact; every bite of fat is loaded with calories.

> The problem is that these calories slip down your throat
> too easily – 100 calories every time you have a few nuts,
> a spoonful of mayonnaise, a small cube of cheese.
> These aren't filling mouthfuls, just fattening ones.

Cutting down fat does not mean cutting down food. In fact, it can mean the exact opposite if you replace fat with carbohydrates. Since carbohydrates have half the calories of fat, it's easy to see that you could eat even more food yet cut down on calories. A win-win situation!

How much more food could you eat? The average American eats close to 40% of his or her daily calories in the form of fat – that's like eating about twelve cups of lard every month! Just picture it...40% of everything you eat next month contained in twelve small cups. That doesn't sound very filling, does it? It's no wonder that most of us eat more calories than we need.

Now cut the fat to nine cups (still plenty) and substitute carbohydrates for the missing fat calories. Instead of three small cups of fat, containing over 5,000 calories, you could have about 25 cups of barley, bulgur, brown rice, beans or lentils.

What a trade-off; every cup of fat you give up could be replaced by more than 8 cups of these filling foods.

Carbohydrates are the careful eater's perfect companion because of their minimal fat content, the fact that they take longer to eat and are very filling. Replacing fat-filled foods with fiber-filled carbohydrates gives you two great choices: Eat more food for the same calories or eat the same amount of food and cut calories. Sounds like a smart choice to us.

Get fat faster

You claim that you watch your calories but can't lose weight? Too much fat could still be the problem. While calories from all foods are used for energy and basic metabolism needs, research suggests that the body does not treat them equally.

It appears that fat can make you fatter not just because it contains more calories per gram, but because calories from fat are converted more easily to body fat than calories from carbohydrate. In other words, the body takes less energy (i.e. uses fewer calories) to convert dietary fat to stored fat. This means that calories from fat may result in greater weight gain than the same number of calories from carbohydrates.

What does this mean to you? Even though caloric intake is the same, the person who eats more fat may end up gaining more weight. If you consume 2000 calories a day, with 40% from fat and 40% from carbohydrates, you may end up with more body fat than the person who also consumes 2000 calories, but eats 30% from fat and 50% from carbohydrates.

When you add this unequal storage efficiency to fat's higher calorie count per gram, it's no wonder that many of us have too much left over. That fat just oozes in and finds a convenient place to settle down – for life. The "minute on your lips, lifetime on your hips" jingle is more than just a saucy slogan!

Mouth control

Start your day with a decent breakfast. Going without food means that your body is not working at its peak metabolic rate and increases the likelihood that you'll eat too much when you finally start. For what's "decent," see the chapter on *"Bread and Breakfast"* for ideas.

Alter your eating in small ways. Put a teaspoon of margarine on only one slice of your sandwich instead of both, save 35 calories. Spread that one slice with light mayonnaise instead of margarine and you'll save another 15.

Finish your noon meal with a brisk walk, not a doughnut.

Eat a snack that takes a while. Both the apple and the glass of apple juice have similar calories, but you'll feel much more satisfied with the whole fruit – and think of the fiber.

Don't snack in front of the refrigerator. Plan what and when you're going to eat. If you decide that you'll have two graham crackers when you come home from work, the chances are good that you will stick with it. But if you arrive home without plans and open the refrigerator door, you may munch through several slices of cheese before you realize what you've done.

Make a pot of low calorie soup (vegetable, tomato, low-salt broth) and have a small cup of it 20 minutes before dinner.

Pour yourself a glass of club soda with a squeeze of lime just before you start making dinner. When you're tempted to sample the food, take a sip instead.

Use high fat foods as condiments, not main events. A bit of grated cheese tossed with rice gives you the flavor you enjoy without the excess calories that a cheese and macaroni casserole would bring.

When you make your food selections, analyze your own diet pitfalls. For example, some people have no problem with eating low calorie regular meals but are tempted with snacks;

others can ignore mid-day munching but have a hard time with small portions at mealtime. Recognize that what works for others may not work for you.

Remember that there is more to dieting than just counting calories or grams. Two foods can have the same number of calories but very different nutritional value. A slice of pizza and a chocolate bar may each have 350 calories and several grams of fat, but the pizza is nutrient dense, providing protein, vitamins and minerals; the chocolate bar has very little other than sugar. Choose wisely in order to get the most out of each bite.

Don't forget that gram for gram, or ounce for ounce, fat has more than twice the calories of either protein or carbohydrate. Keeping an eye on how much fat you eat will help you maintain your ideal weight.

Definition: "Lowfat living means putting less fat into your body and taking more fat out of your body."

Snack attack

Understanding your taste and texture preferences is important when it comes to weight control, and particularly helpful when it comes to snacking. Think about having a snack right now; what pops into mind? A bowl of ice cream? Pretzels? A pickle? Applesauce? Raisins? A bagel? The taste of these very different snacks makes them tempting to different people.

Look again at the list and consider texture – smooth ice cream and applesauce, crunchy pretzels or pickles, chewy raisins and bagels. You're likely to find one of these much more satisfying than the others.

If "sweet and smooth" is your idea of heaven, don't eat "sour and crunchy" and pretend you're pleased. If you do, you may eat the sour and crunchy snack first, then go back and have what you really want. Understanding and controlling your snack attack will help you save calories.

Tub o' Lard Award

Ah, chicken – the perfect diet food. When you want to cut calories, there's no question that chicken can be a good choice. However, it can easily become the vehicle for hundreds of extra calories when smothered in high fat toppings. **Chicken Tarragon** is a truly terrible example.

Six chicken breasts (with skin, of course) are covered with 2 sticks of melted margarine, 1 cup of sour cream and 1½ cups of cheddar cheese. Each person will get **670 calories and 54 grams of fat** from this little jewel. It's hard to imagine that you could even taste the chicken under all that grease.

Incidentally, this recipe came from one of those fund-raising cookbooks. While they often have excellent recipes, very many of them are overloaded with fat, so read carefully. Remember, charity begins at home!

The 3000-calorie low fat diet

We have heard people complain that they have cut the fat from their meals but still can't lose weight. Sometimes an analysis of their eating habits shows a common misunderstanding. Because their food is now low in fat, they think that they can eat as much of it as they want. Unfortunately, life isn't that simple. While fat is the most concentrated source of calories, all foods contain calories and calories do add up.

> You've switched to light cream cheese, with half the calories; does that mean you can spread a layer ¼-inch thick on your bagel? The only mayonnaise in the house is the reduced fat variety; are your sandwiches soggy with it? You can do the right thing and cut the fat, but if you still eat too much you won't lose weight.

Consider the healthy bran muffin. Because one bran muffin may be good for you, two aren't necessarily better. While the muffin is a better nutritional choice than a doughnut, both have calories. When you're cutting calories, make every one count. The reason to choose the muffin over the doughnut is to get extra vitamins, minerals and grains for the same number of calories.

We like potatoes and encourage people to add them to their meals. An average baked potato, with skin, has 100 calories, a great value for what you're getting. However, an average potato is about 4 ounces. Eating a 16-ounce baked potato in exchange for leaving off the sour cream isn't part of a weight-loss plan. Because potatoes are rich packages of nutrients and very low in fat doesn't mean that they have no calories.

Don't misunderstand us; high-carbohydrate foods should remain your first choice for healthful, weight-loss eating, because of their nutrient value and because they fill you up. We just want to remind you that because a food is low in fat, and even good for you, doesn't necessarily mean that it's low in calories. 3000 healthy calories are still 3000 calories.

Stormy weather

For many people, winter months are tough ones for losing weight. When you come inside from a chilly, wet day the first thing you look for is comfort, often in the form of something to eat. Unfortunately, that fresh salad that was so appealing in the summer just doesn't seem to do it on a cold, dark night. Now you want a big bowl of something warm and hearty, maybe a piece of pie for dessert. The result is that winter months can easily lead to too many calories.

Even your clothes conspire against you as you bundle up in bulky sweaters and jackets, thereby disguising extra eating.

You must learn to balance your food intake. A hearty, high calorie main dish served by itself almost guarantees that you will eat too much. However, if you add low calorie foods to the same meal, you can eat less of the calorie-dense food and still feel satisfied. Precede a bowl of chili with a light salad; sip a cup of hot broth before you dig into the creamy casserole; steam extra vegetables to go with smaller squares of lasagna. By filling up on more low calorie foods and fewer high calorie ones, your daily intake will stay under control.

If you're disappointed when you lose only one pound each week, it might help to take a look at a pound of margarine and congratulate yourself on what you just got rid of. Remember, slow and steady wins this race!

What's to drink?

We heard of a person who gained weight on orange juice! While on a strict, self-imposed diet, he decided to cut solid food way down, just drink orange juice and watch the pounds melt away. As time went by, he couldn't understand why he wasn't losing the pounds he'd expected to; in fact, he was gaining weight. He finally admitted he was drinking six quarts of orange juice every day. At 440 calories per quart, he was in calorie overload even before he ate any solid food.

Many people toss down a glass of juice without thinking of the calories. While juice is certainly a better nutritional choice than a glass of cola, too much of it can be a problem to the calorie-watcher. Try diluting it with sodium-free seltzer or learn to appreciate the taste of straight water. Several glasses of water a day are recommended for everyone, not just dieters.

Juice, 8 oz.	Calories
Grape	155
Cranberry*	145
Apricot	140
Pineapple	140
Apple	115
Orange	110
Grapefruit	95
Vegetable*	45
Tomato	40

*usually labelled as "... Cocktail"

Exercise

Move it!

Although the intent of this book is to discuss the role of fat in the diet and show how to live with less of it, the role of exercise in a healthy lifestyle cannot be ignored. Exercise can make you feel better, look better and help you stay in better overall health. Federal fitness goals for this decade include getting people to engage in moderate exercise for 20 minutes, three times a week.

Regular exercise is beneficial for both body and mind. It can improve blood circulation and make your heart stronger so it works more efficiently. It can help the lungs develop greater capacity, a recognized measure of fitness. It can help tone muscles in legs, thighs and abdomen, so you feel stronger and look more attractive. It can strengthen bones and help fight osteoporosis. It can help control weight, reduce stress and improve your psychological well being.

A regular exercise program is as individual as you are. To stick with it, you need to choose an activity that suits you. The American Heart Association suggests several factors to keep in mind: your health and physical capabilities, your interests (sociable? loner?), your proficiency, the equipment and facilities needed and seasonal adaptability. Exercise habits should be maintained year round, so you may want to try a combination of different activities. Scheduling and convenience will play a large role in your decision; if you have to drive across town for your aerobics class you'll soon find a reason not to go. The final factor to consider is the most important one: You must enjoy what you've chosen or you won't continue.

In addition to starting, or re-starting, a regular exercise program, you should increase the physical activity in your daily routine. Change your attitude toward normal movement and look for opportunities to increase it. There are many little ways to add more activity to your daily routine. Think active: bend, reach, stretch, trot up and down stairs, in other words, move. Going up three floors in an elevator doesn't use up very many calories!

Off balance

Weight maintenance requires a balance between calories taken in and calories used up. The body is very efficient and doesn't want to let any calories get away; if you have calories left over because of inadequate activity, they get stored as fat; that's weight gain. If you use up more than you take in, that's weight loss. This concept is very simple, yet so many of us try to "beat the system." The simple fact is that you need to burn off 3500 calories more than you take in to lose one pound.

Shifting the balance to use up more calories is best done not by severe calorie restriction but by combining a reduced calorie intake with increased energy expenditure – a fancy way of saying cut your food and get more exercise! For long-term weight control, don't ignore the second part of the balancing act, get more exercise.

Exercise not only burns up calories, but also builds muscle tissue, which burns calories at a faster rate than fat does. It helps trim inches so you look slimmer, regardless of your weight. Note that you can end up with fewer inches but the same number of pounds, because muscle weighs more than fat. If you're exercising regularly, the way your clothes fit will tell you more than your scale.

Remember that any amount of exercise is helpful in weight control. Just 15 minutes of moderate exercise can use up 100 calories per day. While this doesn't sound like much, if you did it for a year, without changing your eating habits, it could help you drop 10 pounds.

Melt that fat

The number of calories burned during an exercise session depends on the degree and length of the activity and on your weight. However, you don't have to wear yourself out; exercising harder or faster for a given activity will only slightly increase the calories spent. According to the President's Council on Physical Fitness and Sports, a 10-minute mile jog burns only 23 calories more than a 15-minute mile walk for a person weighing 154 pounds. A better way to burn up calories is to exercise longer and/or cover more distance.

Listed below are approximate calories spent **per hour** of exercise. These numbers are for a 150 pound person; a lighter person burns fewer calories, a heavier person burns more. (From *"About Your Heart and Exercise,"* American Heart Association.)

Activity	Calories/hour
Walking, 2 mph	240
Walking, 3 mph	320
Walking, $4\frac{1}{2}$ mph	440
Bicycling, 6 mph	240
Swimming, 25 yds/min	275
Jogging, 7 mph	920

Maybe you think that it's not worth it – an hour of bicycling to get rid of one piece of cake? Don't worry, there is an additional benefit. Once you get your metabolism "revved up" the body may continue to burn calories more efficiently for some time, so it's not just the actual exercise period that counts.

Are you desk-bound for eight hours a day? You can still incorporate more movement into your day. Everything helps. Studies of finger-snappers, pencil-twiddlers and foot-tappers (in other words, people who fidget), show that they can burn significantly more calories than their non-moving co-workers.

Take a walk

Walking is gaining in popularity as a recommended exercise. It is an aerobic exercise that can condition the heart and lungs and contribute to weight maintenance or loss. It burns calories and jogs your metabolism. It can be done anywhere, anytime, by almost anyone, and at almost no cost (except for good shoes). Millions of people walk for exercise just because it is so convenient and easy to do. Even if you find reasons not to participate in other activities, it's hard to come up with a good excuse for not taking a walk!

To ensure a successful walking program, choose a time, find a place, get your shoes and get going. Pick a time of day that suits you: early (get the day off to a good start), after lunch (give yourself a refreshing break), before dinner (ease away from the pressures of a busy day). It's up to you.

Find a place that is suitable for brisk walking. Strolling through a crowded city street is not what we're talking about; however, some cities have very successful mall-walking programs where the local mall opens up a few hours before the stores open, giving people safe, flat, weatherproof, uncrowded areas for walking. Check it out in your area.

As with any exercise program, you should start your walk by warming up with gentle stretches and slow walking. Don't just open the door and charge up the hill at full speed. When you're finished, cool down by walking slowly. If you want more information on walking as exercise, contact your local branch of the American Heart Association for some excellent brochures.

Note: Before you start any regular exercise program, check with your doctor for advice on a program which suits your needs and your physical condition. This applies even if you are considering a simple walking program and is particularly important if you have been leading a sedentary lifestyle.

Fat and Cholesterol

Mono, poly and misleading

"I know I shouldn't eat saturated fat, whatever that is; I think it's in butter so I'm baking with vegetable shortening instead, but the label says it's partially hydrogenated...is hydrogen bad for me? I've been eating polyunsaturated fat so I won't have a heart attack but now I think it causes cancer; I could switch to those monounsaturates that the Greeks eat – hope they taste good. At least I know cholesterol is a no-no so I'm buying lots of safflower oil to deep fry my fish, which I read is good for me because of its omega – that must be that Greek oil again. Hmm, I think I'm finally getting this figured out!"

Does this describe how you feel? The public has been bombarded with messages about fat and cholesterol, many of them confusing and some of them conflicting, tempting many people to throw up their hands and forget the whole thing. It's enough to frustrate anyone, and for someone who is not even sure about the distinction between fat and cholesterol, it can be very discouraging. We'll explain what they are, where they are and how you can cut them down.

Remember that our basic interest is in cutting total fat. One of the main points to appreciate is that when you cut your total fat consumption, you will also cut your consumption of saturated fat and, usually, cholesterol. So even without a clear understanding of the different fats, you can make one change, cut total fat, and know you're heading in the right direction.

Before getting into more details, take this short quiz to see what you know about saturated fat and cholesterol.

1. Which has more saturated fat – 100% pure vegetable shortening or 100% pure vegetable oil?

2. Are saturated fats found in animal or vegetable products?

3. The label says the crackers contain no cholesterol and are made with partly hydrogenated vegetable oil – is this a "heart-healthy" product?

4. Which has more cholesterol – safflower oil or vegetable shortening?

5. Chicken and beef have approximately the same amount of cholesterol per serving, true or false?

Answers to quiz

1. Vegetable shortening. Shortening is made from vegetable oil which has been hydrogenated to solidify it, thus making it partially saturated.

2. Both. Saturated fats are found primarily in animal products but a few vegetable fats and many commercially processed foods also contain them.

3. No. Hydrogenated oil, used to increase shelf life, is not a heart healthy ingredient because of the increased saturation. Also, the vegetable oil might be highly saturated palm, palm kernel or coconut oil.

4. Neither has cholesterol because they're both vegetable products. Cholesterol is found only in animal products.

5. True. Both chicken and beef have between 80 and 95 milligrams of cholesterol per 3½-ounce serving. The chicken has less saturated fat.

Fat translation

The different kinds of fat and their impact on your health is indeed a confusing subject. Some foods have high saturated fat and high cholesterol (ice cream); some have high saturated fat and no cholesterol (palm oil); some have low saturated fat but high cholesterol (shrimp); some have low saturated fat and no cholesterol but high total fat (peanut butter). Sorting out the various statements about how much and what kind of fat to eat is very difficult. Here is an extremely brief explanation of terms.

Fat is composed of triglycerides, so named because they contain three ("tri") molecules of fatty acids, compounds which are basically long chains of carbon and hydrogen atoms. These fatty acids are saturated, monounsaturated or polyunsaturated, depending on their biochemical makeup. If there's no room for any more hydrogen, then the fatty acid is saturated. If there's room for more, the fatty acid may be monounsaturated or polyunsaturated, depending on how much more hydrogen it can accept.

> Note that although the fat itself is generally classified as either saturated, polyunsaturated or monounsaturated, this is not strictly correct. Fats contain a combination of all three fatty acids; this combination determines whether the fat is considered saturated, polyunsaturated or monounsaturated.

Vegetable oils which start out primarily unsaturated may become more saturated by a process of hydrogenation. Additional hydrogen atoms are forced into the unsaturated chain, changing its structure and making it more saturated (and stiffer). For example, when an oil that is only 9% saturated is partially hydrogenated to make margarine, it may become 11% saturated in tub form and 16% saturated in stick form. The more saturated a fat is, the harder it is at room temperature. Think about how soft chicken fat is compared to pork or beef fat – that's because it is less saturated.

Saturated and monounsaturated fatty acids can be made by the body so a dietary source is not needed. Polyunsaturated fatty acids are called essential fatty acids because the body cannot manufacture them, therefore a dietary source is essential. However, the amount required appears to be quite small (some say 1-2% of our daily calories, about one tablespoon per day of almost any polyunsaturated fat).

Cholesterol

Cholesterol is a waxy, fat-like substance which is made by the body and consumed in the diet. It is made in sufficient quantity by the body for normal functions, including the manufacture of hormones, bile acid and vitamin D. **Blood** cholesterol is made in the liver and absorbed from the food you eat. **Dietary** cholesterol is in the food you eat. Both saturated fats and cholesterol-rich foods raise the blood cholesterol level. Conversely, unsaturated fat, when substituted for saturated fat, appears to help lower cholesterol levels.

Cholesterol in food is neither "good" nor "bad." Once it is in the body, however, it gets linked up with proteins to be carried through the bloodstream. The most abundant fat-protein packages are LDLs (low density lipoproteins) and HDLs (high density lipoproteins).

LDLs contain the largest amount of cholesterol in the blood and are responsible for depositing it in the artery walls, thereby earning the label of "bad" cholesterol. HDLs contain a small amount of cholesterol and carry it away from body cells and tissues to the liver for excretion from the body; that's "good" cholesterol. If you have difficulty remembering which is which, try this: LDLs are "lethal" and HDLs are "healthy."

The National Cholesterol Education Program (NCEP) has issued guidelines for levels of **blood** *cholesterol.* **Desirable:** *less than 200 milligrams per deciliter (mg/dl);* **Borderline-High:** *200-239 mg/dl;* **High:** *240 mg/dl and above.*

Sources of cholesterol and fat

Dietary cholesterol is found only in animal products. Despite advertising claims, vegetable products such as peanut butter and vegetable oils do not contain cholesterol. The fact that their labels say the product is cholesterol-free is just a marketing gimmick to encourage you to buy it. (See *"Shop Smart"* chapter for more.)

Animal products (e.g. meat, dairy products, eggs) are the most common source of **saturated** fatty acids, but they are also found in hydrogenated oils, chocolate, coconut and palm oils. The "tropical" fats, palm oil, palm kernel oil and coconut oil, tend to confuse many health-conscious consumers. Despite the misleading name, and their plant origin, these oils are hard fats and are actually highly saturated.

Tropical fats are found in many processed foods, used because of their long shelf life and lower cost: cookies, crackers, breads, some cereals and frozen foods, coffee creamers and imitation sour creams.

Good sources of **monounsaturated** fatty acids include canola (or rapeseed) oil and olive oil. Oils that are high in **polyunsaturated** fatty acids include safflower, sunflower, soybean and corn. An omega-3 fatty acid is a type of polyunsaturated fatty acid found in fish that appears to have beneficial effects in lowering cholesterol levels.

The chart on the next page shows relative amounts of saturated, polyunsaturated and monounsaturated fatty acids in different oils and fats. Just remember to use any fat, even "good" ones, in moderation – fat is still fat!

Recommended **dietary** *cholesterol intake: no more than 300 milligrams per day.*

Saturated sources

The following list of common oils and fats will help you understand their relative amounts of saturation. Note that all these fats have approximately the same total fat content (between 11 and 13.6 grams per tablespoon), but the percent of saturated fat differs widely (numbers are rounded to equal 100%). The last on the list, canola oil (or rapeseed oil), is the newest addition to cooking oils.

Fat	% sat'd	% poly	% mono
Coconut oil	87	2	11
Palm kernel oil	82	2	16
Butter	62	4	34
Beef fat (tallow)	52	4	44
Palm oil	50	10	40
Pork fat (lard)	41	12	47
Chicken fat	31	22	47
Vegetable shortening	28	28	44
Cottonseed oil	27	54	19
Margarine	18	33	49
Peanut	18	33	49
Soybean	15	61	24
Olive	14	9	77
Corn	13	62	25
Sunflower	11	69	20
Safflower	10	77	13
Canola	6	32	62

This may come as a sorry surprise: The fat in chocolate is about 60% saturated (3% poly, 37% mono), about 6 grams in an ounce of baking chocolate. Cocoa powder is a better choice in baking since most of the fat has been removed.

Hidden killers

The most dangerous hidden fat is saturated fat, because of its role in raising blood cholesterol levels. The US Department of Health and Human Services states that saturated fat raises your blood cholesterol more than anything else in your diet.

Currently Americans consume about 17% of their total calories in the form of saturated fat. Dietary guidelines from the National Cholesterol Education Program recommend no more than 30% for total fat intake, divided as follows: less than 10% saturated, up to 10% polyunsaturated, and 10 to 15% monounsaturated fat.

Where will you find hidden saturated fat? In the All-American Diet of ground beef meals, deep fried foods, dairy products, hot dogs, bacon, lunch meats, eggs, butter, doughnuts, cookies, cake and ice cream.

This does not mean that you have to give up all of your favorite foods. Many experts now believe that the most important thing to do is cut down total fat consumption since there is a direct correlation between total fat and saturated fat. As total fat consumption goes down, saturated fat intake will also decrease. This means that one of the easiest ways to cut saturated fat is to find lower fat variations of foods you already enjoy.

> When you replace a cup of whole milk with skim milk, total fat (8 grams) and saturated fat (5 grams) both drop to less than half a gram. Similarly, with cottage cheese, replacing a cup of regular cottage cheese with 1% means that total fat drops from 10 to 2 grams, saturated fat drops from 6 to 1½ grams.

With meat, saturated fat content is again correlated with total fat. If you switch from prime rib to sirloin steak, total fat drops from 30 to 9 grams, the saturated fat from 13 to 4 grams (in 3½ ounces cooked). Lean cuts of meat can be almost as low in saturated fat as dark poultry meat.

In addition to choosing low fat variations of high fat foods, replace highly saturated cooking fats, such as butter, with less saturated fats wherever possible. Both monounsaturated and polyunsaturated oils are excellent substitutes, as long as they are used in moderation.

Although it is not the same as saturated fat, dietary cholesterol also can raise your blood cholesterol level. Because of this, dietary guidelines include a recommendation to cut cholesterol intake as well as total fat. In an attempt to follow this advice, some people decide that they should focus only on lowering their cholesterol intake, assuming that their total fat intake will automatically decrease. True or false?

> Replace a cup of butter with a cup of polyunsaturated oil in your favorite cake recipe. By removing the butter, you decreased your cholesterol and saturated fat intake, but how about your fat consumption? No change; the cake still ended up with a cup of fat in it.

> A recipe for baked chicken browns unskinned chicken in two tablespoons each of margarine and polyunsaturated oil. The cholesterol content is low, the total fat content is not.

Obviously, cutting cholesterol doesn't necessarily cut total fat. Now let's turn the question around: Will cutting total fat cut cholesterol intake? Yes. If you make that cake recipe with half as much oil, then both cholesterol and fat are decreased. If you brown the chicken in just a few teaspoons of margarine instead of butter, you will cut both fat and cholesterol.

Don't get overwhelmed with details about exactly how much saturated fat and cholesterol are in certain foods. If you cut the total amount of fat you eat the result will be a decrease in saturated fat, dietary cholesterol and calories. The best of all worlds!

An ounce of prevention

Research to date shows that there are basically two ways to reduce blood cholesterol levels. One is to modify one's lifestyle, including eating habits, and the other is to take medication. Treatment begins with dietary modification.

Fat down: Reduce major and obvious sources of saturated fat and cholesterol in the diet. For many, cutting total fat will be a good start toward this goal. Losing some pounds, if you're overweight, may also lower your cholesterol level, and the easiest way to do that is to trim the fat.

Fiber up: Increase consumption of carbohydrate and fiber-rich foods. Vegetables, fruits and grains are very low in saturated fat and contain no cholesterol. Additionally, some of them contain soluble fiber, which appears to decrease cholesterol levels.

The US Department of Health and Human Services says it most simply: Eat less total fat; eat less saturated fat; eat less cholesterol; eat more starch and fiber; lose weight, if overweight. We can't make it any clearer!

Tub o' Lard Award

The guidelines say to eat more vegetables. While we certainly encourage this, it doesn't mean you can smother the vegetable in fat, as in this **Saturated Turnip**.

The recipe starts with 3 pounds of healthful turnips, steamed and mashed. Unfortunately, they are then mixed with 2 cups of heavy cream and 2 tablespoons of butter, resulting in a dish of turnips, saturated fat and cholesterol. Total damage: **300 calories and 33 grams of fat** per person.

We'll bet your mother didn't make mashed turnips like that!

Choices: Cheese

Fat-watchers tend to keep a sharp eye on cheese, with good reason, since it contains both saturated fat and cholesterol. Most high fat cheeses shown here contain 5 or 6 grams of saturated fat per ounce and have a cholesterol content between 25 and 30 milligrams per ounce, so individual values are not listed.

Cheese, 1 ounce	Calories	Grams of fat
Havarti	120	11
Cream cheese	100	10
Cheddar	115	9
Gruyere	115	9
Colby	110	9
American processed	105	9
Swiss	105	8
Gouda	100	8
Blue	100	8
Brie	95	8
Parmesan	110	7
Mozzarella, whole milk	90	7
Camembert	85	7
Neufchatel	75	7
Velveeta	85	6
Cheez Whiz	75	6
Feta	75	6
Mozzarella, part skim	70	5

4 ounces, ½ cup

Ricotta, whole milk	215	16
Ricotta, part skim	170	10
Cottage, creamed	115	5
Ricotta, low fat	120	4
Cottage, 1%	80	1

Good Food Guidelines

Nutrition by the numbers

The health-conscious consumer has a problem in today's society. To eat nutritiously it sometimes seems that you need to have a PhD in "Advanced Food Combining." You're told to eat less fat, more fiber, not too much salt, minimal alcohol, extra calcium, reduced sugar, no caffeine, etc. etc. Even something as basic as an apple has problems: One article says to keep the peel on for fiber, the next says to take the peel off because of pesticides.

How can you possibly follow all these statements and still eat your favorite foods? For that matter, how can you follow all these statements and eat anything? The best way to survive this deluge of health information is to avoid going to extremes. While an awareness of healthful eating habits is obviously worthwhile, some people get overly concerned about examining each mouthful – counting every calorie, keeping track of every gram of fat, analyzing every bite for vitamins.

Nutrition is a complex subject and the more we know of it the more complicated it appears. Recommended values change, foods gain and lose favor in the public eye, reputable health educators have honest differences of opinion as to the merits of certain foods. At the same time, there is widespread agreement on general good habits, such as our emphasis on eating less fat.

The best advice we can give is to remember **three** simple words, **four** food groups and **seven** dietary guidelines.

261

Three simple words

The three simple words are **moderation, variety and balance.**
Much of our book deals with this approach to eating, so we
won't go over them again. Proper nutrition is a matter of incor-
porating and balancing many different nutrients. Just switch
your focus from "the numbers game" to a balanced diet containing a wide variety of foods, eaten in moderation.

Four food groups

The four food groups are **meats, milk products, breads and
grains, fruits and vegetables.** A balanced selection from these
groups should give most people the nutrients they need, particularly if choices are made with the seven dietary guidelines in
mind. These are discussed later in this chapter.

The 1990 US Dietary Guidelines recommend the following daily
amounts for each food group:

Two to three servings of meat, fish, poultry, eggs, nuts,
dry peas or beans,

Two to three servings of milk, cheese or yogurt,

Six to eleven servings of grains, including bread, cereal,
rice and pasta,

Five to nine servings of fruits and vegetables (three to
five vegetables, two to four fruits).

Don't be alarmed at the large number of servings for grains,
fruits and vegetables. Consider half a cup of pasta, half an English muffin, half a cup of grapes or a cup of raw leafy greens –
not too much food, yet each of these represents one serving.
Watch your servings of meat, poultry and fish; a recommended
portion is approximately the size of a deck of cards. Think of
that the next time you sit down to a big steak dinner!

Four food groups exercise

If you don't have any idea of how well you follow the food groups, it wouldn't hurt to keep an informal tally for one week. Draw up a piece of paper with five columns on it. Label four with the different food groups, label the fifth with "other."

Every time you eat something, write it down in the appropriate column – not the amount, not the calorie count, not the grams of fat, just the item itself. The fifth column is where you put alcohol and high-fat, high-sugar snacks, the so-called empty calories. No, you can't put potato chips in the vegetable column or croissants in the grain column!

Note significant foods only. For lasagna, check "grain" and "meat." Do the same for a tuna salad sandwich. If you grab a chunk of cheese to eat with your apple, fill in the "fruit" and "milk" columns. Don't list everything in a combination meal, just the main ingredients. If you try to list every slice of tomato, every tablespoon of Parmesan cheese, every ½ teaspoon of margarine, you'll give up.

Eat the way you normally would; this is not the time to try cutting out certain items. After all, the idea is to see what you really eat. After a few days it will become obvious if you're neglecting some food groups and overdoing others, particularly the empty calorie group. You may find some surprises if you have been simply assuming that you eat a balanced diet.

Note that there are no recommended daily servings for oils, margarine, mayonnaise, sweets and alcohol. Most weight-loss programs avoid the empty calories of sweets and alcohol entirely and many limit fats to three servings per day. A serving is one teaspoon, or 4 grams of fat. That's not much. If you're interested in weight control, watch these extras carefully.

Seven dietary guidelines

Dietary guidelines are helpful in this modern world with its many thousands of food items to choose from. They have been issued, and re-issued, for years by various health organizations. In 1988, *The Surgeon General's Report on Nutrition and Health* provided support for the 1985 US Dietary Guidelines. In 1989, the National Academy of Sciences published similar recommendations. In late 1990, the third edition of *Nutrition and Your Health: Dietary Guidelines for Americans* was jointly published by the US Departments of Agriculture (USDA) and Health and Human Services (HHS).

The guidelines may remind you of statements your teachers and parents told you years ago (*"Don't eat too much," "Have something from each of the basic food groups"*), but they continue to make sense. Smart shoppers following the recommendations on calories, fat, fiber, sugar and salt will have an easier time picking healthful choices off the shelves.

The 1990 US Dietary Guidelines are as follows :

1. Eat a variety of foods.

Include daily servings of fresh fruits and vegetables, add whole grain cereals and breads to your shopping list, make casseroles featuring dried beans and peas, sample the new lowfat frozen desserts – in other words, be adventurous. See p. 262 for recommended daily servings from the different food groups.

2. Maintain healthy weight.

The 1985 guideline said to maintain "desirable" weight. The 1990 guideline takes the emphasis off appearance and puts it on health. See *"Why Bother?"* chapter for the relationship between too much weight and heart disease, cancer, diabetes, high blood pressure and more.

3. Choose a diet low in fat, saturated fat and cholesterol.

If you've read this far, you already know this one!

4. Choose a diet with plenty of vegetables, fruits and grain products.

This guideline is consistent with evidence that supports the health benefits of diets containing more complex carbohydrates and a variety of fiber-rich foods. See the next page for more information on fiber.

5. Use sugars only in moderation.

Sugars and foods that contain large amounts of them supply energy but are limited in nutrients. You can reduce the sugar in most recipes by at least a third, without harming the recipe; use the natural sweetness of fresh fruit and juices to make a satisfying and healthful treat. Watch out for excess sugar in commercially prepared foods, particularly those that are advertised as being low in fat.

6. Use salt and sodium only in moderation.

Although no specific limit for daily sodium consumption is given, many of us eat more salt and sodium than necessary and a reduction will benefit those whose blood pressure rises with excessive salt in the diet. If you feel you should make a change, cut down gradually and use herbs for added flavor. Salt intake may be a problem if you buy an abundance of prepared foods or eat out at fast food places.

7. If you drink alcoholic beverages, do so in moderation.

Alcohol has no fat but has many empty calories and lacks nutrient value. Moderation is defined as no more than one drink a day for women and no more than two drinks a day for men. One drink equals twelve ounces of beer, five ounces of wine or one and a half ounces of distilled spirits.

Fiber for your health

One of the dietary guidelines tells us to eat foods with starch and fiber. A higher fiber intake may help protect against colon cancer, modify gastrointestinal disorders, regulate blood sugar levels and lower blood cholesterol levels. Since our primary emphasis is on fat, we recommend fiber-rich foods for yet another reason: They are very low in fat and are therefore a desirable addition to a lowfat lifestyle.

Simply stated, fiber is the part of plant foods that humans can't digest. To say fiber includes cellulose, hemicellulose, lignins, pectins and gums is probably more than you want to know. However, you should be aware that these different types of fiber are divided into soluble and insoluble groups, and have different functions in the body.

Soluble fiber is found in dried beans and peas, lentils, barley, oatmeal, oat bran and some fruits and vegetables such as apples, oranges and carrots. Insoluble fiber is found in wheat bran, whole grain cereals and breads, and many fruits and vegetables, especially those with edible skins.

The average dietary fiber intake has been reported as being between 10 and 20 grams of fiber per day; most recommendations suggest between 20 and 35 grams per day. Trying to keep track of exact grams of fiber is very difficult, since many food products don't list fiber content, and those that do don't distinguish between soluble and insoluble. In addition, estimates of fiber content vary. The easiest course is to eat a variety of high fiber foods in order to get both types of fiber.

Remember to think "whole" – whole vegetables (unpeeled where possible), whole fruits with skin, whole grain breads and crackers, whole wheat pasta. You'll find that this is an easy way to add fiber to your diet.

As a first step to adding more fiber to your diet, analyze how much you're eating now. How often do you eat the following (seldom or never, once or twice a week, three to four times a week, almost daily)?

> Several servings of breads, cereals, pasta or rice,
> Starchy vegetables like potatoes, corn, peas, or dishes made with dry beans or peas,
> Whole grain breads or cereals,
> Several servings of vegetables,
> Whole fruit with skins and/or seeds (such as berries, apples, pears).

The best answer for all of the above is "almost daily," according to the USDA. It's probably safe to assume that most people are not able to answer this way, but if some of your answers fall in the "seldom or never" category it's time to make changes.

> Eat a high-fiber breakfast cereal (read the label!); have an orange instead of a glass of juice; make your lunch sandwich with whole wheat bread instead of white; choose bean soup over cream soup; snack on a fiber-rich cracker instead of saltines; throw a handful of marinated kidney beans, carrots or raw broccoli into your salad; add more potato to your dinner plate instead of a second helping of meat; eat an apple for dessert.

Once again, we strongly suggest that you eat a balanced and varied diet, without going overboard on any single food group. If you're not used to eating fiber-rich foods, don't add too much at once since sudden excess fiber can be hard for your system to handle.

Watch the processing. An apple has four grams of fiber, a glass of apple juice has none. A baked potato with skin has four grams of fiber, ½ cup of peeled, mashed potatoes has one.

A final reminder

Dietary guidelines recommend that no more than 30% of your total daily calories should come from fat. The chart below shows the maximum amount of fat you should eat at different calorie intakes to stay within the 30% limit for the day. Remember your grams and teaspoons!

Daily calories	Fat calories	Grams of fat	Teaspoons
1200	360	40	10
1500	450	50	12
1800	540	60	15
2100	630	70	17
2400	720	80	20

Resources

Valuable sources of information have included government publications, national health organizations, food industry associations and individual companies. Some of the major sources are listed here.

Publications

Diet, Nutrition and Cancer Prevention: A Guide to Food Choices, US Department of Health and Human Services. NIH Publication 87-2878, 1987.

Eating on the Run, Evelyn Tribole, MS, RD. Life Enhancement Publications, 1987.

Eating to Lower Your High Blood Cholesterol, So You Have High Blood Cholesterol, US Department of Health and Human Services. NIH Publications 87-2920, 87-2922, 1987.

Fast Food Checkers, LiteStyler Systems, 1989.

Fast Food Facts, Marion Franz, RD, MS. DCI Publishing, 1987.

Food Values of Portions Commonly Used, 15th edition, Jean A.T. Pennington. Harper & Row, 1989.

High Blood Cholesterol in Adults, National Cholesterol Education Program, National Heart, Lung and Blood Institute. NIH Publication 88-2925, 1988.

Journal of the American Dietetic Association, miscellaneous issues, 1988-1990

Journal of Nutrition Education, miscellaneous issues, 1988-1990

Nutrition and Your Health: Dietary Guidelines for Americans, 2nd edition. USDA Home and Garden Bulletin 232. GPO, 1987.

Nutrition and Your Health: Dietary Guidelines for Americans, 3rd edition. USDA Home and Garden Bulletin 232. GPO, 1990.

Nutritive Values of Foods, USDA Home and Garden Bulletin 72. GPO, 1986.

On Food and Cooking, Harold McGee. Charles Scribner's Sons, 1984.

The Surgeon General's Report on Nutrition and Health, summary and recommendations. Warner Books, 1989.

Miscellaneous resources

American Cancer Society – check local branch for brochures

American Dietetic Association, 216 W Jackson Blvd, #800, Chicago, IL 60606

American Heart Association – check local branch for brochures

American Institute for Cancer Research, Washington, DC 20069

FDA Consumer magazine – available in public libraries

US Government publications, including many from the Department of Health and Human Services, Department of Agriculture, National Heart, Lung and Blood Institute and The President's Council on Physical Fitness and Sports

Note: The Consumer Information Center has a catalog of government publications (most free or very low in cost) dealing with nutrition, exercise and general health. Look for it in your local library or write to Consumer Information Center, PO Box 100, Pueblo, CO 81002

Association and company literature

My appreciation goes to the following associations and companies whose publications have provided recipe inspiration and nutritional data. If you wish to receive additional information on how to use their food products, write to the Consumer Affairs Department of each organization. Since many of them offer several different brochures, your best bet is to send a business-size, self-addressed, stamped envelope and request consumer information on low fat cooking.

American Lamb Council, 6911 S. Yosemite Street, Englewood, CO 80112

Association for Dressings & Sauces, PO Box 720299, Atlanta, GA 30358

Beef Industry Council, 444 N. Michigan Avenue, Chicago, IL 60611

California Iceberg Lettuce Commission, PO Box 3354, Monterey, CA 93942

California Tree Fruit Agreement, PO Box 255383, Sacramento, CA 95865

Calorie Control Council, 5775 Peachtree-Dunwoody Road, Suite 500-D, Atlanta, GA 30342

Dannon Information Center, PO Box 593, White Plains, NY 10602

Egg Nutrition Center, 2301 M Street NW, #405, Washington, DC 20037

Kellogg Company, PO Box 3599, Battle Creek, MI 49016

Kraft General Foods, Technology Center, 801 Waukegan Road, Glenview, IL 60025

National Dairy Council, 6300 N. River Road, Rosemont, IL 60018

National Pasta Association, 2101 Wilson Boulevard, #920, Arlington, VA 22201

National Turkey Federation, 11319 Sunset Hills Road, Reston, VA 22090

Oregon Dairy Council, 10505 S.W. Barbur Boulevard, Portland, OR 97219

Pam Cooking Spray, American Home Food Products Inc, 685 3rd Avenue, New York, NY 10017

Pork Industry Group, 444 N. Michigan Avenue, Chicago, IL 60611

Puritan Oil, PO Box 15697, Cincinnati, OH 45215

Sunkist Growers Inc., PO Box 7888, Van Nuys, CA 91409

The Potato Board, 1385 S. Colorado Boulevard, #512, Denver, Co 80222

The Quaker Oats Company, 847 W. Jackson, 5th Floor, Chicago, IL 60607

USA Dry Pea and Lentil Council, 5071 Highway 8 West, Moscow, ID 83843

USA Rice Council, PO Box 740121, Houston, TX 77274

Index

A Lowfat Lifeline for the '90s was prepared using Xywrite and Ventura Publisher. The typeface is ITC Cheltenham; body text is set at 9.5/12. Cheltenham was originally designed in the 1890s by Bertram Grosvenor Goodhue, the contemporary ITC revision in 1975 by Tony Stan.

Designed by Ron Parker, Lowfat Publications; typographic consultation was provided by David Vereschagin of Quadrat Communications, 50 Alexander St., #1901, Toronto, Ont M4Y 1B6.

The cover was designed by Robert Howard, 111 East Drake Rd., #7114, Fort Collins, CO 80525.

Typesetting was performed on a Linotronic 200 by Editing & Design Services, 30 East 13th Ave, Eugene, OR 97401.

Printing was done by Thomson-Shore, Inc., 7300 West Joy Road, Dexter, MI 48130.

The paper used is 55 lb Huron Natural, a recycled paper, produced by the Glatfelter Corp.